Rule

MW00979833

1. No using money or trading restricted items

2. No scamming or changing passcodes

3. No deleting account or getting it banned or friending random.

Steps:

1. Earn Money

2. Make neons

3. Do good trades with allowed items

Passwords:

Ocea:

282828 ac

CC: Vancouver _Oceania Viche_

Welcome to ~~scribble~~

(-?)

THE ARTS CLUB
ANTHOLOGY

$150 → 1 hr

THE ARTS CLUB
ANTHOLOGY
50 YEARS OF CANADIAN
THEATRE IN VANCOUVER

EDITED BY RACHEL DITOR

PLAYWRIGHTS CANADA PRESS
TORONTO

LIBRARY AND ARCHIVES CANADA CATALOGUING IN PUBLICATION

    The Arts Club anthology : 50 years of Canadian theatre in Vancouver
/ edited by Rachel Ditor.

Summary: In time for the Arts Club Theatre Company's fiftieth anniversary,
    this anthology collects six of the most cherished and popular plays that
    have captivated audiences for the past five decades.
ISBN 978-1-77091-218-2 (pbk.)

    1. Canadian drama (English)--British Columbia--Vancouver. 2. Canadian
drama (English)--20th century. 3. Canadian drama (English)--21st century.
4. Arts Club Theatre Company--Anniversaries, etc. I. Ditor, Rachel, editor of
compilation II. Arts Club Theatre Company

PS8315.7.V35A78 2014   C812'.54080971133   C2013-908492-4

We acknowledge the financial support of the Canada Council for the Arts, the Ontario Arts Council (OAC), the Ontario Media Development Corporation, and the Government of Canada through the Canada Book Fund for our publishing activities.

Canada Council Conseil des arts
for the Arts   du Canada

ONTARIO ARTS COUNCIL
CONSEIL DES ARTS DE L'ONTARIO
an Ontario government agency
un organisme du gouvernement de l'Ontario

Ontario Media Development
Corporation

CONTENTS

INTRODUCTION

I love working with writers. No matter what kind of insight may come out of a discussion, a writer goes away and comes back with material that is better and more inventive than anyone could have anticipated. Good writers don't take dictation from a dramaturg, or anyone; they translate workshops and feedback into action and process it through the marvellous idiosyncrasies of their imaginations and intellect. Since 2001 I have been the literary manager and dramaturg at the Arts Club Theatre in Vancouver, British Columbia, having had the great pleasure and privilege of working with playwrights as they craft new plays for our company. And with nearly one hundred new plays produced over the company's history, including only six for this anthology was difficult.

None of these productions would have existed, however, were it not for the passion of Artistic Managing Director Bill Millerd and his unflagging support and promotion of BC artists. The 2013–2014 season marked our fiftieth anniversary, and forty-two of those years have been led by Bill. Under his leadership the company has grown from a small theatre above a bar in an old gospel hall in downtown Vancouver to one of our country's largest theatres, programming between fifteen to eighteen plays a season across three venues—the intimate two-hundred seat Revue Stage; the four-hundred-and-fifty seat Granville Island Theatre; and on Granville Street the six-hundred-and-fifty seat, beautifully restored proscenium house, the Stanley Theatre—on top of the three-play touring season that travels British Columbia. Canadian theatre may still be young, but fifty years of steady growth is a significant achievement anywhere. Much of this is thanks to visionaries like Bill and former board chair Stan Hamilton, but equally important are people who have been toiling behind the scenes here for decades, like technical director Craig Fulker, stage managers Louis Bournival and Caryn Fehr, designers Marsha Sibthorpe and Ted Roberts, and artist liaison Stephanie Hargreaves.

To honour the immense work that goes into every production, I've endeavoured to give the reader a glimpse into the processes behind the work in the introductions to each of the plays. The fun bits. The hard moments. Stories from the front lines of play development. In several places I've asked the writers a set of questions that I often wish I could ask an absent playwright. The answers could inform choices for the rehearsal hall or simply add illuminating context for the reader. Of course, the feel of each rehearsal process is unique to the artists assembled, but in every case it never fails to move me to see actors commit so fully to a new script and give such specific life to previously unimagined worlds. This is the tricky bit with theatre, coming to life in its final and intended form only when it is spoken aloud. Or sung. My hope is that you will come away with a greater insight into play creation—learning a little more about the playwrights and their insights into process and production, perhaps launching you on a greater exploration of the plays from our west-coast writers—and with that knowledge read these plays aloud and feel in your bones the rhythms and nuances of the people on the page.

At the back of this anthology you'll find a complete list of new plays premiered by the Arts Club Theatre over our fifty years. Any number of them would be equally worthy of inclusion here, and my thanks go to Annie Gibson, publisher of Playwrights Canada Press, for making the tough choices that I couldn't bear to make.

At the time of writing we're just wrapping up this season of celebration and work has begun in earnest on our newest building on West 1st in the middle of the thriving waterfront Olympic Village neighbourhood—an auspicious launch for our next fifty years. This anthology presented me the opportunity to talk with Artistic Managing Director Bill Millerd about his thoughts on the past and future of new plays at the Arts Club.

RACHEL DITOR: What do you advise people about developing and producing new work?

BILL MILLERD: My advice is to have patience. Developing new work takes time. Time for the playwright to write and rewrite. Producing new work requires patience to make sure you do what is best for the play.

RD: Why the commitment to BC artists? Why not Canadian in general?

BM: I feel a sense of commitment to those who live in British Columbia—who have committed themselves to contribute to the artistic life of the province, to be part of the cultural fabric of the people who live and work here.

RD: How do you see the future of new plays at the Arts Club evolving?

BM: My interest now is in finding playwrights of different backgrounds and experiences. I want to further the development of the teen playwrights that are being nurtured through our LEAP teen playwriting program.

RD: When do you know that a new play is "good," or ready? At what point do you know if it will work?

BM: Upon first reading I will have a sense of whether the play has promise. A reading is important in getting a sense of the strengths of the play. But I won't really know if a new play is "good" until it is produced.

RD: What has doing new plays taught you? As an artistic director, as an artist.

BM: One of the biggest thrills for an AD is producing a new work that is both an artistic and popular triumph, but, most importantly, that the new play is being performed for an appreciative audience. The true worth of the play will be revealed over time once it receives additional productions.

All of the plays in this anthology have had an impact on the Arts Club and the development of theatre in Vancouver. The first piece, Sherman Snukal's *Talking Dirty*, was the first new play that enjoyed an extended run with the company. I love it now for its authenticity—a true distillation of the boomer generation in Vancouver at a time when the city's youth were making their mark on the culture. This is a picture of Vancouver then, written in the voice of its time. *The Matka King* by Anosh Irani presents a completely new voice to this mix. I love its fearlessness, its theatricality. From the start of the show we're in a different land and simply expected to keep up. For people who want something new, something unexpected, something to surprise them in the theatre—this is what surprise looks like. Anosh Irani was inspired by the work of Morris Panych, and though *The Dishwashers* and *The Matka King* have nothing in common on the surface, underneath they are tied by an uncommon audacity paired with a philosopher's mind, and a fascination with life at the margins. Panych's craftsmanship with narrative is undeniable in this play. Who else could bring such humour and depth of feeling to the foul dish pit of a posh restaurant? The adaptation of Carol Shields's *Unless* theatricalizes Reta's inner struggle with ideas of goodness and loss. In doing so it attempts to answer the tricky question of translating a first-person novel to the stage by allowing Reta to directly address the audience through monologue. This script is a great study of the challenges of translating exposition to action. Reta's struggle with motherhood is both specific to her loss and common to all parents, and I know of no better playwrights who capture the highs and lows of parenting with as much naked truth and comedy as the Mom's The Word Collective. *Remixed* is the best of their best, and a lively ride on both sides of the footlights. Sometimes all-star teams work, and sometimes egos get in the way. *Do You Want What I Have Got? A Craigslist Cantata* brings together three all-star writers of mine who knocked it out of the park with this unique musical want ad. Amiel Gladstone, Veda Hille, and Bill Richardson's vision of our search for connection in the online universe is touching and funny, and gets right to the heart of our need for community.

The theatre community in Vancouver has changed a lot in just the last twenty years that I have been here, and even more over the last fifty. The community has grown, the work is diverse and inventive, and it is finding resonance beyond the mountains with an international audience. These six plays are a part of a much larger conversation about Canadian theatre, and many voices prominent in BC are missing from this collection, but I encourage you to search them out. Stories like Yvette Nolan's post-apocalyptic *The Unplugging*; or Hiro Kanagawa's Christmas play, *The Patron Saint of Stanley Park*; or Michele Riml's look at gay rights and the church in *Poster Boys*; or any of the visually and textually inventive works from the Electric Company. The chance to share with readers even just the six western plays in this anthology brings me right back to what it felt like to be a child showing off a prized rock collection, all the excitement and pride—look, look, look at these beautiful, unique creations. Aren't they fabulous?!

Rachel Ditor
Literary Manager, Arts Club Theatre
Vancouver, British Columbia
2014

TALKING DIRTY
BY SHERMAN SNUKAL

INTRODUCTION TO *TALKING DIRTY*

I have a photo on my office door, a black-and-white picture of a group of actors around a table in our rehearsal hall. It's 1980 and everyone has long hair and a cigarette burning away, smoke curling up and caught in the sunlight streaming in the rehearsal-hall windows. A different era. Gabrielle Rose looks like a mischievous waif; a young Norman Browning is earnestly studying the page in front of him; the director, Mario Crudo, cuts a handsome profile; and down centre, with his back to the camera, slouching slightly, is playwright Sherman Snukal. Much of the cast is turned towards him, and, knowing Sherman, I suspect he was talking at lightning speed, in the middle of an impromptu monologue, providing animated insight into the choices he made on the page.

His play, *Talking Dirty*, changed the course of the Arts Club's history. It was a huge success, playing for months, and then going on to tour across the country. It gave Bill Millerd the confidence and passion to produce more new plays by BC writers, and he's never wavered from that course. Twenty-five years later, to mark the anniversary of this turn in the company's history, a visionary former board chair, Stan Hamilton, and his wife, Kathy, made a generous donation that launched our Silver Commissions project. That program continues today to fund the commissioning of two to three new plays every season. And, at the time of writing, one hundred percent of the completed commissions have been produced by the Arts Club.

This anthology wouldn't be complete without the addition of Sherman's play. And how interesting to look back on the sexual mores of the late '70s and early '80s to see how much has changed, and how much has remained the same.

RACHEL DITOR: Is there a trick or insight about getting the play "right"?

SHERMAN SNUKAL: The trick to getting *Talking Dirty* right, or any naturalistic comedy right, is to play it honestly. Never play it for laughs. If the comedy is any good, the humour is there. The laughs that count arise naturally from character and situation. You can throw character and situation to the wind to get a few easy laughs. But you'll lose the integrity of the play and likely the audience as well.

RD: Did you learn something working on this play? Did it teach you something about your craft?

SS: Rehearsing *Talking Dirty* I abandoned any thoughts that a play is a literary artifact. I learned that a play is only complete and alive when it is performed. The written word is the starting point of theatre, never the finish line. A corollary of this is that the playwright is only one part of a large collaborative team dedicated to performance.

These are hard truths for a young playwright to swallow. Especially after years of solitary toil spent endlessly reworking precious lines. But as Shakespeare said, "The play's the thing." And he was talking about performance, not a play script.

RD: What was the genesis of this play?

SS: Many years ago, before *Talking Dirty* was written, before marriage and children, before most of my life was lived, I had an apartment in Kitsilano in an old house that had been divided into apartments. On weekend nights parties sprung up throughout the house. Sometimes partygoers, after too much beer or grass or out of boredom or curiosity, wandered into the wrong apartment.

The next morning there were stories to be told.

I thought one of these stories might make a play. And so through the alchemy of the theatre and its inhabitants an anecdote told over Sunday brunch became a play that spoke to Vancouver about itself.

Talking Dirty was first produced at the Arts Club Theatre, Vancouver, on October 13, 1981, with the following cast:

Michael: Norman Browning
Dave: Dana Still
Beth: Sheelah Megill
Karen: Gabrielle Rose
Jackie: Alana Shields

Director: Mario Crudo

Characters

Michael Kaye: Early to mid-thirties.
Dave Lerner: Early to mid-thirties.
Karen Sperling: Late twenties.
Beth Gordon: Late twenties.
Jacqueline Lemieux: Early twenties.

Time

The present. A weekend in May.

Place

Vancouver.

Setting

Michael's apartment, the living room. The apartment is in an old house that has recently been reworked as a trendy apartment block.

On the left, a door to the hall. Down right, a window looking out onto the street. Up right, the entrance to the dining room. At the back, the entrance to the kitchen, and doors to the bedroom and bathroom. The kitchen and the dining room are connected by an unseen passageway that allows free movement between the two rooms.

At the right, a large piece of antique furniture serves as a bar and also holds the stereo equipment. A couch to the right of stage centre. A coffee table in front of the couch. A bonsai tree on the coffee table. To the left of the couch, a small end table, lamp, and comfortable armchair. A desk and bookcase at left.

Scene One

About twelve-thirty on a Saturday afternoon. MICHAEL *is sitting on the couch working. His notes and books are on the coffee table in front of him. After a moment, he puts down his book and takes a sip of coffee. He then turns on the stereo, and, taking his coffee mug and a dirty ashtray, enters the kitchen. There is a knock on the door.* MICHAEL *returns from the kitchen with a bottle of wine. He pours himself a glass and returns to the couch. There is another knock.* MICHAEL *turns off the stereo and answers the door.* DAVE *is there. He is holding a small package.*

MICHAEL: Dave.

DAVE: Mike. How you doing?

MICHAEL *and* DAVE *give each other a hug.*

MICHAEL: Jesus. It's been a while.

DAVE: No kidding.

MICHAEL: What are you doing here?

DAVE: I'm a "conventioneer." Can you believe it?

MICHAEL: Come in. When did you arrive?

DAVE: Last night.

MICHAEL: You should have called. I would have picked you up.

DAVE: Ah. Things were up in the air. I was going to go. And then I wasn't going to go. And then when I did go I had to take an afternoon flight, which means I arrived just in time to go to meetings all last night. I shouldn't be here right now. A thousand lawyers in the same room. The body rebels. The mind rebels. I was losing the ability to think.

MICHAEL: You've come to the right place. I haven't thought about anything in years. No Lynn and the kids?

DAVE: In Toronto. Minding the family estate.

MICHAEL notices the box. DAVE waves it at him. Then he throws it at him.

For you. A new ball.

MICHAEL: Thanks. Never say die, eh Dave?

DAVE: I've been practising. I've got a feeling after twenty years I'm going to win the championship.

MICHAEL: Don't count your chickens. You want some wine?

DAVE: Sure. Mike.

DAVE shows off his ensemble.

MICHAEL: Very nice.

DAVE: Intelligent, successful, well-dressed, but short.

MICHAEL: Not short, Dave. Compact. More man per cubic inch.

DAVE: What counts in a man is density. Density and taste. Mike. *(showing his label)* Harry Rosen. Top of the line.

MICHAEL: Very nice. Very lawyer.

DAVE: Mike.

DAVE points to the floor.

MICHAEL: What?

DAVE points again.

What?

DAVE: Gucci. Two hundred and thirty dollars.

MICHAEL: Hudson's Bay. Forty-eight fifteen.

DAVE: On sale. Saved thirty bucks.

MICHAEL: Regular price. Includes tax.

MICHAEL hands DAVE his wine.

DAVE: Functional.

MICHAEL: You forget you have them on.

DAVE: Cheers. *(takes a sip)* Not bad. Are you working this afternoon?

MICHAEL: Someone's coming over for a meeting but it's not for a while.

DAVE: By the way, your philosophy department made the *Globe and Mail* last week.

MICHAEL: Yeah?

DAVE: Something about the new head you got in January. He's some sort of hotshot?

MICHAEL: Kant scholar. Big jerk.

DAVE: You still making enemies of your department heads?

MICHAEL: What do you think? He hates my guts. I hate his. A very uncomplicated bit of social interaction. Thank God I've got tenure. Maybe I should have been a lawyer.

DAVE: Then you'd have partners. And they can also be a big pain in the ass. Such is life.

MICHAEL: I'll drink to that.

DAVE: I like the new place. How long has it been?

MICHAEL: About six weeks.

DAVE: Very academic. Still have your bonsai, I see.

MICHAEL: Yup. Still hasn't grown.

DAVE: *(to the tree)* Don't worry about it. Short trees have more personality. Hey. Where's Beth?

There is a loud buzz from the kitchen.

MICHAEL: That's my oven. Saturday afternoon. Beth is probably shopping. You want something to eat?

DAVE: Nah. Just ate.

MICHAEL exits to the kitchen.

MICHAEL: *(off)* Where you staying?

DAVE: The Four Seasons.

MICHAEL: *(off)* Very nice.

DAVE: And the two dozen hookers wandering around out front is that special touch that makes everything so much nicer.

MICHAEL: *(off)* A big tourist attraction.

DAVE: Yeah. I noticed the traffic jam taking in the sights.

    MICHAEL returns with his lunch.

MICHAEL: Well Dave, not that you're interested, but for a small fee you can take some of that scenery up to your room.

DAVE: What's that?

MICHAEL: Whole-wheat bread. Crabmeat. Edam cheese. Throw it in the oven. Heat it up. Voila. You sure?

DAVE: Nah. . . Full. . . Maybe just a bite. . . Not bad. Last night I watched three Japanese tourists purchase some of that scenery you were talking about. They bought six.

MICHAEL: Six?

DAVE: Six. The yen is strong. The dollar is weak. I'll have a little more.

MICHAEL: I could make you up one.

DAVE: Nah. Forget it. I'm not hungry. Mike. Do you ever wish you were Japanese?

MICHAEL: No. Do you?

DAVE: No. Yes. Lately I've been thinking it might make things a lot easier. Things are different over there in the Land of the Rising Sun.

MICHAEL: What are you talking about?

DAVE: I'm talking about geisha girls. I'm talking about the Liberal Party. I'm talking about feeling like the straightest married man in all of Ontario.

MICHAEL: Is something bugging you, Dave?

DAVE: Ah, I don't know. It's as though sex is some sort of perk. If you've been a lawyer for a while, if you've got a good reputation, if you're successful.

Well then, it only stands to reason that you join the Liberal Party and grab a little something on the side. You remember my partner?

MICHAEL: Sure.

DAVE: Well Jim Bannerman and the Liberal Party are like this.

MICHAEL: You're not just talking politics, are you?

DAVE: I see Jim every day. Lynn and I have dinner with him and his wife at least once a month. Their kids and our kids play hockey in our living room. Now get this. In March when we had that late blizzard and I had to get a room downtown, guess who and his girlfriend had a room just down the hall?

MICHAEL: Really?

DAVE: Really, really. I was going to be discreet and pretend I didn't see him but Bannerman ambles over and introduces me to his bimbo. Cool as a cucumber. Like they spent the evening playing Crazy Eights and eating popcorn. It's been going on for over two years. A very sophisticated liaison. Every couple of months Bannerman and bimbo get away for a romantic weekend. This January it was Maui. Pretty nice for some people.

MICHAEL: I guess.

DAVE: I'm twice the lawyer he is. He'd be out on the goddamn street if it weren't for me. All the best accounts are mine. Everybody knows that. So I've been thinking. This is Vancouver, right?

MICHAEL: Right.

DAVE: And my home's in Toronto. Right?

MICHAEL: Right.

DAVE: So?

MICHAEL: So?

DAVE: So I'm away.

MICHAEL: Away?

DAVE: Away from Lynn and the kids.

MICHAEL: Oh. Right.

DAVE: Yeah. Why the hell not? So that's what's been bugging me. Not very bright, is it? What do you think?

MICHAEL: Look, Dave. I haven't been married for eight years, but I know how it must be. If you feel you have to.

DAVE: I don't have to. I just want to.

MICHAEL: Well if you think it might be good for you.

DAVE: I don't think it will be good for me. It'll probably be terrible for me. What's the matter with you? You used to have an answer for everything.

MICHAEL: You know I understand.

DAVE: What do you mean, "understand"? I haven't done anything. There's nothing to understand.

MICHAEL: Well, if you were to do something. Then I'd understand.

DAVE: Well, I probably won't. I'm only thinking about it.

MICHAEL: It's your decision.

DAVE: I know it's my decision.

MICHAEL: I can't make your decision for you.

DAVE: I don't want you to make my decision for me. I want to know how you feel.

MICHAEL: It's not my place, Dave. Look, I'm here. I'm your friend. Whatever you decide to do is fine with me.

DAVE: Terrific, wonderful. Good friend.

DAVE crosses to the bar and pours himself some wine.

Sorry, Mike. You got any grass? I wouldn't mind some grass.

MICHAEL: Sure.

DAVE: I was just thinking out loud. My eighteen-year-old self got the best of me. Who am I kidding? Right? It's not me.

MICHAEL exits to the dining room.

Married eight years and you get an itch. The trick is not to scratch.

There is a knock on the door.

MICHAEL: *(off)* Will you get that, Dave?

DAVE: Yeah.

DAVE answers the door. BETH is there. She is holding a cardboard box and a painting.

BETH: Dave.

DAVE: Beth.

BETH: When did you get in?

DAVE: Last night. You look terrific.

BETH: And you look very prosperous.

DAVE: I am prosperous.

BETH: You're not all here.

DAVE: Only the neurotic half. I left the better half in Toronto. Lynn doesn't like conventions.

BETH: The legal one? At the Four Seasons?

DAVE: With the lawyers loitering in the Garden Lounge. And the hookers loitering at the door.

BETH: Be good, Dave. You're a lawyer, not a travelling salesman.

DAVE: Haha.

BETH: A friend of mine was at the session this morning.

DAVE: Yeah. What's her name?

BETH: Earl Telford.

DAVE: Bright woman taking a man's name in the legal profession. I'll say hello if I bump into him.

BETH: How are Lynn and the boys?

DAVE: Lynn's great. Going to exercise class three times a week. She's going back to work in the fall. She's got kids. Now she wants money. The boys are almost human. I got Josh and Danny skating last winter. And Sean is talking and making a mess of everything. I think we spoil the shrimp rotten. How's work?

BETH: Grade nine this year. Lots of boys. Are all fifteen-year-olds completely obsessed with sex? How were you at that age?

DAVE: I was great in crowds. I could bump into a different pair of breasts every five seconds.

MICHAEL enters.

MICHAEL: Hi honey. I thought I heard you. *(a kiss for BETH)* What's all this?

BETH: It's yours. You left it when you moved out. I thought you might want it back.

DAVE stands up.

MICHAEL: Yeah. Thanks. *(noticing DAVE's reaction)* Well, isn't this great? Dave's going to be in town for a few days.

DAVE: Yup. Dave's in town and in the dark.

BETH: There's another box in the car.

MICHAEL: I'll get it.

BETH: I can manage.

BETH exits.

DAVE: When did this happen?

MICHAEL: About six weeks ago.

DAVE: I just acted like an idiot in front of you.

MICHAEL: You didn't act like an idiot.

DAVE: Why didn't you tell me?

MICHAEL: You know how you get.

DAVE: What does that mean? How the hell do I get?

MICHAEL: Think.

DAVE: I'm a little irked. That's all. What is it with you? Is three years the limit of your involvement with a woman? What are you—God's gift—that you have to spread yourself around? Make up your mind and settle down like the rest of the human race.

MICHAEL: I didn't see any sense in getting into this long-distance. . . Look, Dave, Beth and I have been living together for over three years. We were thinking of buying a house together. And Beth needs a car. And I need dental work. And then there were going to be mortgage payments for God knows how long. And then, of course, given all this mutual financial involvement and human nature, we'd get married and have kids. It's inevitable, isn't it? And then what would we be? Some sitcom in the suburbs. Me and Beth and Ginger and Skip and a big black Lab that craps all over our backyard.

DAVE: Don't be so high and mighty. You're talking about my life. C'mon, Mike. Any eighteen-year-old can give me that crap. You can do better than that.

MICHAEL: Every second Sunday we go to Beth's parents' for dinner. Her dad's this charming old jock who sits around drinking Scotch and sneaking cigarettes and getting a little loaded, and telling me how he bogeyed five and parred fifteen and who died last week and how the market's going to do next week. After dinner her mother, who is the nicest woman in the world but who talks too much and occasionally reminds me of Beth—which scares the shit right out of me—very graciously talks philosophy with me. Kahlil Gibran and Alan Watts and the meaning of life and also the meaning of marriage and just when are Beth and I going to settle down and make it all legal. And it's warm and safe and snug in that living room. With the fire in the hearth and the crocheted throws on the furniture and the chocolate mints in the china dish on the coffee table and all of us sitting around chatting like that wonderful family in the telephone commercial, waiting around for that long-distance call from that other wonderful family sitting around the fire thousands upon thousands of miles away. But, Dave, from Sunday to Sunday, nothing ever changes, and it gets so warm and close in that living room that I feel like I can't move and if I don't get the hell out of there my life will be frozen in maple syrup forever.

DAVE: Why should you get away with it? You're not a kid. You grow old. Your life gets smaller. It's life. There's nothing anyone can do about it.

MICHAEL: You know my history. Nothing ever seems to last.

DAVE: I thought you felt differently about Beth.

MICHAEL: I do.

DAVE: So split. That's taking the bull by the horns.

MICHAEL: We haven't split up. Just because we no longer live together doesn't mean that we've split up. We've managed to work something out.

DAVE: Oh?

MICHAEL: Well there's always more than one way of looking at things, isn't there? If you want to look at it in the worst possible light, well then, yes, we're both screwing around. But that's not the only way of looking at it.

DAVE: Uh-huh.

MICHAEL: I'm not denying there's sex. There's always sex. It's a biological law. There's nothing anyone can do about it. But I don't think sex is central.

DAVE: Sure.

MICHAEL: Look, Dave. It was my idea. Okay? We have an arrangement. Some nights we see each other. Some nights we don't. We're playing it by ear. In another month or so a decision will be made.

DAVE: Can I say something?

MICHAEL: Shoot.

DAVE: Don't be a jerk.

MICHAEL: Wave your finger at me, Dave. That's just what I need.

DAVE: And in the meantime you're single.

MICHAEL: In a manner of speaking, yes.

DAVE: So how's the single life?

MICHAEL: I'm used to having Beth around. I'm on my own only I'm not really on my own. Some days I wake up by myself. Some days I wake up with Beth. Some days I wake up with someone else. It's confusing.

DAVE: Oh, boo hoo.

MICHAEL: I'm not complaining.

DAVE: Uh-huh. And?

MICHAEL: And?

DAVE: How's the sex?

MICHAEL: What do you want? The play-by-play?

DAVE: C'mon.

MICHAEL: Initially it was terrible. Christ, I'd been with one woman for over three years.

DAVE: Yeah, I suppose. But you persevered?

MICHAEL: What did you want me to do? Give up?

DAVE: A good Boy Scout. And now?

MICHAEL: I'm doing all right.

DAVE: You're a great raconteur, Mike. Anyone ever tell you that?

MICHAEL: What do you want, Dave?

DAVE: Nothing. Just wondering if all single men find their sex life as boring.

MICHAEL: I'm not saying it's boring. It's not boring. Look. Dave. I've been with the same woman for more than three years. During that time I've thought about other women. Who wouldn't? And some of those other women have thought about me. I know that. And now, to be perfectly honest, I have the opportunity to do something about what I've only been thinking about.

DAVE: And all I'm asking is how's it been?

MICHAEL: How do you think?

DAVE: What does Beth think of this arrangement?

MICHAEL: She had her reservations. But lately she's beginning to come around.

DAVE: You giving her in-class tests?

MICHAEL: She's enjoying her independence.

DAVE: Who's this Earl guy?

MICHAEL: Who?

DAVE: Earl Telford.

MICHAEL: Just a friend.

DAVE: You know him?

MICHAEL: We've never met. Beth met him swimming. Very buddy-buddy.

DAVE: But she has been seeing other guys?

MICHAEL: What do you mean "seeing"?

DAVE: What do I mean "away"?

MICHAEL: Yes.

DAVE: What do you think about it?

MICHAEL: I don't think about it.

DAVE: What do you mean "you don't think about it"?

MICHAEL: *(intensely)* I mean I don't think about it.

DAVE: Oh. You don't think about it.

MICHAEL: What do you want me to do? Think about it? We have an arrangement. If I'm entitled, Beth's entitled. Why the hell should I let myself get upset?

    BETH enters carrying a box.

BETH: Hello again.

    MICHAEL moves to help her.

MICHAEL: Where'd you park? Burnaby?

BETH: I couldn't get the hatchback open. I had to drag this over the back seat.

DAVE: Michael just told me.

BETH: Yes.

DAVE: You look terrific.

BETH: What did you expect? A red mark on my cheek? My hair falling out in clumps?

DAVE: Ha ha. Very funny. Still have your sense of humour. I was just wondering how things are going.

BETH: Thanks for your concern. It's really not necessary.

DAVE: Good. So. You're having a great time?

MICHAEL: Dave.

BETH: Everything's fine, Dave.

MICHAEL: That's all I said.

DAVE: You think you're typical?

BETH: What?

DAVE: There are some women. . . I mean, I know some who wouldn't be so fine. They'd be full of hate and resentment.

BETH: Is something bothering you?

DAVE: Just wondering about human nature.

BETH: What about it?

DAVE: Maybe there's no such thing.

BETH: You're shocked by our behaviour, aren't you?

DAVE: Surprised, that's all. You're both handling it so well. That's great. Good for you. But I've only seen you two as a couple, never as an arrangement. And I'm a traditional guy. It's kind of confusing. I gotta go. They run that convention like a summer camp. If they don't see me for half an hour, they'll have a search party out combing the woods. You free tonight, Mike?

MICHAEL: For sure.

DAVE: Nine thirty?

MICHAEL: Fine.

DAVE: See ya then. Bye-bye, Beth. Terrific.

MICHAEL: See ya, buddy.

DAVE leaves.

BETH: Well? How was I?

MICHAEL: What?

BETH: Was I cool and casual enough? Sophisticated, enlightened, the woman of the world you've always wanted?

MICHAEL: Beth.

BETH: What's bugging Dave? He seemed very. . . something.

MICHAEL: I just told him about us.

BETH: It seemed like something else. . . Oh. Never mind. It's probably me. Talking about our arrangement always makes me paranoid.

MICHAEL: You're not paranoid.

BETH: Want to bet?

MICHAEL: Dave is away.

BETH: Away?

MICHAEL: He's thinking of getting laid.

BETH: Ah. That explains it.

MICHAEL: He's just thinking about it. He probably won't do anything about it. Dave's always been terrible with women. I even had to get him together with his wife. Lynn was an old girlfriend of mine.

BETH: Very generous. Are you planning on offering my services this time round?

MICHAEL: In Dave's mind he's a sexual loser. A little fooling around may be good for him. A weekend affair. It happens all the time. What's the big deal?

BETH: Big deal? No big deal?

MICHAEL: Lynn doesn't have to know.

BETH: Not terribly original but it'll do. . . Was that what you told him?

MICHAEL: I didn't tell him anything. It's not my place. I'm Dave's friend. Whatever he does, I'm here. I understand. . . What would you have done?

BETH: If Dave was my best buddy and he's as happily married as he seems I would have tied him up until he got this silly idea out of his system.

MICHAEL: *(getting up)* Right.

> MICHAEL *takes a basketball from one of the boxes.*

Thanks for bringing everything over. What prompted this?

BETH: I was cleaning up. It's not my stuff.

MICHAEL: *(picking up the painting)* I thought you liked this.

BETH: I do. But it's yours. I thought you'd like it back.

MICHAEL: Thanks.

MICHAEL examines the wall. He jokingly places the painting against the door.

Here?

BETH shakes her head no. MICHAEL tries a few other places.

BETH: Better.

MICHAEL enters the kitchen.

You remember we're going to Ted and Anne's on Wednesday.

MICHAEL: *(off)* I've got it marked down. How's Ted doing? He likes being a principal?

BETH: "Likes" is not the word. An intelligent career move, as they say in the staff room.

MICHAEL returns with a tool box.

MICHAEL: We're not going to spend another evening listening to them ramble on about sailing. Their boat and their brass and their teak and their heads. *(mocking)* "We've two heads. Sleeps six. Had a lovely little sail up to Secret Cove." I wish to hell they'd stop talking about that boat and take us for a sail on the damn thing. How the hell can Ted afford it? What do they pay principals anyway? I don't know why I bothered getting a Ph.D. I should have gotten a degree in education and joined the local yacht club.

BETH: It's a co-op. They own it with three other couples. And the only reason Ted and Anne went on about sailing was to prevent you from monopolizing the evening by ranting and railing about first-year students who can't read or write. Ted is a high-school principal, after all. I think he showed a lot of restraint.

MICHAEL: Oh? Do I often embarrass you in public?

MICHAEL kisses BETH.

BETH: *(flirtatiously)* You playing basketball at three?

MICHAEL: *(moving away)* Term's over. No more games until the fall. *(with painting)* Here?

BETH: You like your art on the ceiling? So?

MICHAEL: Karen's coming by. We're collaborating on a paper. Milton. How's this?

BETH: Mike, ever hear the expression "eye level"?

MICHAEL: You do it.

BETH: What do you know about Milton?

MICHAEL: Nothing. Karen needed my background in transformational grammar.

BETH: Didn't that kind of paper go out of style years ago?

MICHAEL: Karen found an obscure journal that was interested. In the English department, one publication is as good as another. They don't read articles. They just count them.

MICHAEL takes a vase from one of the boxes.

This is not mine.

BETH: I wasn't sure.

MICHAEL: There's enough of this crap. Whose car did you borrow?

BETH: No one's. I bought one. It's just out front. The little red Rabbit. Now I can drive to Grandma's house.

MICHAEL: You didn't say anything.

BETH: Did I have to?

MICHAEL: No. Was that the down-payment money?

BETH: Part of it.

MICHAEL: It's your money.

BETH: And I need a car. Besides, it takes two incomes to buy a house these days.

MICHAEL: At least. . . It makes a hell of a lot of sense, Beth. Really. Good luck with it. *(gestures at wine)* Want some?

BETH shakes her head no.

So. How does your little red Rabbit run?

BETH: It doesn't. It limps if I'm lucky. It won't start. And when it does, it stalls. And then it won't start again.

MICHAEL: I'll take a look at it.

BETH: It's better now.

MICHAEL: It may happen again.

BETH: Actually, I'm on my way to a friend's. He said he'd have a look at it.

MICHAEL: Didn't know Earl was so handy.

BETH: He feels responsible. He was the one who advised me to buy the car in the first place.

MICHAEL takes a hammer and moves to the wall to hang the painting.

MICHAEL: Well then it's only right that he should shoulder the blame if your little red Rabbit turns out to be a little red lemon... You've been seeing a lot of Earl?

BETH: Yes.

MICHAEL: Still very buddy-buddy?

BETH: More than that.

MICHAEL: *(turns to the wall and begins to hammer in the nail for the painting)* Spatial relation isn't for me. I'm too verbal. Play me Scrabble and I'll wipe you out. Jigsaw puzzles, on the other hand, drive me crazy. Earl, I'm sure, will go far. I see the Liberal Party in his future.

BETH: I don't think the picture is straight.

MICHAEL: *(letting it out)* Well what do you expect anyway? I'm a philosopher, for Chrissake. Not a goddamn interior decorator!

BETH adjusts the picture.

Thanks for your help.

BETH: No charge... Well, I should be going.

MICHAEL: Why don't you join Dave and me tonight?

BETH: I'm sorry, Mike. I've made other plans. Earl's throwing a party.

MICHAEL: Ah. Beth.

BETH: Yes.

MICHAEL: Don't forget your vase.

There is a knock on the door. KAREN enters.

KAREN: I'm early. I know I'm early. You don't mind, do you? I'll just flop down here out of the way. I won't make a peep. These shoes have got to go. Italian women must have the smallest feet in the world.

BETH: Hello, Karen.

KAREN: Beth. Hello. I'm interrupting.

I know I'm interrupting. I'm sorry. Truly sorry. Michael, I'm leaving. Barefoot. These shoes will cripple me. Don't worry about me. I'll just pad up and down your hall.

MICHAEL: Relax.

BETH: I was just on my way out.

MICHAEL: Let me take your coat.

KAREN: Would you mind hanging it up? It cost me an arm and a leg. We're working on this paper together. I need Michael's background in transformational grammar.

BETH: So Michael said.

KAREN: I'm *Paradise Lost.*

MICHAEL: And I'm Past Participles. You must have heard of us. The famous vaudeville team.

MICHAEL exits to the kitchen with the tool box.

KAREN: Did I walk in at a bad time?

BETH: No.

KAREN: You sure? I can still make myself scarce.

BETH: I'm sure.

KAREN: You are coming to our tennis lesson tomorrow?

BETH: I'll be there. Where do you get the time for all your exercise?

KAREN: Do I exercise that much?

BETH: If you're not playing tennis, you're playing squash. And if you're not squashing, you're running in the rain just to clear your head.

KAREN: You're just as bad.

BETH: No I'm not.

KAREN: Maybe so. But you don't need to. You're one of those lucky women. You're thin by nature. By nature I'm a tub. I was born fat and stayed fat for twenty years. Thank God for Weight Watchers and racquet sports. They've made my life bearable.

BETH: Karen, I've never known you as anything other than thin. All you do is talk fat.

KAREN: Really? I talk about my weight a lot?

BETH: I'm sorry. I didn't mean it that way.

KAREN: Yes. Well. Weight-wise things are under control. And I guess generally things are moving forward.

    MICHAEL enters.

However, at present, as I was just about to tell Michael, the shits. But I'll bore you with that after our tennis lesson. Michael, where did you get this hideous vase?

BETH: It's mine.

MICHAEL: She got it from me. It was a birthday present.

BETH: I like it very much.

MICHAEL: And I know you do.

KAREN: Look at that. Two birds with one stone. Sorry, sorry.

MICHAEL: Karen, how about some wine?

KAREN: Michael, you are a lifesaver. Beth? How about you?

BETH: No. I really should be going.

KAREN: *(quietly to BETH)* Beth, you know I play squash with Earl.

BETH: Yes. He says your game is improving.

KAREN: Very cute in white.

BETH: Really?

MICHAEL moves to KAREN with her wine.

KAREN: I've always had this thing for lawyers. My father's a lawyer. Ah, Michael. Thank you. *(to BETH)* You look terrific. Have I told you that? *(a sip)* Nice. I must look a mess. *(to MICHAEL)* I hope you've done your homework.

MICHAEL: Yes. And you?

KAREN: Busy little bee.

BETH: I'll leave you two to it.

KAREN: Why don't we go for brunch after tennis tomorrow?

BETH: I'm spending the afternoon with my parents. It's Mother's Day.

KAREN: Dammit. I'll be by that phone for an hour trying to get through.

BETH: Good luck with the paper. Don't forget Wednesday. Ted and Anne's.

MICHAEL: Right.

BETH leaves.

KAREN: I'm losing a friend.

MICHAEL: Don't be ridiculous.

KAREN: I know it. I'm losing a friend. I don't blame Beth. The way I behave around her I wouldn't like me either.

MICHAEL: What do you mean?

KAREN: Oh nothing. You know me. I get flustered and ramble on. Beth's certainly looking well. When I broke up with Danny I put on twenty pounds and my hair got so frizzy that I wore a scarf on my head for months. Stunning. Absolutely stunning. And it's only six weeks since you split up. She's certainly doing something right.

MICHAEL: *(standing by the window)* We haven't split up.

KAREN: Whatever, Michael. Whatever. What are you looking at out there?

MICHAEL: Beth's been having car trouble.

KAREN: *(crossing to the window)* Oh, she's fine. Peppy little thing, isn't it? Whose is it?

MICHAEL: Beth's. She got it the other day.

KAREN: Oh. . . With what? I thought every spare penny went for that house she wanted.

MICHAEL: Do you have those notes?

KAREN: Big step.

MICHAEL: You've been working hard.

KAREN: Beth forgot her vase. . . It grows on you.

MICHAEL: Let's start with background material. Perhaps some very general information to put Milton and *Paradise Lost* in perspective.

KAREN: A little intellectual history.

MICHAEL: Right.

KAREN: For the Renaissance poets there were two major poetic forms: epic and tragedy. Milton divides the epic into two species: the diffuse epic in twelve books, like *The Iliad* and *The Odyssey,* and the brief type for which *The Book of Job* is the model. Could I have some more wine?

MICHAEL: Sure.

KAREN: I've had a terrible day. Melvin called from Whitehorse. He won't be coming down this weekend. Or any weekend for that matter. He's decided to spend his time entirely in the North. Melvin's found his heart's desire in the Land of the Midnight Sun.

MICHAEL: I'm sorry to hear that.

KAREN: I lost Melvin to the call of the wild. *(taking her wine)* Thanks. There's this teacher in Watson Lake. From what I gather, Melvin heard her howling at the Arctic moon on more than one occasion, but last night he succumbed and tracked her spoor across the frozen tundra. Now they're yelping together and I'm out in the cold. I'm writing the Territorial Council an anonymous letter about Melvin Preschuk, their flying dentist. I think he's made every white woman above the sixtieth parallel. To be perfectly honest, Michael, the only reason I became involved with Melvin in the first place was because I thought, flying or not, a dentist is a dentist. Was I wrong. I should have taken a chance on that attractive but sleazy Greek restaurateur. . . In high school I was the kind of girl who got firsts in everything but physics. I was never very attractive or popular. Too fat to be attractive. Too bright and bitchy to be popular. I think those miserable three years made me far too cautious about sexual matters.

MICHAEL: All of us feel, at one time or another, that we're not as sexually adventurous as we hope.

KAREN: On the other hand, as you well know, I'm not a careful, conventional, introverted woman. I've been finding that the older I get, the less discreet I become.

MICHAEL: And that's very admirable, Karen. Trying to overcome your background that way.

KAREN: I know it sounds silly but it's been good for me. You should try it. It would be good for you. Oh, I know you talk a good game, Michael, but really, deep down, you're very unadventurous.

MICHAEL: Oh, am I?

KAREN: Don't be defensive.

MICHAEL: I'm not being defensive. I'm just trying to understand what you mean by "sexually unadventurous." Are you talking technique? What I do when I do it. Are you talking taste? Who I do it to and why. Or are you talking totals? How many I do it to and how often.

KAREN: I was talking timidity, and don't be such a philosopher.

MICHAEL: So. There were two major poetic forms in the Renaissance: epic and tragedy.

KAREN: Most Renaissance critics regard the epic as the greater form. This is the result of the epic's larger intellectual scope. Of course things have changed. I'm no longer an awkward, plain teenager. I'm an attractive, successful career woman. Do you find me attractive?

MICHAEL: Of course I find you attractive.

KAREN: Don't humour me.

MICHAEL: I wasn't humouring you. You're very attractive.

KAREN: As an object of sexual desire?

MICHAEL: Only good breeding and an appreciation of high fashion prevents me from ripping the clothes from your body.

KAREN: Thanks.

MICHAEL: Karen. We're friends.

KAREN: And you're a hypocrite. Last Christmas.

MICHAEL: You were missing Melvin. I was missing Beth. It was the festive season. We were just exchanging greetings. Besides, nothing happened.

KAREN: That faculty party.

MICHAEL: It was spring. The trees were budding. Everything was in blossom. More season's greetings. . . I was drinking brandy.

KAREN: Michael, if that drunk, obnoxious, funny-looking man hadn't stumbled by. . .

MICHAEL: That drunk, obnoxious, funny-looking man just happens to be the pumpernickel head of the philosophy department, and in his more lucid moments he is one of the world's foremost Kant scholars.

KAREN: You're very good at confusing the issue, aren't you?

MICHAEL: I think the most important thing for you to remember, in terms of the paper, is that a theory of transformational grammar must begin by making a fundamental distinction between linguistic competence and linguistic performance.

KAREN: You're a very reasonable man, Michael.

MICHAEL: Well, reason before passion, don't you think?

KAREN: Not always. Sometimes it isn't reasonable to be reasonable. Sometimes we just have to say to hell with reason, to hell with obligation. I'm going to do what I damn well please and everything and everyone be damned.

MICHAEL: Linguistic performance is the actual use of language in concrete situations, as opposed to linguistic competence, which is the speaker's knowledge of his language.

KAREN: Arrangements like yours usually mean the end. They're the way decent, honest people fool themselves into thinking they still have something left. You and Beth have been making each other miserable for months.

MICHAEL: I was finding the relationship claustrophobic. I needed more freedom.

KAREN: And now you have it.

MICHAEL: Yes.

KAREN: And Beth has it.

MICHAEL: Yes.

KAREN: And I have it.

Short pause. MICHAEL doesn't respond.

Okay. . . We get along so wonderfully. I thought it would be a shame to waste it. When you really think about it, it does make so much sense. . . Traditionally the epic begins at a low point in the middle of the action. In *Paradise Lost* the low point is the point furthest from God. . . Michael, our friendship is something very special to me. I would hate for this little "episode" to cause it any lasting damage. . . I'll read you some of this. You should have an idea of how it sounds. "Of man's first disobedience, and the fruit / Of that forbidden tree whose mortal taste / Brought death into the world, and all our woe. . ." Well, perhaps Milton said it all. I don't know what came over me. I'm really very, very sorry.

MICHAEL: *(moving to KAREN)* You're right. It does make a hell of a lot of sense. And we do get along very well. I'm not saying we can do everything we want. That would be adolescent. On the other hand, the limits to human behaviour are a lot less strict than some people make out. And what could the difficulties be? Especially if we're intelligent and educated, and we try to be as frank and as candid as possible.

MICHAEL kisses KAREN. While in the embrace KAREN moves the vase from the couch to the floor.

Scene Two

About nine thirty on Saturday evening. MICHAEL *and* DAVE *are standing over a wastepaper basket at stage right.* DAVE *is holding a glass of wine.* MICHAEL's *wine is on the desk at stage left.*

MICHAEL: I don't believe this. I really don't believe this.

DAVE: I don't care what you believe.

MICHAEL: I was here. I was in the room. I saw it. It went right in. Swoosh. And you're going to stand there and tell me, right to my face, that it bounced.

DAVE *takes a Nerf ball from the wastepaper basket.*

DAVE: It bounced. Bounce. And it doesn't count.

MICHAEL: Dave, tell me. How did I miss it? Was the sun in my eyes? Maybe it was the blond in the stands. Maybe this is all a bad dream and you're not here at all.

DAVE: Don't give me your philosophy, Mike.

MICHAEL: Okay, Dave. Explain it to me.

DAVE: You blinked.

MICHAEL: Right.

DAVE: You blinked when it bounced. No complicated explanation. Everyone blinks.

MICHAEL: You're cheating, Dave. You're cheating your best and oldest friend. And I'm disappointed in you as a friend and a human being.

MICHAEL *takes the Nerf ball from* DAVE.

But I can see why you're a very successful lawyer.

DAVE: Take it over.

MICHAEL: I don't want to take it over. I want the point.

DAVE: Take the point.

MICHAEL: I don't need you to give me the point. I deserve the point.

DAVE: And it's yours if you want it.

MICHAEL: Well I don't want it. I won't take it over and I won't take the point.

DAVE: Take it over. That strikes me as a reasonable compromise.

MICHAEL: Forget it.

DAVE: Four–one.

MICHAEL: Five–one.

DAVE: Four–one.

MICHAEL: It should have been six–one. But we decided that since it's so hard to tell whether a Nerf ball bounces that it's five–one, Christ almighty.

MICHAEL is about to throw. DAVE breaks his concentration.

DAVE: What time does this thing start?

MICHAEL: I told you. Ten thirty. All I could get were tickets for the second show.

MICHAEL is about to throw.

DAVE: Game's to ten, right?

MICHAEL: Seven.

DAVE: Seven. Right.

MICHAEL hesitates.

Okay. Take your shot. You're delaying the game.

MICHAEL: Jesus.

MICHAEL throws. He sinks it.

DAVE: Fluke.

MICHAEL: You're a sweet guy, Dave. Anyone ever tell you that?

They exchange places.

DAVE: Yeah. Lynn tells me that all the time. Okay, Dave. Relax. Don't think. Let the ball find the target.

DAVE throws. He misses.

Shit. If this were Tokyo my life would be so much simpler. It would be stupid though. A wife, children, a family. To risk it all over a piece of ass. Idiotic.

MICHAEL returns the ball.

Have I ever won at this?

MICHAEL: Once. Nineteen seventy. I had a broken wrist.

DAVE: Very funny. What is it? A buck a point?

MICHAEL: Two bucks a point and a five-dollar bonus to the winner. And it was your idea to play for money.

DAVE throws. He misses.

DAVE: I'll take it over.

MICHAEL: What?

DAVE: I'll take it over.

MICHAEL: Why?

DAVE: The music threw me off.

MICHAEL: What music?

DAVE: The music from the party down the hall.

MICHAEL: Dave.

DAVE: It's louder over here. And just as I was about to throw there was a sudden increase in volume.

MICHAEL: I didn't hear it.

DAVE: Well that stands to reason, doesn't it?

MICHAEL: Why?

DAVE: Because if you can miss seeing a Nerf ball bounce then you can sure as hell miss hearing a burst of music burst.

MICHAEL: What are you saying, Dave? That sometime today I've had a cerebral hemorrhage?

DAVE: Okay, okay. I'll take it over.

MICHAEL: Don't take it over. Take the point.

MICHAEL gives DAVE the ball.

DAVE: No, no. I want to be fair. Don't be a big shot, Mike. I only want what I deserve. You know, you and Bannerman should get together. You've got a lot in common. You've both managed to work out very nice arrangements. Christ, if Lynn had so much as an inkling that I'd been with another woman she'd be out on the town making the Blue Jays to get even.

MICHAEL: Christ.

DAVE throws. He sinks it.

DAVE: I'll win this game yet. So three more shots this round?

MICHAEL: Two more. You've taken three.

DAVE: Yeah. Well, live and learn. You know who I've been thinking about all weekend? Brenda Lipton. The last of my single life. I went out in style. What the body of Brenda Lipton had that made it so unique was economy. Now don't get me wrong. I'm not talking petite. She was a big girl, was she not?

MICHAEL: Taller than me, I think.

DAVE: Yeah. Tall and long. Just the way I like them.

MICHAEL: You and Paul Simon.

DAVE: Brenda was a wonderful girl, right?

MICHAEL: Right.

DAVE: Nothing but the essentials. An absolutely no-bullshit body. Long legs. Firm bum. Nice big boobs.

MICHAEL: Dave. Spare me.

DAVE: Mike. First of all, I've got good taste and a way with words. And second of all, you've got a present. All I've got is a past. She was a gymnast or a contortionist or something?

MICHAEL: A dancer.

DAVE: A dancer. Right. And double jointed, and she could do things I still remember. With her head facing one way and my head facing another.

MICHAEL: Like a Japanese woodcut. One time I put my back out.

Pause.

DAVE: I'd forgotten about that. But that's all right. Now I remember. You went out with her first. You set me up. You were a good friend. Like always. Thanks for reminding me, I appreciate it.

MICHAEL: I'm sorry. I thought you remembered. It seemed like that kind of conversation. C'mon, take your shot.

DAVE: What do I owe you?

MICHAEL: Forget it.

DAVE: Don't tell me to forget it. What do I owe you?

MICHAEL: Eight bucks.

DAVE: And the bonus makes thirteen. Here's twenty. Go water your bonsai. You got any more wine?

MICHAEL: I'm out. How about a Scotch?

DAVE: *(a nod)* When does that show we're going to get out?

MICHAEL: I don't know. Midnight, I guess.

DAVE: Let's not hang around. There's a party I'd like to catch.

MICHAEL: Sure.

DAVE: *(taking his drink)* All I have is an address, but I told some of the Vancouver guys I'd drop round to say goodbye.

MICHAEL: What's the matter? You don't like my Scotch?

DAVE: I'd like soda.

MICHAEL: It doesn't need soda. Try it.

DAVE: I like my Scotch with soda.

MICHAEL: Dave, I'm telling you, it's Glenfiddich. It doesn't need soda. Just have it neat. If you don't like it I'll get you soda.

DAVE: Christ.

MICHAEL: Look, Dave, why ruin good liquor? If you're going to drown it in soda you might as well throw in Kool-Aid and drink it holding your nose.

DAVE: And you don't judge. What is all this Scotch business? I don't like Scotch; I've never liked Scotch. Jim Bannerman drinks Scotch. The Liberal

Party drinks Scotch. I'm a Canadian, goddamn it! I drink rye. And proud of it. It's good for every occasion. You want to drink cheap—Three Star and ginger. You want to drink every day—CC and soda. You want to drink special—Crown Royal on the rocks. Don't give me this Glenfiddich crap. No wonder this goddamn country is falling apart!

    DAVE *drinks.*

MICHAEL: Well?

DAVE: Where's your Kool-Aid?

MICHAEL: There's soda in the fridge.

    DAVE *exits to the kitchen.*

(calling to DAVE*)* I'm going to shave.

DAVE: *(off)* Yeah.

    MICHAEL *exits to the bathroom.* DAVE *returns. There is a pause before a knock on the door.* DAVE *gets it.* JACKIE *is there.*

JACKIE: Hello.

DAVE: Hello.

JACKIE: My name is Jacqueline Lemieux.

DAVE: Dave Lerner.

JACKIE: Hi David. I'm a friend of Jim's. Jim Loadman? Blond guy down the hall?

DAVE: Yeah?

JACKIE: Jim's throwing this huge party. Wall-to-wall people. And it's only nine thirty. Listen. I don't know how to say this. This is going to sound strange no matter what. I'm a member of an organization called Kinergetics. Does the name Kinergetics ring a bell?

DAVE: No.

JACKIE: Kinergetics began here in Vancouver about two years ago and lately it's been really catching fire.

DAVE: You're selling something?

JACKIE: Very funny. Actually Kinergetics is very mainstream. Lots of professional people and people in the arts and media. Suzy Brissenden? She's a sculptor. Had a show at that gallery on Pender Street. Some very unusual pieces.

DAVE: I'm from out of town.

JACKIE: Becky Selig? She was with the Royal Winnipeg Ballet for ten years.

DAVE: I'm from Toronto.

JACKIE: Becky's the driving force behind Kinergetics.

DAVE: What's Kinergetics?

JACKIE: It's a movement place.

DAVE: A movement place?

JACKIE: People go there to move. By themselves. In couples. In groups. They move together. They touch each other. They relax. It's very therapeutic.

DAVE: Uh-huh.

JACKIE: Bernard Hedley. He's an older man, been painting for over forty years, kind of a mentor figure for me. He suggested I take it. Bernard thinks there's an intimate connection between body awareness and visual imagination. I think it's helping. Tuesday I went up like Baryshnikov and I came down like a ton of bricks. And tonight, just when I thought I was through with it, my back is killing me again. And, like I said, it's wall-to-wall people down the hall. So what I'm wondering is, can I lie down? I'll just be ten minutes.

DAVE: Sure. The bedroom's this way.

JACKIE: Now you're really going to think I'm a nutcase. My chiropractor recommended it. He's very progressive. And it's been written up in some very prestigious medical journals by some of the world's most famous orthopaedic surgeons. I've sworn off beds. I use the floor.

DAVE: The floor?

JACKIE: We spend a third of our life lying down. Why shouldn't a lying posture be as important as standing posture? All I need is six square feet.

DAVE: Floor space is waste space.

JACKIE moves to the floor.

JACKIE: I've always liked the name David.

DAVE: David and Goliath.

JACKIE: David Macfarlane. Do you know him?

DAVE: I don't think so.

JACKIE: Architect. From Toronto. What do you do?

DAVE: I'm a lawyer.

JACKIE: Bill Maguire?

DAVE: Sorry.

JACKIE: He's my partner in movement class. Bill's a very sensual man as well as being a very successful lawyer. I don't think I've ever met a man with more eclectic tastes. Lawyers are often surprising.

JACKIE stretches.

Don't let me interrupt.

DAVE: No problem. *(after a beat)* So. How do you like it down there?

JACKIE: It's a very comfortable rug.

DAVE: Persian. They're very comfortable.

JACKIE exercises.

I've slept on the floor. In the past. I still do. Not as often as I like. You know how it is. You're a successful lawyer. You get busy. You don't have time to sleep on the floor.

JACKIE: I've been thinking of giving up beds permanently.

DAVE: Uh-huh.

JACKIE: It's healthier.

JACKIE exercises. DAVE watches.

DAVE: You're right. Healthier. Nice jeans.

JACKIE: *(indifferent)* Calvin Klein.

DAVE: They fit well.

JACKIE: Size eight. . . Those are very unusual shoes.

DAVE: You think so? Gucci.

JACKIE: Very nice.

DAVE: Size eight and a half. D.

MICHAEL enters.

Ah, Mike. Jackie, this is my buddy, Michael Kaye. This is his place. Mike, this is the lovely and charming Jacqueline Lemieux.

JACKIE: Hello.

MICHAEL: Hi.

DAVE: Jackie was at a party just down the hall. She has a bad back but there was no place to lie down there. So she's going to use your floor for a while.

MICHAEL: Sure. What seems to be the problem?

JACKIE: Muscle inflammation. Lumbar region. It needs support. I strained it at Kinergetics. That's a movement place. People go there to move.

MICHAEL: Uh-huh.

JACKIE: I'll just be ten minutes.

MICHAEL: That's fine. Will you excuse us?

DAVE: We'll just be a sec, Jackie.

MICHAEL and DAVE move away from JACKIE.

MICHAEL: What's she doing here?

DAVE: Don't worry about it.

MICHAEL: We're going out.

DAVE: We've got lots of time. The woman is in a lot of pain.

MICHAEL: Why on my living-room rug?

DAVE: Why not? She helps the decor.

JACKIE: *(calling to MICHAEL)* I like your art.

MICHAEL: What?

JACKIE: Is that a Dondell?

MICHAEL: That's right.

JACKIE: It must be one of Jack's older pieces. What do you do, Michael?

MICHAEL: I teach philosophy at the university.

JACKIE: Aesthetics is my interest. What's your field?

MICHAEL: Philosophy of language.

JACKIE: Words and things.

MICHAEL: In a manner of speaking.

DAVE: And you, Jackie? What do you do for a living?

JACKIE: I paint. So I notice good art when I see it.

DAVE: Have you had any shows?

JACKIE: I'm just starting out.

DAVE: I've got a friend who's an artist. It's a tough life. Only the best make a living at it.

JACKIE: Money's not everything. Besides, I'm optimistic.

MICHAEL: That's the spirit.

JACKIE: Hope springs eternal.

MICHAEL: You can't rush these things.

JACKIE: You shouldn't.

MICHAEL: It's all developmental.

JACKIE: A slow, painful process. Ow.

MICHAEL: What is it?

JACKIE: Muscle spasm.

MICHAEL: Oh. Can I get you something?

JACKIE: I have some Darvon at Jim's but I've taken a few already. I'll just have to grin and bear it. . . There is something. Can you pop my back? My chiropractor does it. It sets me up for hours.

MICHAEL: I've never done this before. What do I have to do?

DAVE: Actually, and I don't want to brag, I have loads of experience.

MICHAEL: That's all right, Dave.

JACKIE turns on her stomach.

JACKIE: Kneel down. One leg on either side of me.

MICHAEL: Yes.

JACKIE: Place your hands really low on my back.

MICHAEL: Really low?

JACKIE: That's right.

MICHAEL: This okay?

JACKIE: Lower.

MICHAEL hesitates.

DAVE: You want me to do it?

MICHAEL: No thanks, Dave.

JACKIE: Now make sure your hands are on either side of my backbone.

MICHAEL: It's hard to find your backbone all the way down here.

DAVE: Right there.

MICHAEL: It's all right, Dave.

JACKIE: Now with the insides of your wrists facing each other and your fingers spread, lean forward with all your might.

MICHAEL: Hang on a second.

DAVE: Like this.

MICHAEL: Dave. Now what?

JACKIE: Just put your weight on your hands and lean forward.

MICHAEL attempts it awkwardly. JACKIE moans loudly.

MICHAEL: How's that?

JACKIE: Not good.

DAVE: Let me try.

JACKIE: It's all right. It helped a little.

DAVE: So, Jackie. Where would you be on this Saturday night if you weren't lying on the floor?

JACKIE: I'm at a party. Jim's. Just down the hall.

DAVE: Oh. Right. Sorry.

JACKIE: I usually work Saturday nights.

DAVE: No kidding? You paint away your Saturday nights? Art's important, Jackie. But all work and no play.

JACKIE: I'm a cocktail waitress.

DAVE: That's interesting. Where do you work?

JACKIE: Creole Pete's.

DAVE: I don't know it.

MICHAEL: Their chicken gumbo is out of this world.

JACKIE: There's nothing like it.

DAVE: It must be a demanding job being a cocktail waitress.

JACKIE: It's all right.

MICHAEL: It gets an interesting crowd.

JACKIE: That's the best thing about it. Meeting all those unusual people.

DAVE: How do you do it? There must be a trick to it. Keeping all those glasses and bottles upright on your tray, not spilling a drop, threading your way through a crowded room.

MICHAEL: Funny. I've never seen you there.

JACKIE: I think I've seen you around.

MICHAEL: Really?

JACKIE: Yes. I think so.

MICHAEL: You do look kind of familiar now that I think about it.

DAVE: Do you hold your tray like this? Or like this?

MICHAEL: Looking for work, Dave? I usually eat there on Wednesday.

JACKIE: I have the section near the windows.

MICHAEL: I'll look for you.

DAVE: Mike, get the lady a drink. Be a good host. You want a drink, don't you, Jackie?

JACKIE: *(to DAVE)* I wouldn't mind some water. Perrier with a twist?

DAVE: Mike.

MICHAEL: Coming up. Excuse me, Jackie.

MICHAEL goes. JACKIE exercises.

DAVE: Jackie.

JACKIE: Yes.

DAVE: It's Saturday night. I was thinking.

JACKIE: Do you know that evolutionarily speaking the backbone is the oldest bone we have?

DAVE: Jackie, listen.

DAVE hesitates.

JACKIE: Yes.

DAVE: I'm from Toronto. Have I told you that?

JACKIE: Uh-huh. Do you travel a lot?

DAVE: Uh. Yeah.

JACKIE: That's a big dream of mine. To have the time and the money to just travel.

DAVE: I've been around. All over the world. One day Toronto. The next Vancouver, LA, New York. Last week I was in London. That's the kind of practice I have. Lots of multinationals. And right now, like I was saying, I'm not in Toronto. I'm away.

JACKIE: "Away"?

DAVE: From Toronto.

JACKIE: Oh. . . I've been to Toronto.

DAVE: Great town. No place like it in the world. And I've seen them all.

JACKIE: It's not my kind of city. All that concrete and cars and people. I like Vancouver with the mountains and the vistas and the natural grandeur.

DAVE: You're right there. You sure as hell don't get your mountains and your vistas and your natural grandeur on the corner of Bay and King. My wife always complains about that.

JACKIE: You're married?

DAVE: Yeah. Married. Eight years. Three boys.

JACKIE: That's nice.

DAVE: Yeah. Terrific.

MICHAEL enters with Perrier.

MICHAEL: Here we go.

JACKIE: Thanks.

MICHAEL: I'm sorry. Can I offer you anything to eat?

JACKIE: No thanks. I'm watching my weight.

DAVE: *(mocking, angrily)* Calvin Klein. Size three.

DAVE exits to the dining room.

MICHAEL: What was all that about?

JACKIE: Your friend's married. He lives in Toronto. With his wife and three kids. He's "away."

MICHAEL: Shit.

DAVE enters.

Dave.

DAVE: Where are those joints?

MICHAEL: Dave.

DAVE: Where are those joints?!

MICHAEL: Right-hand drawer.

DAVE returns to the dining room.

JACKIE: He made his move as soon as you left. You're not married, are you?

MICHAEL: No.

JACKIE: I didn't think so. You don't have the *ambiance*.

MICHAEL: Look, Jackie. Things are getting a little complicated. Maybe you should. . .

JACKIE: I like your place, Michael. It makes its statement. Sophisticated, intelligent, but not uptight.

JACKIE opens the door to the bedroom and peeks in.

MICHAEL: Jackie.

DAVE: *(off)* Matches!

There is a knock on the door.

MICHAEL: What?

MICHAEL answers the door. BETH strides into the living room.

BETH: Hello.

MICHAEL: Hello.

JACKIE: Hello.

MICHAEL: Oh. Beth, this is Jackie, uh. . .

JACKIE: Lemieux.

MICHAEL: Lemieux. Jackie, this is Beth Gordon.

JACKIE: Hi.

BETH: Hello.

JACKIE lies down on the rug.

MICHAEL: Jackie has a terrible problem with her back. I just met her ten minutes ago. She was at a party down the hall. She needs a place to lie down. Dave and I are just on our way out. He's in the dining room toking up.

DAVE: *(off)* Where are the goddamn matches?

MICHAEL: See. Well. How's the car?

BETH: No better. Stall, start, stall, start. It stalled just now and I couldn't get it started. I'm amazed I get anywhere at all.

MICHAEL: You should speak to your dealer about that car.

BETH: Either I get a replacement or they return my money.

MICHAEL: Exactly.

BETH: If only I could run my life on that straightforward a basis.

MICHAEL: Jackie, would you mind?

JACKIE begins to get up.

BETH: What is it, Michael? Do you think I'll embarrass you in front of your guests?

JACKIE lies back down.

I just came from my parents'.

MICHAEL: Ah. How are they?

BETH: Mother invited me over for *tea.*

MICHAEL: Right.

BETH: I haven't seen very much of her lately. It wasn't very pleasant. I told Mother not to worry. You and I just needed some time to work the kinks out of our relationship. Mother said that she and Father have been happily married for over thirty years and they never once used the word "relationship." I said times have changed. People aren't the same. Pressures are very different. We have an arrangement. We're going to work things out. "Arrangement" bothered Mother. She said that except for its musical use, the term "arrangement" shouldn't be used in polite society. She asked me if it was one of your words. I said it was.

MICHAEL: Would you like me to give her a call?

BETH: She doesn't want to talk to you. She wants to wash your mouth out with soap.

MICHAEL: Jackie.

JACKIE gets up, takes her glass, heads for the hall, then, remembering her glass, returns to the kitchen.

BETH: Actually, to be honest, in spite of everything, she still seems to be fond of you. She invited you to dinner tomorrow night. I said you couldn't make it.

MICHAEL: Why?

BETH: Because I don't want to sit around the table with my family, on Mother's Day, in the house where I grew up, and pretend that everything is hunky-dory between you and me knowing all the while that I'm seeing you and Earl, and you're seeing me and God knows how many other women. I haven't felt as guilty since I was eighteen and hiding my pills and lying to my parents about just what I was doing out until four in the morning. Jesus Christ, I'm thirty years old and I feel like a teenager. I don't know what I'm doing. Half the time I don't know whether to laugh or cry. This goddamn arrangement. Smiling at each other and pretending we're these sophisticated, enlightened people. It makes me nauseous.

MICHAEL: I thought we decided not to have this conversation.

BETH: You decided. I capitulated.

MICHAEL: I seem to remember it as a mutual agreement. . . Beth. There's no point in rehashing things. Talking about it only makes us both upset.

BETH: Talking about it makes me upset. . . It's just another philosophical conversation to you.

MICHAEL: Now is not the time.

BETH: I don't know how you can live like this. Sweeping everything under the rug. What is it with you? The only position you're happy in is sitting on the fence.

MICHAEL: Okay, okay. Let's talk.

BETH: I don't want to talk. I want to scream and yell and break things over your head.

MICHAEL: That won't solve anything.

BETH: It will make me feel a hell of a lot better.

MICHAEL: Beth, what is it you want from me?

BETH: I love you. I want you to make up your goddamn mind.

DAVE enters with an unlit joint and some matches.

DAVE: Hi, Beth. Want some of this?

BETH: No thanks.

DAVE: Mike?

MICHAEL turns away. DAVE talks to BETH.

How are you doing? You're looking terrific as usual.

BETH: Thanks, Dave.

DAVE: Why don't you join us tonight?

BETH: I'm sorry, but I have other plans.

DAVE: That's too bad. It would have been nice to spend some time with you.

BETH: Thank you, Dave. I appreciate that.

BETH crosses to the door, then moves to the phone.

May I use your phone?

MICHAEL: Of course.

BETH looks through the Yellow Pages.

You looking for anything in particular?

BETH: I'm calling a cab.

MICHAEL: Take my car. We don't need it.

BETH: No.

MICHAEL: Why not?

BETH: I don't want it.

MICHAEL: Okay, okay. Let me look at your car.

BETH: I don't need your help.

MICHAEL: Beth, please. This isn't doing any good. I don't have to see Dave tonight. He'll understand. You and I can have that talk.

BETH: Why bother, Michael? You'll put things off and I'll give in. We're not the best of people, are we? You're scared and I'm weak. But that's who we are. We might as well make the best of it.

BETH looks through the phone book. MICHAEL crosses to DAVE.

MICHAEL: *(hurrying DAVE across the stage)* Give her a hand.

DAVE: What?

MICHAEL: Give her a hand with the car.

DAVE: I don't know anything about cars.

MICHAEL: *(to BETH)* Dave will give you a hand.

DAVE: I'll have you going in no time.

BETH leaves.

MICHAEL: Just try, will you?

DAVE goes. After a moment MICHAEL moves to the window. JACKIE enters.

JACKIE: Resentment, resentment, resentment.

MICHAEL: What?

JACKIE: Resentment. Your ex-girlfriend's reaction. You can't let it get you down. We do what we have to do. If people resent and can't forgive that's too bad for them. We just have to accept it as one of the consequences of doing what we want to do.

MICHAEL: Jackie, I'd really like to be alone.

JACKIE: Jeffrey Fiskin. Psychotherapist. Very eclectic. Jung, Freud, theatre games, body work. Once he made me listen to *Blonde on Blonde* for an entire afternoon. When's the last time you spent four hours listening to Bob Dylan? Jeffrey Fiskin is a very perceptive man. I recommend him wholeheartedly.

MICHAEL: Jackie, I don't know you. You've been lying on my living-room floor for the last half hour. I just had a falling out with my best buddy over your lumbar region. You saw what happened between me and my girlfriend or whatever she is. Now don't you think it's time for you to leave?

JACKIE: I throw up. Every couple of weeks. Things are going along smoothly. Then, all of a sudden, vomit. I'm sweating. I can hardly move. I feel like I'm going to die. Jeffrey says it's a hysterical reaction. He says I'm still trying to deal with Burnaby. It's really nothing that unusual. Just your run-of-the-mill suburban malaise. Environmentally I was being understimulated. Artistically I was being underutilized. Intellectually I was being underexercised. But you must have heard it all before. It's the same old story. I was born there. And I went to school there. And I met a guy there. And I was going to raise a family there. And then it hit me. I was going to live and die knowing only Burnaby. But Burnaby's not me. And I'm not Burnaby. So now, every couple of weeks or so, when Burnaby rears its ugly head, I throw up and feel like I'm going to die.

JACKIE stifles a belch.

MICHAEL: You're not going to throw up now, are you?

JACKIE: I'm not going to throw up. I haven't felt as good in months. Too much Perrier water. Can I use your bathroom?

JACKIE exits to the bathroom. Pause. There is a knock on the door. KAREN sticks her head into the apartment.

KAREN: Hello.

MICHAEL: Karen. Hello.

KAREN enters. She is carrying a bouquet of flowers and a bottle of wine.

KAREN: I was driving by and I saw the light. Well, to be frank, I bought the flowers and the wine first. I was hoping you'd be home and luck was with me. Narcissus. It's all over for the tulips and the daffodils. Nice. Aren't they? I stole them. Figuratively. There's this Chinese grocery on South Granville that has the freshest flowers and the cheapest prices.

KAREN offers the flowers to MICHAEL.

MICHAEL: Thank you.

KAREN: You know me and sexual stereotyping. *(with wine)* The talk of the English department. A full-bodied red with a pleasing bouquet. Also politically correct. From the now-socialist France. Also, as French wines go, very cheap.

KAREN offers the wine.

MICHAEL: Thank you.

KAREN: I thought we might go for a walk. It's a lovely night. We could have the wine on the beach.

MICHAEL: Sorry. My best and oldest buddy is in from Toronto. He'll be back any second.

KAREN: Oh. Well then. I hope my behaviour this afternoon. . .

MICHAEL: No. It's not that.

KAREN: Really, Michael, I don't know what came over me.

MICHAEL: Karen, please.

KAREN: To become so anxiety-ridden and uptight and unresponsive at such a time. It couldn't have been much fun for you. I owe you an apology.

MICHAEL: You're making far too much of it.

KAREN: Don't demean me by making light of it.

MICHAEL: Right. Sorry.

KAREN: I've always hated the kind of woman who behaves that way. I hope you don't think that I'm the kind of woman who's incapable of having a casual affair with a good friend.

MICHAEL: I don't think that, Karen. I know that you're capable of having a casual affair with just about any man you set your mind to.

KAREN: Yes. And having a hell of a good time while I'm at it.

MICHAEL: Well, then, that goes without saying, doesn't it?

KAREN: I guess I was feeling a little guilty.

MICHAEL: Well, sometimes it gets the better of us.

KAREN: It's a disgusting emotion. And there's absolutely no place for it in this situation. Michael, I've thought about my behaviour this afternoon. I understand it. Both emotionally and intellectually. I really have come to grips with it. And I can assure you that that kind of neurotic episode will never happen again.

MICHAEL: Good. Then the afternoon wasn't a complete waste of time. . . I didn't mean that, Karen. What I meant was that when people are friendly with each other and like each other and are curious about each other, well, then, sometimes, they do things to each other that maybe they should do only to others.

KAREN: I'm not looking for an intense emotional involvement. What I have in mind is a very casual, very informal, adult affair. No demands. No responsibilities. Just good, clean fun. Nothing will change between us, Michael. Nothing. Except that we'll sleep together on a regular basis.

MICHAEL: Karen, I'm sure you're aware that people sometimes convince themselves they feel one thing when really they feel something completely different. And then sometimes we blow things up out of all proportion because, perhaps, we're reacting to the past. Danny, Melvin the flying dentist. So I think it would be best if we waited a few days to find out how we really feel. Okay?

KAREN: Okay.

MICHAEL: I'll call you Monday.

KAREN: Okay. Just think about it, Michael. That's all I ask.

JACKIE enters from the bathroom.

JACKIE: Michael, I'm seeing Jeffrey on Thursday. Oh, hi. . .

KAREN: What do you do, Michael? Give out lottery tickets as door prizes? Give every tenth woman a free pair of pantyhose?

MICHAEL: Jackie and I met this evening under the most unusual circumstances. Jackie was at a party down the hall.

JACKIE: At Jim Loadman's? He's a foreman at the Alberta Wheat Pool, but most people know him as a shortstop. In the Industrial League? Last year he was voted most valuable player.

KAREN: You must keep track. How do you do it? Steal the labels from their panties and display them, mounted like butterflies, in a large red album?

MICHAEL: Jackie has a terrible problem with her back. There was no place to lie down at the party.

JACKIE: Wall-to-wall people.

MICHAEL: So I let her use the floor.

KAREN: Christ!

KAREN turns away. MICHAEL throws JACKIE a look. JACKIE exits to the bedroom.

MICHAEL: Karen, listen. . .

KAREN: There are so few decent men around these days. They're all fags or running around after eighteen-year-olds.

MICHAEL: I'm sure you haven't exhausted all the men in the city.

KAREN: Michael, you are so damn blind about everything. I've been screwing myself silly for months. Christ, if something good doesn't happen soon I'll start making it with my students. Michael, I know you. I understand you. It'll work. I know it will. Goddamn you, Michael. Why do I have to demean myself like this in front of you?

MICHAEL: I'm sorry. I didn't know you felt this way. Or maybe I did and conveniently ignored it. You were free. I was free. At the time there seemed no reason not to. It was a mistake, Karen. Let's not make it worse.

KAREN walks to the door. She turns.

KAREN: By the way, Michael, have you ever met Earl? He is one of the most dynamic, charming, attractive, tall, broad-shouldered, smouldering dark-eyed men I have ever had the pleasure of being in the same room with. What is it about men of that age? They have a drive—an energy—that men lose when they hit thirty.

MICHAEL: It's called "naïveté" and they're well rid of it.

KAREN: I think he's putting it to your girlfriend. It's the first intelligent thing Beth has done since you moved out. Face it, Michael. It's over between you two.

MICHAEL: I hurt you. Now you hurt me.

KAREN: That's about it.

DAVE enters.

DAVE: Hello.

KAREN: Hello. Goodbye.

KAREN goes.

DAVE: Who was that?

MICHAEL: Karen Sperling. How's Beth?

DAVE: I don't know. Karen Sperling. What does she do?

MICHAEL: She teaches English at the university. What do you mean "you don't know"?

DAVE: I mean "I don't know."

MICHAEL: Did she get going all right?

DAVE: Yeah. Maybe her choke is sticking. Maybe her carburetor is lousy. Don't ask me about cars.

DAVE enters the kitchen to clean his hands.

MICHAEL: But you saw her drive away?

DAVE: *(off)* Yes.

MICHAEL: Did she say where she was going?

DAVE: *(off)* This Earl fella. He's throwing a party.

MICHAEL: Right.

DAVE returns from the kitchen, wiping his hands with a paper towel.

DAVE: I know it's none of my business, Mike. But do you know what you're doing?

MICHAEL: I know what I'm doing. I know exactly what I'm doing. I don't know what the hell I'm doing. What am I doing?

DAVE: Jeez, Mike. I don't know what to say. I haven't been single for eight years, but I know how it must be. Look. If you want to get married and have kids, that's fine with me. And if you want to put an ad in the paper and make it with three bald women and a fox terrier twice a day, that's also fine with me. Because, you see, Mike, I'm your friend, and whatever you do I'll never judge and I'll never advise and you're all on your own. Doesn't help much, does it, best buddy? Where's the lady with the backbone?

MICHAEL: In the bedroom.

DAVE: *(mocking)* Joseph Stalin. Do you know him? He's a Russian dictator but he has a marvellous sense of humour. The mountains and the vistas and the natural grandeur. It's all bullshit. I usually eat there on Wednesday. I have the section near the windows. I'll look for you.

MICHAEL: I thought you were just horsing around. I didn't think you were serious.

DAVE: You didn't?

MICHAEL: No. . . Well. . . Maybe I did. I don't know. I guess I just wasn't thinking. You know how you are with strange women. It was obvious you weren't going to get anywhere. I don't know, Dave. It felt like ten years ago and I guess I did what I always did. I'm sorry.

DAVE: Yeah?

MICHAEL: Dave, I mean it.

DAVE: Too fucking late.

MICHAEL: Where are you going?

DAVE: To that party. Stalin's friend was strike one. I'm told I get three.

MICHAEL: Dave, think about it.

DAVE: Eight years, Mike. Eight years is a long time. Eight years is no joke.

DAVE walks to the door.

MICHAEL: Okay, Dave. Go on. You deserve it. You're a successful lawyer. You've put in your time. It's coming to you. Go ahead. Join the Liberal Party and get your piece of ass.

DAVE: I don't know where you get off talking to me like this. We're no different, you and me. Just because you don't say "tits and ass," just because you say "arrangement," just because you're full up to here with all this crap of sexual chic doesn't mean you're not just another horny guy looking to get laid.

MICHAEL: I know that, Dave, okay? All I'm saying is acting on it doesn't make it any better.

DAVE: And you know something else? Being up front about your failings doesn't make them any better. When you've got BO, you've got BO. The solution is not to tell your girlfriend you smell bad and you want an arrangement. The solution is to take a goddamn bath. Jesus Christ, Mike, you're driving Beth crazy.

MICHAEL: Yeah.

DAVE moves to the door.

Don't be an idiot.

DAVE: You haven't been doing without. I have. I haven't had any of it. And I'm going to get some of it. Even if it damn well kills me.

MICHAEL: Dave, it's exciting and romantic. It's one hell of a rush. I'm not going to deny that. But getting laid is not a detachable event. Acts have consequences and they're never the ones you want or the ones you expect. Dave, just take it from me. It's not worth it.

DAVE: Thanks for the sermon. I'll keep it in mind.

DAVE moves to the door. MICHAEL gets him in a headlock.

MICHAEL: *(facetiously)* Dave, please. Don't make me tie you up.

DAVE: *(having none of it, intensely)* Let go.

MICHAEL releases DAVE. DAVE walks to the door.

MICHAEL: I'll see you tomorrow?

DAVE says nothing and goes. Pause. MICHAEL moves to the desk, finds a number in the phone book, and dials.

Hello. . . Who am I speaking to please. . . ? Listen, you don't know me, Earl, but we have a friend in common. Beth Gordon. . . That's right. It's Michael Kaye. . . Yes, Earl, and I've heard a lot about you too. Is Beth there. . . ? I wouldn't worry about it, she's probably having car trouble. . . I'm sure it's not your fault, Earl. . . Could you have Beth call me when she arrives. . . ? What? She did. . . ? Sure. I'll hang on. . . Beth. Mike. . . I want to talk to you. What do you think I want. . . ? Yes. Of course, it's very important. . . Yes. I know where you are. . . Oh. I see. You think this is easy for me, do you. . . ? Beth, what the hell are you talking about? You're the one who walked out of here without. . .

BETH has hung up.

Beth? Beth? Fuck!

Short pause. Then MICHAEL takes his jacket from the closet and writes down EARL's address. JACKIE enters from the bedroom.

JACKIE: Did everyone leave?

MICHAEL: *(startled by JACKIE)* Oh my God. . . Not everyone. I was just on my way out.

JACKIE: Michael, this wonderful thing happened. I was trying to get comfortable on your bedroom floor when something in my back popped. I feel just terrific.

MICHAEL: Jackie, the time has come for you to quietly fold your little tent and leave my apartment.

JACKIE: You look very tense and anxious.

MICHAEL: I am.

JACKIE: I know just the thing.

JACKIE attempts to give MICHAEL a back rub.

MICHAEL: What do you think you're doing?

JACKIE: You'll feel like a new man. I promise.

MICHAEL: Jackie.

JACKIE: I thought you were interested.

MICHAEL: I was.

JACKIE: What happened? Was it something I said? I talk too much. I know I talk too much.

MICHAEL: Jackie, why is it you don't want to leave this apartment?

There is a loud knock on the door.

JACKIE: That's why.

JACKIE hurries to the door and looks through the peephole. There is another loud knock.

MICHAEL: Who's that?

JACKIE: Phil.

She quickly slips the chain and locks the door. There is another very loud knock.

He's a big dumb jock and he's very drunk.

The door is shaken violently.

MICHAEL: What does he want?

JACKIE: He's my husband. He thinks we're screwing. He wants to beat the piss out of you.

The shaking continues. The door frame gives way. Blackout.

Scene Three

About eleven thirty Sunday morning. KAREN and DAVE are sitting on the couch. Their arms are around each other.

DAVE: I was thinking body oils. Rose, lavender, peach blossom. I cover you in it then I sniff you all over. Then you cover me in it. Then you sniff me all over.

KAREN: I was thinking hot tubs. We could watch the water gurgle.

DAVE: Then there's always leather.

KAREN: I have just the thing. It's not leather but it'll do. An old-fashioned corset. It cinches up. No bottom half. Black garter belts.

DAVE: Actually I was thinking leather thongs.

KAREN: David.

DAVE: I'm enlightened. I tie you up. Then you tie me up.

KAREN: You're crazy.

DAVE: A movie. Starring you. And me. It begins. You're naked. Covered in oil. Tied to the bed with leather thongs. I enter. Also naked. But not covered in oil. I look at your naked, oiled, tied-up body. I give a fiendish ha-ha. Ha-ha. I turn my back to look at the other five women in the room.

KAREN: Well excuse me.

DAVE: But you're hot and sweaty and the oil has loosened the thongs. You squirm free and quick as a wink, while my back is turned, you overpower me.

KAREN: Good for me.

DAVE: Wait a minute. You're no better than me. You're just as twisted. You bind me with leather, douse me in oil, peach blossom, and then, with one of your perverse little giggles. . .

KAREN giggles.

You sadistically sniff me all over.

KAREN: Oooh. . . Then.

DAVE: Then?

KAREN: *(standing up)* Your body a quivering mass on the floor, I leave.

DAVE: You leave?

KAREN: I leave. But I return in a moment clad in my crotchless corset.

DAVE: Wunderbar!

KAREN: And carrying a twelve-foot bullwhip.

DAVE: Oh my God!

KAREN: But by this time you have slithered free.

DAVE: *(standing up)* Slither, slither, I grab the whip from your oily hand and raise it above my head.

KAREN: When suddenly you catch sight of my liquid pools.

DAVE: Liquid pools?

KAREN: Eyes.

DAVE: Ah.

KAREN: We embrace passionately and make convulsive, oily love.

DAVE: All over the bedroom floor. We don't worry about the wall-to-wall.

KAREN: What do we care? It's just some sleazy motel.

DAVE: Then I order in some beer and pizza and the two of us, content and happy, watch the last two periods between the Leafs and the Canadiens.

KAREN: Let's go, sex fiend.

DAVE: Let's wait another five minutes.

KAREN: You left him a note. You'll call him this afternoon.

DAVE: Five minutes. It's important. I may not see him for another year. I still don't like the looks of that door. And all this dirt.

KAREN: An accident.

DAVE: Could be. I'll have another look around.

    DAVE enters the dining room.

KAREN: Where is my purse?

DAVE: *(off)* Oh my God!

KAREN: David! David!

DAVE returns with the remains of the bonsai.

DAVE: The bonsai is no more.

KAREN: You scared me half to death.

DAVE: Bad joke. Sorry, sweetie.

DAVE gives KAREN a kiss. MICHAEL enters.

KAREN: Michael.

DAVE: Mike, how are you?

KAREN: What is wrong with your eye?

MICHAEL: It's nothing.

DAVE: What do you mean "nothing"? That's a beaut.

KAREN: What happened?

MICHAEL: Last night this big guy breaks down the door, knocks over my bonsai, and punches me in the face. I got in a good one though. Adam's apple. He was a nice deep blue here for five minutes. I really don't want to talk about it. What are you two doing here?

DAVE: I just dropped in to say goodbye.

KAREN: We've been trying to phone you all morning.

DAVE: There was no answer.

KAREN: We've been knocking on your door.

DAVE: There was no answer.

KAREN: But the door was unlocked.

DAVE: So we just walked in. . . . Karen and I . . . Met.

KAREN: Actually, we've become quite good friends.

DAVE: Actually, a little more than friends.

KAREN: Actually, David's right.

DAVE: Life. Figure it out.

KAREN: People. Figure them out.

DAVE: That Vancouver guy. It was Earl. Imagine that.

KAREN: I remembered David from your apartment.

DAVE: Karen was the only person I knew. Next to the guys.

MICHAEL: Wasn't Beth there?

DAVE: She was there. I just didn't see much of her. She was there for a second. Then she was gone.

KAREN: Just swallowed up by the crowd. Never to be seen again.

DAVE: So many people. All trying to get at each other. We hit it off right away.

KAREN: Thank God for that. There is so little time. David is leaving for Toronto first thing in the morning. We won't be able to spend any time together until he gets back from England.

MICHAEL: I didn't know you were going to England.

DAVE: I can't believe I didn't tell you. Four months. For the federal government. I wasn't supposed to tell anyone. Very hush-hush.

MICHAEL: What about your affairs in Toronto?

DAVE: No problem. I'll sublet my apartment and Bannerman will look after my practice.

MICHAEL: *(at phone)* Isn't that Bannerman one hell of a nice guy?

KAREN: We're going to spend two weeks together in September.

MICHAEL: Really? Two weeks?

DAVE: Yeah. Two weeks.

MICHAEL dials.

KAREN: We should go.

DAVE: What's your rush?

KAREN: I want to luxuriate over brunch.

DAVE: We have lots of time. I want to talk to Mike.

KAREN: Have you seen my purse?

DAVE: Don't worry, sweetie. It's around.

MICHAEL hangs up the phone.

MICHAEL: It's not like Beth to disappear on a Sunday morning.

KAREN: Have you tried Earl's?

DAVE: Stop worrying. She'll turn up.

MICHAEL: I've been trying to get in touch with her all morning.

KAREN: She's playing tennis.

MICHAEL: What?

KAREN: We had a tennis lesson this morning.

MICHAEL: How long does it go?

KAREN: She'll be another hour at least.

DAVE: Well then. Let's have some coffee with Mike. Mike?

MICHAEL: Uh. Sure.

KAREN: What about our brunch?

DAVE: It's happening. We'll just visit for a little while. Karen, please.

KAREN: I'll put the kettle on.

DAVE: Thanks, sweetie. You get things started. I'll finish things off.

DAVE gives KAREN a domestic little kiss.

MICHAEL: There should be some apple strudel in the fridge if you want to warm it up.

KAREN: I'll find it.

KAREN goes.

DAVE: Well? What do you think?

MICHAEL: Huh? What about?

DAVE: Jesus Christ, Mike. This is the morning after the night before. This is the first time in eight years that I've got a night before to talk about. I'm enjoying this. Talking about it. It's exciting just talking about talking about it. Aren't you even happy for me?

MICHAEL: I hope you had a nice time.

DAVE: Ferocious. Absolutely ferocious.

MICHAEL: Ferocious?

DAVE: Did you ever go to bed with a member of the English department? Do it. I recommend it wholeheartedly. I don't want to tell tales out of school but a wild, impetuous, passionate night. And after eight years of married life I was ready for it.

KAREN: *(off)* I need a pan for the strudel.

MICHAEL: Under the stove.

DAVE: Have you known Karen for a long time?

MICHAEL: Three, four years.

DAVE: She's a good friend?

MICHAEL: Pretty good.

DAVE: She always like this?

MICHAEL: Like what?

DAVE: No hassle, exciting, fun, good times.

MICHAEL: I guess.

DAVE: Nice girl.

MICHAEL: Dave.

DAVE: Yeah.

MICHAEL: Two weeks?

DAVE: We had a great time. We really got along. . . Christ. I don't know.

KAREN sticks her head into the living room.

KAREN: David, could you give me a hand with the coffee?

DAVE: Sure, sweetie.

KAREN goes.

I don't know, Mike. I just don't know.

DAVE exits to the kitchen. Giggles and laughter off.

KAREN: *(off)* Stop that, David. We have to make the coffee.

She enters.

It's not as bad or as simple as it seems. I'll admit that last night I was angry and vindictive and the only reason I came on to David in the first place was to get back at you.

DAVE: *(off)* Where's the coffee?

MICHAEL: In the fridge.

KAREN: I never thought he'd turn out to be such a sweet, nice man. I never thought I'd have such a wonderful time.

DAVE: *(off)* Found it.

KAREN: I wasn't expecting it. I wasn't expecting that I was doing what I was doing. It started out one way but it ended up another.

DAVE: *(off)* This coffee is going to win me a golden cup.

KAREN: Yesterday afternoon. I was desperate. I made a mistake. It's best forgotten. No one need ever know anything.

MICHAEL: I haven't had time to think about this.

KAREN: You're doing very well.

MICHAEL: What if something comes up?

KAREN: Lie.

MICHAEL *shakes his head.*

You should never have gone to bed with me in the first place if you weren't willing to lie about it.

MICHAEL: Karen, I should never have gone to bed with you period.

DAVE: *(off)* Should I cut up the strudel before I heat it up?

KAREN: *(calling)* No.

DAVE: *(off)* Three fifty?

KAREN: *(calling)* I'll be there in a second. *(to MICHAEL)* Michael, you're gracious and honest and well-intentioned and it doesn't mean one damn thing. If you cause pain you cause pain and all the heartfelt talk in the world doesn't make one bit of difference.

DAVE: *(off)* Tinfoil?

KAREN: Coming.

KAREN returns to the kitchen. Short pause. There is a knock on the door. MICHAEL answers it. BETH is there.

MICHAEL: Beth. C'mon in.

BETH: Mike, what happened to your eye?

MICHAEL: It's nothing.

BETH: Let me see.

MICHAEL: It's nothing. Really.

BETH: What happened?

MICHAEL: I'll tell you all about it later. Sit down. Please. I've been trying to get in touch with you all morning.

BETH: I went for a walk. It's such a beautiful morning.

MICHAEL: How was it?

BETH: It did the trick. Mike, we have to talk.

MICHAEL: I know that. Beth. I. . .

But KAREN enters with the plates and silverware on a tray.

KAREN: Michael, do you have any cinnamon? Beth.

BETH: Hi, Karen. I didn't know you were here.

KAREN: Just getting some coffee and pastry together.

BETH: I see.

KAREN: You didn't go to tennis?

BETH: No. Neither did you.

KAREN: Sunday mornings.

BETH: Yes.

KAREN: Great party last night. I felt like a kid again.

BETH: We weren't expecting that many people.

KAREN: Oh no. I liked the crush. I was putting coffee on. But maybe you and Michael. . .

BETH: Don't leave on my account. Perhaps I'm the one who should go?

KAREN: No, no, no. Michael's been trying to get in touch with you all morning.

BETH: Really?

KAREN: Yes. Oh silly you. I was just on my way to an absolutely decadent brunch. I only dropped in for a moment. Not five minutes ago. With an old friend of Michael's. He's an absolutely wonderful man. We just popped round to say goodbye. The mad fool has to go to England for four months. *(calling)* David. We've had a marvellous, glorious twelve hours. I'm still reeling. *(calling)* David, there's someone who wants to say hello. *(as DAVE enters)* There you are. I believe you two know each other.

DAVE: Hi, Beth.

BETH: Dave.

DAVE: Old friends.

MICHAEL: Dave's going to England for four months. These bachelor lawyers. The world's their oyster.

BETH: I hope Dave doesn't get indigestion.

DAVE: Ha-ha. The job's in London. For the federal government. Very hush-hush.

BETH: Dave, I wish you hadn't told me. I'm a terrible security risk. I'm sure I'll be spilling the beans to all the wrong people.

DAVE: Very funny.

KAREN: David's flying back here when he returns from England. We're going to spend two weeks together in September. Just the two of us.

BETH: Just the two of you. That's very romantic. You're going to be a very busy man these next four months.

DAVE: You know me. Pressure. I thrive on it.

KAREN: Beth, coffee? Another cup, serviettes, oh my God, the strudel.

KAREN exits to the kitchen.

BETH: You're out of your mind.

DAVE: Yeah. Well. Only in BC, and I've made my peace with it.

DAVE exits to the kitchen.

MICHAEL: I tried, but he's an adult.

BETH: I doubt it.

MICHAEL: Beth.

BETH: Mike, I'd like to apologize for that phone call.

MICHAEL: Forget it.

BETH: And for my behaviour last night.

MICHAEL: Someone hurts you, you hurt them back. It's human nature.

BETH: Yes. I've done a lot of that. I think we should call it quits.

MICHAEL: Why. . . ? Earl?

BETH: No, Michael.

MICHAEL: Why then?

BETH: I want it all. A husband, a family, a home for my family. The whole banal, bourgeois package. That's what I want. That's who I am. So let's just forget the whole damn thing because I'm not going to let you or anyone else make me feel guilty about it any longer.

MICHAEL: Beth, listen.

BETH: No. Let me finish. When you started talking "arrangement," I should have told you to get lost. But I was too scared of losing you. Of being out in that meat market looking for a man. Jesus Christ, I'm thirty. What if I didn't meet someone for a while? And even if I did, I wasn't going to get married and have kids with someone I just met. And goddamn it, Mike, I was hoping you'd come through.

MICHAEL: And I have come through. That's what I've been trying to tell you. Beth, you're very special to me. I love you very much.

BETH: And I resent the hell out of you. Sometimes I don't even like you. God knows I don't respect you the way I used to. And there's no sense in even talking about trust.

MICHAEL: The arrangement was a big mistake. I know that now. But we can get over it.

BETH: These last few months. They're not marks on paper. They're here with us.

KAREN enters with strudel.

KAREN: Here's the strudel. And I found some melon. *(reacting to MICHAEL and BETH)* Why don't I cut this in the kitchen?

KAREN returns to the kitchen.

MICHAEL: I've been a big jerk. But that's over with. History. It's best forgotten. Beth? Let's give it another chance. There's more to us than these last few months.

BETH: I know that.

MICHAEL: We can do it. I've got all this garbage out of my system.

BETH: It doesn't work that way. Why are you doing this to me?

MICHAEL: We'll get it straight. You'll see.

BETH: Mike, please.

MICHAEL: All right, then. We'll have dinner tonight. We'll go to that little Portuguese place you like so much.

BETH: No.

MICHAEL: Tomorrow then? Beth? Please.

BETH: Okay, Mike. We'll talk.

DAVE enters with the coffee. KAREN follows with the strudel.

KAREN: Here we go. David will pour the coffee. This is an absolutely perfect melon. Did you pick this, Michael? Well, you certainly have a way with fruit. I go crazy in produce sections. I don't know whether to pinch or prod or sniff or squeeze.

DAVE: Sniff?

KAREN: Pineapples.

DAVE: Yeah? You sure? Where do you sniff them?

KAREN: All over, David. Where do you think?

BETH: Just the top.

KAREN offers DAVE some melon.

DAVE: None for me. I'll stick to strudel. Carbohydrates. They keep you young.

KAREN: And ruin your appetite. We are going for brunch. It's melon or nothing. Wonderful coffee.

DAVE: I told you. *(a sip)* Delish. *(another sip)* Delish, delish, delish. A little time, a little effort. And God rewards.

MICHAEL: Quite the spread you put on, Karen. Thank you.

KAREN: David warmed the strudel.

DAVE: And cut the melon. And got the plates. And made the coffee. Delish, delish, delish.

There is a knock on the door. MICHAEL answers it. JACKIE is there. She is carrying two small pieces of luggage.

JACKIE: Free at last, Michael. Free at last. Oh. Does that eye hurt?

MICHAEL: It's fine.

JACKIE: I'm sorry. I didn't know you had people over. Hello, David.

DAVE: Hi.

JACKIE: I just came by to say I'm sorry. And Phil's sorry too. He's swallowing now.

MICHAEL: Good.

JACKIE: Here's a cheque for fifty dollars for the door.

MICHAEL: I can't take this.

JACKIE: Please. It'll make Phil feel better.

MICHAEL: Thanks.

JACKIE: I've made my decision. I'm leaving Phil. *(to the group at large)* Phil's my husband.

DAVE: And he mangled the door?

JACKIE: Yes.

KAREN: And hit Michael?

JACKIE: Yes.

BETH: Why?

JACKIE: Jeffrey Fiskin thinks it's Burnaby, but I think. . .

MICHAEL: *(cutting JACKIE off)* I'll tell you all about it later. Nice seeing you again, Jackie.

BETH: Mike, why are you being so rude? Do you want some coffee, Jackie?

JACKIE: *(walking to the couch)* No thanks. Someone's supposed to be picking me up out front. Anyway, Jeffrey's diagnosis is Burnaby, but I think Jeffrey is full of it. *(sitting down)* Jeffrey's my psychiatrist. Very eclectic. I've been puking for months. Jeffrey blames it all on Burnaby. But I knew it couldn't just be Burnaby. I knew it was also Phil Lemieux. Phil and I got married just out of high school but we've been drifting apart ever since I started throwing up. I've been dancing and painting and meeting all these interesting people. And Phil, well he's been working at the Wheat Pool and going through a dozen beers a night and playing baseball like a maniac. Just generally being your basic veg. Last night at Jim's—Jim Loadman? Phil's foreman at the Pool—I told Phil I wanted the freedom to experiment. We had this big fight and my back started to act up. And then I met Michael and David. Nothing happened. But Phil didn't know that. I've been in Burnaby arguing all night. I realize now that Phil is a very little person and that some people just can't handle change. He resents and he won't forgive. Well, I'm bigger than that. This is all I took and it feels just great. That's what I was thinking when I walked in. Goodbye, Burnaby. Goodbye, Maalox. Free at last, Michael. Free at last. *(moving to MICHAEL)* I'm sorry you had to be a part of all this.

MICHAEL: It's all water under the bridge.

JACKIE: Guess I better be going. Bernard's picking me up out front. He always gets lost in Burnaby. Besides, I didn't want him to run into Phil. Bernard Hedley, he's been painting for more than forty years, kind of a mentor figure for me. Well, I'm moving in. He's got this boat, close to forty feet, in a month he's going to sail the inside passage to Alaska. I'll be his deckhand.

DAVE: Bon voyage, Jackie.

JACKIE: I guess I owe you an apology too, David. I wasn't straight with you either.

DAVE: Forget it.

MICHAEL: You should wait for Bernard out front.

DAVE: Mentor figures are very impatient.

MICHAEL: Forty years waiting for a protege like you. He must be getting antsy.

JACKIE: I just want you to know I respect you.

DAVE: Thanks.

JACKIE: You were honest about your wife in Toronto. I should have been as honest about Phil down the hall.

KAREN: Wife.

DAVE: Shit.

JACKIE: And family. Three boys.

KAREN: Where is my goddamn purse?

DAVE: Karen, don't be like that.

KAREN: Why didn't you have the guts to tell me the truth?

DAVE: Some women don't like to get involved with married men.

KAREN: I don't give a damn about your marital status. I hate being lied to.

DAVE: I'm new to all this.

KAREN: That makes everything just fine.

DAVE: I thought it would make things easier.

KAREN: You both knew, didn't you? Lovely. Just dandy. I love being treated this way. It does wonders for my self-esteem. And what's all this crap about two weeks away from it all?

DAVE: I'm serious. I'm looking forward to it.

KAREN: *(moving into the dining room in search for her purse)* Bring your wife and kids. We'll get a family rate.

DAVE: *(following KAREN into the dining room)* I'll work something out. I promise.

KAREN: *(off)* Forget it, David. I don't need you. There are twelve nineteen-year-olds in my first-year section who would like nothing better than to tie me up and douse me in oil. Where is my goddamn purse?

> JACKIE, *sitting, moans loudly and puts a hand to her stomach.* KAREN *enters.* DAVE *follows.* KAREN *continues her search for her purse.*

DAVE: Karen, can't we handle this in a civilized manner? Let's talk about it. We'll go to the Four Seasons. We'll have that brunch.

JACKIE: Don't go there. You'll never get in.

DAVE: Sure we will.

JACKIE: Not today. The place will be just packed.

DAVE: So we'll go someplace else. Now get lost!

BETH: Dave, unless you have reservations I'd forget about brunch. ·

DAVE: What's so special about. . . Oh shit.

MICHAEL: What is it?

JACKIE: It's Mother's Day.

KAREN: Charming. Absolutely charming. That would have made for a very interesting brunch. Why can't I find anything when I need it?

JACKIE: This is all my fault. I'm so sorry. I'm not stupid. I'm really very sensitive. It's because I never saw them as a couple. It didn't make sense to me. So I didn't know to be quiet.

MICHAEL: It's all right, Jackie. It's not your fault.

JACKIE: But David, you must understand.

> DAVE *turns away. She talks to* MICHAEL.

When things make sense to me I'm really very perceptive. I'm very astute. When I saw you and her together, *(gesturing to KAREN)* I knew right away something had been cooking. Because you two make sense together. And that's another reason I got things. . .

MICHAEL turns away. JACKIE trails off and sits down. She clutches her stomach.

BETH: What kind of sense did you and Karen make together?

Short pause. KAREN laughs loudly.

KAREN: Last night Michael and I were having a disagreement over Milton. This mindless muffin walked in on it. She obviously took our heated discussion of *Paradise Lost* to be sexual recrimination. . . I really don't see how you can take this space cadet from Burnaby seriously.

BETH looks at MICHAEL. MICHAEL turns away.

Michael, you are such a fool.

MICHAEL: I didn't see any point in telling you.

BETH: When?

MICHAEL: Yesterday afternoon.

KAREN: The one and only time.

MICHAEL: We did something very stupid. It was a big mistake.

KAREN: I really can't understand just how or why it happened. It was just one of those things. It means nothing. It's best forgotten. We both had an absolutely miserable time.

BETH turns away. KAREN follows.

You had that silly, fatuous arrangement. Beth? Oh, damn it!

JACKIE: Does anyone have some Maalox?

MICHAEL walks towards BETH.

DAVE: You and Karen?

MICHAEL: Dave.

KAREN: I'll leave without my purse. I'll walk. Hitchhike. I don't care. *(remembering)* Oh right.

KAREN exits to the bathroom.

DAVE: Shit. The first time in eight years of marriage and on Mother's Day, for fuck's sake. You shoulda said "no" to me right from the start. That's what a friend would have done. That's what I needed to hear. You shouldn't have been such a sophisticated, with it, enlightened son-of-a-bitch.

KAREN: *(off)* I can't believe my luck. Three men in one weekend. *(entering with her purse)* I'm not down. I'm out.

KAREN moves to go.

DAVE: Ten years later and I'm still getting your cast-offs. Eh, best buddy? And for what? To feel like a big man. Like the successful lawyer.

KAREN: *(at door)* Excuse me, David. I didn't quite hear that. What did you call me?

Short pause. DAVE doesn't relent.

DAVE: Forget it.

KAREN: Well, David, "cast-off" may very well be apt. But I think you should know that I found your conversation inane—delish, delish, delish. Your stature second-rate—I don't know where you got the idea that women would forget about your height if you talked about your density. We're interested in men, not precious metals. And your performance, unusual to say the least. Sniff, sniff. I think you'd rather inhale than orgasm. The only reason I put up with all these failings was because I wanted to inflict some pain on a former friend who had recently, as you so aptly put it, cast me off.

KAREN leaves. MICHAEL walks to DAVE. Puts his arm on DAVE's.

MICHAEL: Dave.

DAVE: Fuck off!!

DAVE pushes MICHAEL away. MICHAEL sprawls into the sofa.

JACKIE: I think I have to puke.

JACKIE runs to the bathroom. DAVE leaves.

BETH: Are you all right?

MICHAEL: I'm fine.

BETH: You sure?

MICHAEL: Yes. I'm fine.

JACKIE returns from the bathroom holding a large bottle of Maalox.

JACKIE: And Jeffrey Fiskin kept saying it was Burnaby. It's an ulcer. It has to be. I'm sorry. . . Well, Bernard must be waiting.

JACKIE takes a swig from the bottle and leaves. There is a short pause. BETH walks to the door.

MICHAEL: I'm sorry.

BETH: Yes. I know.

BETH leaves. MICHAEL sits for a moment, forces himself to get up, takes a sip of his coffee, and turns on the stereo. He looks out the window. The lights fade.

The End.

THE MATKA KING
BY ANOSH IRANI

INTRODUCTION TO *THE MATKA KING*

The Matka King was an important show for both Anosh, the playwright, and myself. For me, it was the first play I directed at the Arts Club. For Anosh it was his debut play. Few writers have the experience of premiering their first work on a large stage; I say experience and not privilege on purpose, and, in truth, I should say ordeal. For a first-time playwright everything that happens in the long process of development and production is happening for the very first time. For example, there is no way to know that witnessing a cast in the process of getting off book is not akin to witnessing a mutiny against the script. In rehearsals we made prototypes of a flying carpet and a twelve-foot-high dancing dream penis and worked intensely on finessing their effects with actor Lois Anderson and our properties master Michael Gall. Anosh saw his ideas fail and fail and fail, literally coming apart at the seams and crashing to the ground before they could soar like magic on the stage.

Because the play was new, and because our collaboration was new, I asked Anosh a lot of questions—for two years. One of the most memorable and illuminating answers he gave was to my question about Top Rani, the lead character, and why he would choose suicide at the end. Anosh explained that to a Zoroastrian who believes in reincarnation, Top Rani was choosing to move on; this wasn't a defeated man, it was a defiant man. This is when I started to think more deeply about what we mean when we say we want new plays—we want new voices. A truly new voice, like Anosh's, doesn't sound like anything that has come before, and it references customs and histories outside our own well-known tropes. Will we even recognize a new play by a new voice when it first crosses our desks? I think back to the story about the dramaturg at the Actors' Theatre in Louisville who first encountered a manuscript by Sam Shepard, and said, "I don't know if this is even a play, but I know this is a writer."

RACHEL DITOR: For future productions, is there a trick or insight you have about getting this play "right"?

Anosh Irani: To keep the play as real as possible. For magic realism to work, the play needs to be firmly grounded in reality. One needs to taste the dirt of the brothel for the surreal parts to have the desired impact.

RD: Do you have a particularly memorable moment from the production?

AI: When the main character, Top Rani, talks about how he was castrated as a ten-year-old boy. When I first wrote that monologue it just came through, and remained more or less unchanged over several drafts. To finally see it realized was a fulfilling moment for me—it was incredibly eerie and moving on stage.

RD: What was the genesis of this play?

AI: I grew up very close to Kamhathipura, Bombay's red-light district. Ever since I was a boy I have been intrigued by the prostitutes, pimps, cops, and the transgenders—the living, breathing machinery of the red-light district. I did not know what function they performed, or that the district represented a flesh market of truly hideous proportions, but the whole place had a theatricality to it that made me stare in wonder. I guess that landscape followed me to Canada, where I started writing plays.

The Matka King was workshopped and given public readings at the Arts Club Theatre's ReACT showcase in 2002 and 2003; the CrossCurrents Festival in 2002 and 2004 at the Factory Theatre, Toronto; and at the On the Verge festival in 2002 at the National Arts Centre, Ottawa. It was first published in *Canadian Theatre Review*.

The Matka King premiered in October 2003 at the Arts Club Theatre, Vancouver, with the following cast and creative team:

Top Rani: Craig Veroni
Guru Gantaal: Marvin Ishmael
Satta: Allan Zinyk
Chandni: Laara Sadiq
Aarti: Anoushka Anderson Kirby

Director and dramaturg: Rachel Ditor
Artistic managing director: Bill Millerd
Puppeteer: Lois Anderson
Set design: Robert Gardiner
Lighting design: Marsha Sibthorpe
Costume design: Barbara Clayden
Sound design: Noah Drew
Stage managers: Chris Allan and Pamela Jakobs
Assistant stage manager: Anne Taylor
Design assistant: Erin Harris

Characters

Top Rani: A eunuch in his thirties.
Chandni: A prostitute in her twenties.
Aarti: A ten-year-old girl.
Satta: A gambler in his late thirties.
Gantaal: A fortune teller of about fifty.

Setting

The play takes place in Bombay at:

a) Top Rani's brothel.
b) Grant Road.

The time is the present.

ACT ONE

Prologue

TOP RANI enters dressed in a sari. His hair is long but tied back. He has bangles on his wrists.

TOP RANI: Come, come, enter my brothel. I have big-big girls for little-little prices. And little-little girls for big-big prices. Cheapest is ten rupees only. Surely you must have ten rupees. If you don't want complete insertion, then simple massage is also there. With happy ending.

Pause.

No? Oh, you enemy of love. You must be married. Is that your wife? Hello, beautiful. The word for tonight is "Legs." Spread the word.

Pause.

Let me show you around. You are in a red-light district called Kamhathipura. There is a small merry-go-round just outside my window. It is operated by a pimp. Every evening, while his whores work, he gives their children free rides. Next to the merry-go-round is a doctor's dispensary. He has written the names of famous diseases on a whiteboard—syphilis, gonorrhea, and TB—none of which he can cure. Then there is Café Andaaz, where the prostitutes collect for their afternoon tea and pretend they are free. But in this city, no one is free. I realized that when I was ten years old. I was sent here by my father to work as a servant boy. I had dreams then. Now I can hardly remember what they were. The truth is there is no such thing as an Indian Dream. If there was, it died the day this city was born. Welcome to Bombay.

One

Grant Road. December 30th. Eight forty-five p.m. Guru GANTAAL *sits on the footpath. A large steel trunk rests in front of him. The sound of a car rushing past. Smoke from the car covers* GANTAAL's *face. He coughs violently.*

GANTAAL: Time for cigarette.

He removes a cigarette from behind his ear and puts it to his lips, but does not light it. The sound of another car going past. He cocks his head forward in anticipation of the exhaust fumes. He exhales in time with the car's expulsion of smoke, pretending that he has blown cigarette smoke.

Cars cause smoking. Smoking causes cigarettes. It is a vicious cycle.

Enter SATTA *on a cycle.* SATTA's *cycle is old and beaten. It has a huge bugle-like horn on it and a large placard that says "God is great but always late."*

A vicious cycle indeed.

SATTA: Guru Gantaal. Please tell me. It's almost nine o'clock.

GANTAAL: Okay. It's almost nine o'clock.

SATTA: Don't do this to me. Tonight, I *have* to win. A lot of money is at stake.

SATTA shows him a fat wad of notes.

GANTAAL: Where did you get that?

SATTA: I sold my *kholi.*

GANTAAL: Sold it? Now where will you live?

SATTA: There's no time to explain.

GANTAAL: Then tonight I will show you something that is very precious to me.

SATTA rubs his hands in anticipation. GANTAAL *opens the lid of the trunk and without looking he puts his hand in. He screams in agony. He closes the lid and shakes his hand as though he has been stung.*

SATTA: What happened?

GANTAAL: My cobra bit me.

SATTA: You have a cobra in there? Is it poisonous?

GANTAAL: Very poisonous. I sometimes forget that the little one is still in there.

SATTA: Shouldn't you be rushing to a hospital?

GANTAAL: What for?

SATTA: It bit you.

GANTAAL: I used to be a snake charmer. Cobras never kill the hand that feeds them. He is just angry that he is locked in this trunk. But if *you* put your hand in, you will need to see a hospital. Anyway, I'm looking for my parrot.

SATTA: A cobra and parrot stay in the same trunk?

GANTAAL: The parrot is fake.

He brings SATTA *closer to him. He opens the lid again.*

Satta, have you heard of any new methods?

SATTA: I have heard of this new method called the Ant Race. It's very effective. You place ten sugar cubes in a row on the ground. Then you keep watch over the next few minutes as ants gather. Whichever cube the ants go to first, that is the opening number of the day. So if they go first to the cube placed fifth in the row, then the opening number is five. The cube the ants go to last, that is the closing number.

GANTAAL: It works every time.

SATTA: What works?

GANTAAL: Your talk of opening and closing numbers is so boring that it has put my cobra to sleep.

SATTA: Snakes can't hear. They're deaf.

GANTAAL: You want the truth? It's not your talk that's putting it to sleep.

SATTA: Good.

GANTAAL: It's your body odour. Your smell is so bad the government will be forced to give you your own area code. Anyway, now I can safely remove the parrot from the trunk. Your smell has knocked out my cobra.

He removes a parrot from the trunk and places it on the lid.

Where is your pack of cards?

SATTA removes a pack of cards from his shirt pocket.

Why a new pack every day? You must have spent a fortune only on buying cards.

SATTA: I have heard that *he* uses a new pack every day. So I must also use a new pack, otherwise we will never be able to predict the numbers.

GANTAAL: It.

SATTA: It?

GANTAAL: Not *him*. It. A eunuch is an "It." That is why the name Top Rani. The Head Queen.

SATTA: He is also called "The Matka King." In which case, he is a he.

GANTAAL: Fine. Let us refer to the eunuch as a he. Now place numbers one to ten in a row.

SATTA places the ten cards on the lid of the trunk.

The parrot will choose one number with its beak. That will be tonight's opening number.

SATTA: But the parrot is fake.

GANTAAL: I am aware of that.

SATTA: Then how will it choose the number?

GANTAAL: Watch.

They both stare at the parrot. GANTAAL makes absurd parrot sounds. The parrot, of course, remains stationary.

It's taking its time.

SATTA: What are you talking about? It's stationary.

GANTAAL grabs the parrot by the neck and bangs it down on the card placed second in the row.

GANTAAL: Number two. Opening on two. The bird has spoken.

SATTA: You banged its face down on the trunk!

GANTAAL: Are you doubting my powers?

SATTA: Yes!

GANTAAL: Good. Doubt gets rid of certainty.

SATTA: What?

GANTAAL: Bet on two. It's almost nine o'clock.

SATTA shakes his head, mounts his cycle, and leaves. GANTAAL places the parrot back in the trunk. The cobra bites again.

(to cobra) Again you have woken up. This time you will be in a deep sleep. The only cobra I know who falls asleep to bad smell: the natural odour of this city.

He keeps the lid of the trunk wide open.

(to sewer in the distance) Beautiful sewer! As natural as a gurgling brook. . . *(to cobra)* Ah, you're getting drowsy. . . *(to breeze)* Oh wafting breeze from the public bathroom, please come in, come in. . . who needs the scent of jasmine when. . .

He looks down in disgust. GANTAAL lifts his foot up and examines his sole. He has just stepped in something. He scrapes it off his foot into the trunk.

(delightfully to cobra) Knockout. It works every time.

He slams the lid shut.

Two

The brothel. December 30th. Eight fifty-five p.m. TOP RANI is seated on a swing that is suspended from the ceiling by long iron rods.

TOP RANI: Matka is a very simple game, okay? At nine o'clock each night, I pick one card. I call that the opening number. At midnight, I pick one more. The closing number. I post each number outside. Within minutes the people of this city will gather to check if they have been able to guess correctly. The tea-stall owner will tell the man on the cycle. The man on the cycle will stop at all the traffic signals and tell the taxiwalas, the taxiwalas will tell their passengers, who will go home and tell their household. All those who have placed bets with their bookies will calculate—up or down? If they guessed the number correctly and bet their weekly pay on it, they will have an extra round of drinks. If they guessed wrong and bet their weekly pay on it. . . they might hang themselves from a ceiling fan.

Pause.

But gambling is not about money. Only amateurs think that. Gambling is about good health. It makes your blood circulate better, you sleep less and are alert, and your heart does not waste its time on love because it is too busy beating out of anticipation.

Enter CHANDNI. She carries a silver tray in her hands. In it is a stainless-steel container that holds a red mixture.

CHANDNI: It's almost nine o'clock.

TOP RANI: Has the matka been washed?

CHANDNI: Yes, Top Rani.

TOP RANI: Is the red mixture ready?

She places the steel container in front of him. She then dips her finger in the red mixture.

CHANDNI: It looks like blood. What's it for?

TOP RANI: *(indicating her red finger)* If you put your finger in my business you *will* get cut.

She turns to leave.

Those flowers in your hair. Are they fresh?

CHANDNI: Yes, Top Rani.

TOP RANI: Are all the daughters ready for the night?

CHANDNI: Except Sudha. She's sick.

TOP RANI: She's falling sick too often. I can't afford to keep her if this continues.

CHANDNI: But she's worked here for many years. She must be looked after.

TOP RANI: This is not a government job.

CHANDNI: What happens if *I* fall ill?

TOP RANI: I will be plunged into darkness. You are the red light of my life.

CHANDNI turns to leave.

Chandni.

CHANDNI: What?

TOP RANI: Make Sudha drink lots of water. Water can cure any sickness.

CHANDNI: Then maybe *I* should drink water. To prevent my legs from spreading.

TOP RANI: Ah, Chandni. . . when I brought you here, you were so young and quiet. But look at you now!

CHANDNI: Thanks to your fine parenting.

TOP RANI: Don't thank me, thank God. It is *in* God's will. When God left this earth, he left a will. In it, he declared that you and six other girls, now your sisters, were to be placed under my care. That is why I say it is *in* his will. By operating this brothel, I'm merely honouring God's wishes.

CHANDNI: Unfortunately, I'm not.

TOP RANI: Why is that?

CHANDNI: God wants me to take these nails and pierce your eyes.

TOP RANI: Must be a different God.

He tells her to leave. She exits.

It's nine o'clock. Time for the opening number.

TOP RANI walks to a small wooden cupboard. He opens the cupboard and removes a pack of cards and a blindfold. He walks to the matka, stands above it, and opens the seal around the pack. He separates the coloured cards from the pack and shows them to the audience.

Jacks, Queens, Kings, and Jokers. They are, by nature, separate from the pack.

He throws them to the floor.

Royalty and commoners do not mix.

Pause.

Before I pull the opening number, I always do something to honour those who have lost their lives to gambling. I call it my auspicious invocation. It is extremely holy.

He spits into the matka.

There. I've paid my respects.

He empties the cards into the matka and blindfolds himself. Then he reaches into the matka and pulls out one card. He takes off his blindfold, inspects the card, and shows it to the audience.

Ten is the opening number. Time to disclose it to the public. It's the ten of diamonds. It means I'm going to find a jewel soon.

Three

Grant Road. December 30th. Ten minutes later. Enter SATTA *on his cycle.* GANTAAL *has fallen asleep.* SATTA *seems angry.*

SATTA: Wake up!

He blows the cycle horn.

Wake up, you. . . !

GANTAAL *gets up with a jerk.*

GANTAAL: Ten! Ten is the opening number!

SATTA: I know that, you fool.

GANTAAL: My dreams are very lucid.

SATTA: Your lucid dreams are of no use if you get the number *after* it is pulled. Where is your parrot?

GANTAAL: Why?

SATTA: I want to kill it! I lost a lot of money.

GANTAAL: So no more gambling for you?

SATTA: I'm betting on tonight's closing number.

GANTAAL: What?

SATTA: It's the last bet of the year.

GANTAAL: Last bet? But today is the thirtieth.

SATTA: Last Matka bet of the year. Tomorrow night, no Matka. On the thirty-first, Top Rani plays Raja Kheench.

GANTAAL: Ah, "Pull the King." The game that nobody has ever won.

SATTA: I know. That eunuch must be cheating. That is why *tonight* will be the biggest bet of my life. Seven thousand rupees.

GANTAAL: Seven thousand!

SATTA: It's all I have left from the sale of my *kholi*. I have a dead tip. Dead accurate. It's for tonight's closing number. The tip comes straight from the hand that washes the matka. Her name is Chandni. She's a worker at Top Rani's.

GANTAAL: Worker. Why don't you use the correct word?

SATTA: Because I have a daughter too. It's a shame, a shame.

GANTAAL: But it's not a shame to use her.

SATTA: I'm not using her. This jeweller whose shop is at Grant Road goes to Chandni very often for his. . .

GANTAAL: Oiling?

SATTA: Oiling-boiling. So Chandni revealed to him that for the last bet of the year, Top Rani does not pull the closing number from the matka. He simply bases closing number according to a whim.

GANTAAL: I'm afraid to ask what the whim of a eunuch can be.

SATTA: Which daughter earns the most money. This year it has been Chandni. She is the first daughter. So the closing number is one.

GANTAAL: Who told you this?

SATTA: My sister-in-law. She sweeps the jeweller's shop. She heard the jeweller discuss this over the phone. That is why I say it is a dead tip. There's no room for mistakes. And I'm not going to place the bet with any bookie-fookie. I'm going straight to the top.

GANTAAL: Top Rani.

SATTA: He gives terrific odds. My plan is foolproof.

GANTAAL: It is the proof of a fool. I am not betting no matter how dead the tip.

SATTA: That's not why I'm here. I want you to look after my daughter while I go and place my bet. I've already made an appointment with Top Rani.

GANTAAL: I am Guru Gantaal! World-renowned fortune teller! I will not look after your daughter! Let your *wife* do it.

SATTA: My wife is dead. I've told you many times.

GANTAAL: Where is your daughter?

SATTA: She's just round the corner drinking a lassi.

SATTA whistles loudly to call her. Enter AARTI.

GANTAAL: *(to AARTI)* What is your name?

AARTI does not respond. She looks shyly at SATTA.

Don't be shy. Tell me your name.

SATTA: Her name is Aarti.

GANTAAL: Did I ask you?

SATTA: Aarti cannot speak. Ever since her mother died. . .

GANTAAL: I. . . I'm sorry.

SATTA: Aarti, I have to go for some time. You stay here and. . . stare at this silly old man.

AARTI holds on to SATTA to prevent him from leaving.

I have to go.

SATTA exits on the cycle. AARTI stares at GANTAAL.

GANTAAL: Of course I'm silly. I'm a real silly man. You are an angel. You don't *need* to speak. Look at your wings. You have such beautiful moon-coloured wings.

AARTI is not impressed. GANTAAL *pretends he hears something.*

Can you hear that, Aarti?

She shakes her head no.

The whispering. That is Aroramanyu. The warrior angel. He wants to tell you what moon colour is.

He pretends to repeat Aroramanyu's words.

Thousands of years ago, the earth was a happy and pure place. Slowly slowly it became bad. First the sins were very small—the worst thing people would do was lie. But then the sins increased. People started robbing, stealing, and beating each other up. Then murder started happening. God got very upset. He got up from his big chair near the sun and put his hand out and grabbed all the bad people in his fist. They were all shouting and screaming and choking. . . and God took them, made this round ball, and put them all in that. That is your moon. But then—all these bad people tried to escape from the moon. So God called his biggest and most powerful angel—Aroramanyu! And to prevent the moon prisoners from escaping, God tore off Aroramanyu's wing.

AARTI does not like this.

He covered the moon with this wing so the prisoners could not escape. When they realized they were trapped, they began to cry and their tears stained this wing. The white wing became a different, translucent colour. That is your moon colour!

Pause.

But do you know *why* he is telling you this?

She shakes her head no.

He is saying that his other wing is for *your* protection. He will send it to you, but only if you ask for it. You can do it. Through your thoughts. Thoughts are more powerful than words. They can travel a longer distance.

Pause.

Open your mouth. Catch your thoughts in your fist.

She grabs unspoken words from her mouth.

And throw them to the moon! Keep looking up.

GANTAAL pulls out a white bedsheet from the trunk and covers AARTI with it. The sheet is old and worn.

He is saying that *this* is other wing. It will always cover you and protect you from harm.

He listens to Aroramanyu again.

What? Oh. Aarti, I have some bad news for you. Aroramanyu says he cannot protect your father. You know why? Because your father is *so* boring, *so* boring. All he talks about is opening number and closing number and opening number and closing number. . . one of these days I will set my cobra loose on that idiot.

The sound of a car in the distance.

Quick, cover your head. *(covering AARTI's head with the sheet)* Smoking is bad for you.

GANTAAL takes the cigarette from behind his ear and puts it to his lips. He sucks in. The car passes by but there are no exhaust fumes.

No exhaust. Must be a foreign car.

Four

The brothel. Ten minutes later. TOP RANI is seated on the swing. But he is unseen. CHANDNI leans out of a window and is selling herself. She is talking to SATTA, who is on the street.

CHANDNI: *Kya,* darling? Ready for action?

SATTA: No. . . I'm here for. . .

CHANDNI: Don't be shy. I will make your Monday a Sunday.

SATTA: But today is Sunday.

CHANDNI: *Kya*, darling, it's only an expression. You want deluxe package or ordinary? In deluxe I make sounds also.

She moans in complete boredom.

SATTA: No, you don't understand. I'm not here for that. No one must see me talking to you.

CHANDNI: Okay. Fry your own onions.

SATTA: I did not mean it like that.

CHANDNI: Then how you meant?

SATTA: I'm here to see Top Rani. I have an appointment.

CHANDNI: Come up. I will open for you.

She opens the door for him.

That's all I ever do. Open.

Enter SATTA, who tries to adjust to the darkness of the brothel. TOP RANI is still on the swing, unseen.

You must be Satta then.

SATTA: Don't tell anyone.

CHANDNI: Man or mosquito?

SATTA: It will look bad if. . .

CHANDNI: If someone sees you with me? What do you expect here, your mother's arms?

SATTA: I just want to meet Top Rani. Please.

TOP RANI: You will.

He is now visible. CHANDNI leaves.

SATTA: I want to. . .

TOP RANI: I know what you want. If it is not a special night with one of my daughters, it is money.

SATTA: I do not need anything. I have come to place a bet.

TOP RANI: What bet?

SATTA: For tonight's closing number.

TOP RANI: Go to a bookie. I do not take bets.

SATTA: I've heard you give better odds.

TOP RANI: How much are you willing to place?

SATTA: Seven thousand.

TOP RANI: Seven thousand. You do not look like you can afford that sum. You must know something I don't.

SATTA: I need to win the money for my brother's operation. He has a hole in his heart.

TOP RANI: And I have one from where I shit. Do not waste my time.

SATTA: I am in heavy debt. Do you know Khalil Bhai?

TOP RANI: You owe that gangster money?

SATTA: Fifty thousand. If I do not pay him. . .

TOP RANI: He will kill you.

    SATTA nods.

I do not accept small bets. If you will increase the amount, I will consider.

SATTA: I'm not begging for money. I'm just asking that you accept my bet. Give me the odds that will allow me to repay Khalil Bhai.

TOP RANI: Why are you so sure you will win? Something is black in the gravy.

SATTA: I have to pay Khalil Bhai by tomorrow morning.

TOP RANI: Then it is rude of me not to grant a dying man his last wish. But the problem still is that the bet is not enough. You will have to raise the stakes.

SATTA: But I have nothing. Absolutely nothing. I promise. I've even sold my house.

TOP RANI: You have nothing. That is not what I have heard.

SATTA: I can assure you that whatever you have heard is wrong.

TOP RANI: Then it is wrong to say that you have a daughter? Chandni!

Enter CHANDNI.

(to SATTA*)* What happened? Suddenly you are silent? Just like your daughter. *(to* CHANDNI*)* What is his daughter's name?

CHANDNI: Aarti.

TOP RANI: Age.

CHANDNI: Ten.

TOP RANI: Colour of hair.

CHANDNI: Dark brown.

TOP RANI: Eyes.

CHANDNI: Black.

TOP RANI: Favourite hero.

CHANDNI: Shah Rukh Khan.

TOP RANI: Best movie.

CHANDNI: *Dil To Pagal Hai*.

TOP RANI: Mother.

CHANDNI: Killed. In riots.

TOP RANI: *(to* SATTA*)* You shake like a leaf. Chandni must be correct. I will accept your bet. If you lose, I get the seven thousand. *Plus* your daughter. She will be well looked after. She will earn more than you do. I know what you are thinking: my daughter will never be a whore. *(pointing to* CHANDNI*)* I'm sure her father thought the same before he drank himself to death. It's what men do. They abandon. And we eunuchs are the ones that are ridiculed.

SATTA: That is impossible. I will never allow it.

TOP RANI: Then it is impossible for me to take your bet. Goodbye.

SATTA turns and walks hastily to the exit.

Fifty-to-one odds.

SATTA stops, but his back is still to TOP RANI.

Fifty to one. Three and a half *lakhs* on a bet of seven thousand. Not only can you repay Khalil Bhai, but you can also buy your *kholi* back. And more.

SATTA faces TOP RANI.

But I agree. A daughter is too much to ask.

SATTA walks up to TOP RANI and hands him an envelope that contains the money and a slip of paper with the number he is betting on.

SATTA: I accept your condition.

TOP RANI: Some people take more time to buy vegetables.

Pause.

If you win, your money will be ready. If not, I will make sure Aarti is here first thing tomorrow morning. It is good. Tomorrow is the last day of the year. Men pay a lot on New Year's Eve.

SATTA exits. TOP RANI gives the envelope to CHANDNI. She exits.

Let me tell you a story. Don't worry, everybody loves stories.

Pause.

Twenty-five years ago, there lived a man named Surya—handsome as the sun itself. Women looked beautiful in his light, baby moons reflecting his own beauty. When they made love to their husbands they cried out *his* name until their throats dried up. The first time I saw Surya, he was tied to a tree, shivering with fear. It was nine o'clock on New Year's Eve and I was ten years old, a servant boy carrying a matka on my head. . . *(points to the earthen pot)* this very matka, to fetch water from a nearby well. Surya had raped one of the men's wives. He would be set on fire for it. Men gathered round the tree and started to take off his clothes to shame him as he had shamed the woman. Once Surya was naked, his innocence was obvious. He was a eunuch.

Pause.

But the men were not satisfied: "If our wives burn for him, he shall burn too." They poured gasoline over him, lit a match, and fled. I ran to the well, filled this matka with water, and tried to douse the flames. I poured water into his mouth. He drank a little, then touched this matka and blessed it. He said: "A king will make you whole." That same day, at the stroke of midnight, *I* became a eunuch.

TOP RANI spots CHANDNI walking towards the door.

Where do you think you're going?

CHANDNI: To a movie.

TOP RANI: What for?

CHANDNI: To watch it.

TOP RANI: You can't go.

CHANDNI: Why not?

TOP RANI: I don't feel well.

CHANDNI: Maybe you have what Sudha has.

TOP RANI: Why? Is she dying?

CHANDNI: She looks like a skeleton.

TOP RANI: Good. The same showpiece over and over is stale.

CHANDNI: Then let me go from this place. I am your oldest prostitute.

TOP RANI: You be grateful that I have given you the chance to put food in your mouth.

CHANDNI: That's not the only thing you've helped me put in my mouth.

TOP RANI: I rescued you from a gutter. Your own father did not think you were worth it.

CHANDNI: I am not worthless. *You* are. I'm going for that movie. The men in the movies have something you don't. Something you never will.

> TOP RANI *walks to the corner and picks out a cricket bat. He circles around* CHANDNI *and makes sure that she notices the bat.*

TOP RANI: Do you know what I wanted to become when I was a boy? A cricketer! A century on my debut in England! I'd look dashing in my spotless white uniform. After the match, the British girls would rush to me and say, "I say, old chap, mister brown boy, can we stroke your bat?" But since I'm from India, I'd feel shy. We are a backward country, we are not used to advances. Then the girls would say, "We have heard your bat is finer than English willow. Would you like to rest it on our pillow?"

> *He grazes the bat along* CHANDNI'S *thighs.*

One day you're a young boy playing cricket staring at the sun. . .

The sun shines very brightly on him. The way he holds the bat suggests he is about to hit CHANDNI.

The next day. . .

Blackout.

Five

Grant Road. Ten minutes later. AARTI *is seated on top of* GANTAAL's *trunk. She still has the sheet draped over her and seems happy. Enter* SATTA. *He is very anxious.*

SATTA: Where is that fool? I can't believe he left you alone. *(to himself)* I can't believe what I have done. How did this happen?

He goes to AARTI. *He holds her.*

Aarti, I will never abandon you. Do you understand? No matter what happens. Remember what your mother used to say—be brave. When times are tough, be brave. If you are afraid, you will lose. If you are brave, you will win.

She wipes the sweat off his brow. He puts his head in her lap. She caresses his face.

Don't worry. Your papa is okay. Your papa is okay. *(looking skywards)* I just wish that your mother would give me a sign that everything will be okay. Please, Shanti. Please. . .

He paces about restlessly. A dog barks once. SATTA *freezes. He listens.*

Did you hear that, Aarti? How many times did the dog bark?

AARTI *holds up one finger.*

Once! Just once! A dog *never* barks once. Dogs always bark twice, or three times. Don't you see what this means? I bet on one. The closing number is *one*. I am right. That dog barked *once*.

Pause.

Oh God, what if it barks again? Don't bark again. Please. Maybe I should find it and kill it. Then it won't bark anymore.

He rushes in the direction of the bark. GANTAAL *enters.*

GANTAAL: Where are you going?

SATTA: To kill a dog.

GANTAAL: What?

SATTA: It must not bark again!

GANTAAL holds SATTA, who is nearly hysterical. He looks at AARTI, who seems afraid. He takes out some coins from his pocket and gives them to AARTI.

GANTAAL: Angel, it is lassi time!

She takes the money and exits.

What is wrong with you? You're scaring the girl.

SATTA: I did it. I can't believe I did it.

GANTAAL: Did what?

SATTA: I placed my bet. This is a question of my life.

GANTAAL: The question of your life is whether you can trust your wife's sister. *She* has given you the tip.

SATTA: I trust her with my life.

GANTAAL: Seven thousand rupees is a lot of money. If you lose, you have nothing. Who will look after your daughter then?

SATTA: Top Rani.

GANTAAL: Satta, that is something even I would not joke about.

SATTA: I'm serious. I owe a lot of money—fifty thousand—to Khalil Bhai.

GANTAAL: Fifty thousand! When did this happen? I thought you played small.

SATTA: My gambling increased after my wife died. If alcohol makes you remember, gambling makes you forget. I have failed in my duty towards Aarti. I have failed. I'm a miserable father.

GANTAAL: You are a bad gambler, but a good father.

SATTA: I've wagered Aarti in a Matka bet with Top Rani.

GANTAAL: What?

SATTA: I've wagered Aarti in a Matka bet with Top Rani.

GANTAAL: What do you mean?

SATTA: I've wagered Aarti in a Matka bet with Top Rani.

GANTAAL: Will you stop repeating? I heard you.

SATTA: I am saying it over and over so that it sinks into my wretched skull!

GANTAAL: I cannot believe it.

SATTA: If I do not repay Khalil Bhai by tomorrow morning, I am a dead man. Who will care for her then? I'm glad her mother is not alive to see this.

GANTAAL: Why didn't you just place the seven thousand?

SATTA: Top Rani refused to accept the seven thousand. The dead tip will not fail me. I know it. The dead tip will not fail me.

GANTAAL: Satta, I don't know what to say.

SATTA: Just tell me I will win!

GANTAAL: Call the whole thing off.

SATTA: My days are numbered. Khalil Bhai has given me a final warning. If I do not pay him by tomorrow, I am a dead man.

GANTAAL: There must be another way out.

SATTA: Like what? Maybe we should ask your parrot.

GANTAAL: Even he will be speechless in this matter.

   Pause.

But I overheard a conversation last night between the parrot and the cobra. Do you want to know what the parrot said?

SATTA: No.

GANTAAL: Good. The parrot said that when he was alive, his name was Polly. He was owned by a fortune teller. Now Polly was a very gifted parrot because he could tell the Matka numbers nine times out of ten. Lots of people came to Polly. "Polly the Punter, Polly the Punter, can you tell us the Matka number?" Then Polly would say the number out loud. The gamblers of this city respected Polly so much they started calling *him* the Matka King. *Until one day. Saala*, there is always *until one day* in everything. When you buy mangos, they taste good *until one day* they taste bad. You wear a pant that you like every day *until one day* you are too fat to wear it. A person is alive *until one day* the person is dead.

Pause.

Where was I?

SATTA: Polly the Punter. . .

GANTAAL: So Polly the Punter and his master were really happy *until one day*. . . people came to kidnap Polly. They held Polly by the neck so he could not scream for help. They squeezed his voice box too hard. All the magic was in Polly's voice box. So Polly turned to stone. Right there in the kidnapper's hands. That is what Polly the Punter told the cobra.

SATTA: Why didn't someone squeeze my voice box? I would not have agreed to Top Rani's wager.

GANTAAL: All will be well. Trust in God.

SATTA: God is great but always late.

GANTAAL: Ssh!

SATTA: I don't care if he hears me. Where was God when my wife died? Hah? Which garden was he tending when those rioting bastards killed her? They were stoning the mill owner who was running for his life. And what happened? They hit my Shanti. I'm ready to accept whatever fate comes my way. You can tell God that.

GANTAAL: I will. But there is one problem.

SATTA: What?

GANTAAL: God does not come to this city anymore. Poor fellow cannot bear the smell.

SATTA smiles.

It is a good omen that you are smiling. No harm will come over your daughter. But I think after tonight's closing number, you will never play Matka again.

SATTA nods.

Now you are relaxed and I am nervous.

He removes a cigarette from behind his ear and looks to the end of the road.

Where is a car when you need one?

Six

The brothel. December 30th. Almost midnight. It is dark. Oil lamps have been randomly placed and lit. It gives the brothel an eerie look.

TOP RANI: I thought if I waited, the king that Surya spoke of would seek me. Throughout history, kings and eunuchs have shared a special relationship. At times of war, eunuchs served as protectors of the kings' harems. For eunuchs were strong enough to keep the women safe, yet unable to make love to them. So in the past, *kings* have needed eunuchs. It was the people of this city who led that king to me. . . when they bestowed upon me the title of the Matka King. I realized it was *me* Surya was talking about. I had to make *myself* whole. So to honour Surya's death, I do not pick an opening number on New Year's Eve. And at the stroke of midnight, this city plays a special game. Raja Kheench: Pull the King. I throw Jacks, Queens, Kings, and Jokers into the matka along with the rest of the cards. It's the one time I want gamblers all across the city to win. For I know that if I pull a king. . .

He picks up a dark grey cylindrical piece of stone, shaped like a phallus. It is wide at the base, but tapers at the top.

. . . I will be a man again. You see this thing?

He holds the phallus like an offering.

It is used to grind masalas. You place a thick slab of stone on the ground. You put the masala on that slab and sit on your haunches. You grind the masala to a paste. It is hard work—you rock back and forth, back and forth, and your limbs ache from squatting. But you do it because you are a servant boy and it is what you are meant to do. But that does not mean you cannot think of other things while you are doing it: of cricket and how you run away when you break someone else's windowpane. That is what gives the masala its flavour—the thoughts of the person at the time of grinding. If you think about dead people, the masala will taste stale. If you are homesick for your village, the masala will taste bittersweet. And your master cannot understand how the masala tastes different every time because the ingredients never change. *(indicating the phallus)* But this is now a part of me. It's almost midnight. Odd time to be doing all this *natak*. Odd time, no? *(blowing out lamp nearest to him)* Odd time to be woken from your sleep to see eyes shining in the dark. *(blowing out second lamp)* Odd time for you to be dragged by people you don't know into your master's kitchen. *(blowing out third lamp)* Odd time for you to hear them say, "You will no longer be a man." *(blowing last lamp out to a blackout)* My hands are tied; my mouth is gagged. I cannot see their faces because it is dark. But I can see eyes.

> *Parts of the kitchen start glowing. At great speed, the oil lamps come on again.*

They all have long hair and wear saris. They hold oil lamps in their palms and circle round and round like an offering. They remove my shirt. As they take my shirt, the bangles on their wrist. . .

> *The sound of bangles clinking rapidly.*

Then they sit on my chest so I cannot move. I see their dark faces. They have colour on their lips, all red-red. In the centre of the forehead, a bindi. They tear my short pants. They turn me around. And put this delightful object inside me. I pass out from the pain of this. . . *(indicates sodomy)* so I do not feel the pain of. . . *(indicates castration)* When I open my eyes again it is midnight. They all shout, "You are pure, you are cured." Where there should be the mark of a man, there is mud. To heal the wound, to stop the bleeding. They put mud. Mud behind also. To heal the wound, to stop the bleeding. Mud, like trees grow from. They take the man from me and give me mud in return. Mud.

> *He dips the phallus in the red mixture that* CHANDNI *had placed in the tray. The phallus now looks blood-smeared. He places it upright on the swing.*

By midnight tomorrow, I must be *worthy* of being whole again. Otherwise I will not pull a king. So I relive the worst moment of my life to purify myself for the best. It is called the Myth of Merit.

He lifts his sari just a little, faces the audience, and slowly sits on the phallus. He is in tremendous pain. Simultaneously, there is the sound of thunder. It starts to rain heavily. He stays there for a moment, regains his composure. He still breathes in and out slowly as the phallus is in him.

It is midnight. . . the last Matka bet of the year.

The matka lies at the foot of the swing. So do the blindfold and pack of cards. He uses his feet to bring the matka directly in front of him. He points to the night sky.

It never rains this time of the year. It means the night sky is weeping. It could be for any one of us, for the sky looks over us all.

He separates coloured cards from the pack, empties the rest of the cards into the matka, and blindfolds himself. Then he puts his hand in the matka and pulls the closing number. He removes his blindfold and stares straight at the audience. He smiles.

Seven

Grant Road. Fifteen minutes later. Guru GANTAAL *is absent but his trunk is on the street. We hear music. Street performers playing the drums, celebrating. Enter* SATTA. *He looks absolutely dejected. He is drenched from the rain. A few moments later,* AARTI *enters. The white sheet still covers her. The sheet is wet. She goes over to him, tugs his shirt, and starts clapping her hands to cheer him up.*

SATTA: Yes, dance, my angel. Dance! It will soon be the New Year! A new beginning for all of us! *(looking skywards)* Look—all the stars are out. Stars are the eyes of all the people who have left this earth. They are watching over us. Look—those are your mother's eyes. I know. . . because I am unable to look into them.

Enter GANTAAL.

GANTAAL: Angel! I'm so relieved to see you!

GANTAAL covers her head with the bedsheet and wipes her dry. While doing so, he talks to SATTA.

I take it all clear? Jackpot?

SATTA: Yes, baba. All clear. Not to fear.

GANTAAL: So where are you going now? To pay Khalil Bhai?

SATTA: Later, later.

GANTAAL: What do you mean later? You don't keep Khalil Bhai waiting.

SATTA: But we are celebrating.

The sound of thunder.

Even the sky is celebrating! It's okay. Everything is okay. Listen to me.

GANTAAL stares at SATTA for a moment. The three of them listen to the sound of thunder. There is also the sound of a convoy of cars approaching.

GANTAAL: Listen to all those cars. . .

The cars get louder.

Never in my life have I seen so many cars on this road. How much commotion! As if anybody cares? Does Aarti care? Does Satta care?

SATTA nervously shakes his head, somewhat distracted. He looks at the cars in the distance, but his mind is clearly somewhere else. The sound gets louder.

This is my home! Don't come and blow smoke in my face and remind me that I am poor! How will you like it if I come to your home and shit? Hah?

The cars are very near and are moving at great speed. SATTA looks very disturbed and nervous. He looks skywards. Suddenly, everything goes quiet. Lights only on SATTA.

SATTA: Aarti, your mother is calling us. . . we must go to your mother. . .

The sound of the cars is heard once again. SATTA yanks AARTI by the hand and jumps into oncoming traffic. The glare of headlights rises on SATTA and AARTI as the cars are only a foot away.

GANTAAL: Aarti!

There is a sickening thud and crash of cars.

End of Act One.

ACT TWO

One

The brothel. December 31st. Sunrise. TOP RANI *reclines on his swing.*

TOP RANI: If you think about it, from the time we are born, we are all prostitutes. From the time we are born. What is the first thing a child learns? To suck. You come from a hole and then you start sucking. It's the skill you acquire first on this earth. So why stop utilizing it? Why is Chandni so good at her work? She never stopped sucking. Prostitution is what we are meant to do. All these other things: doctors, lawyers, accountants, these are inventions that deviate us from our true destiny.

Enter CHANDNI. *She has just woken up. She walks with her legs slightly apart.*

CHANDNI: I'm so sore.

TOP RANI: It's a good sign you still get sore. Men don't want the well too deep.

CHANDNI: No one's forcing them to fetch water.

Pause.

Why are you smiling?

TOP RANI: Today is a special day.

CHANDNI: I forgot. Raja Kheench. You'll make lots of money.

TOP RANI: Pull the King isn't about money.

CHANDNI: What if you *do* pull a king? You will lose everything you own when people come to collect their winnings.

TOP RANI: By that time, I will not care about money. I will not care. . .

CHANDNI: Why do you always act so strange just before the New Year?

TOP RANI: Aah, Chandni, Chandni. You have come a long way. *We* have come a long way. Come. Talk to me.

CHANDNI: I have work to do. Otherwise you will remind me that you picked me up from the gutter.

TOP RANI: Not today. Today, I just want my daughter next to me. Come. Press my feet. You'll feel better.

CHANDNI sits on the floor with his feet in her lap.

You're a very lucky girl.

CHANDNI: Yes, I've been saved from the gutter.

CHANDNI starts pressing his feet too hard.

TOP RANI: With some love. What are feet if they are not pressed with love?

CHANDNI: I cannot make out whether you are happy or sad.

TOP RANI: And people cannot make out if I am man or woman. It is sad that a *hijra* is made by what he doesn't have. I have to show people what they can't see. That is why you are lucky. You can show your breasts because you have them and it is what people want. But people are repelled by what I don't have. Chandni, you are one country. You take off all your clothes and tell me: "Look, look, I have this terrible nuclear bomb. It will destroy you." And I am the country that laughs in your face. I simply lift my sari: "Look, look, I have this terrible nothing." And of the two countries, *you* will surrender.

CHANDNI: I surrendered a long time ago.

Pause.

Will I ever be free?

TOP RANI: You can't be free. You have to charge.

CHANDNI: Will I ever be able to say no if I don't want to press your feet?

TOP RANI: No.

CHANDNI: Even though I'm your first daughter?

TOP RANI: That's why I hold you so close. You're my number one prostitute.

CHANDNI: I'm proud, so proud.

TOP RANI: You have my blessing.

CHANDNI: I don't want your blessing.

TOP RANI: *(holding her chin in his hand)* Then what do you want, Chandni? You have everything. You have nice breasts, a home, a family. You have *me*. Don't you love me?

CHANDNI: With all my heart.

TOP RANI: Sometimes a heart can be the wrong colour. What is the colour of your heart, Chandni?

CHANDNI: The colour of your sari.

TOP RANI: Purple?

CHANDNI: My heart is bruised.

TOP RANI: I love colours. They're so. . . colourful.

CHANDNI: Can I wear your sari?

TOP RANI: Of course. But you will never leave here with it.

CHANDNI: Then I don't want it.

TOP RANI: Now don't sit there with a black face.

CHANDNI: If my future is black, my face will be the same colour.

TOP RANI: And the future is shaped by betrayal.

CHANDNI: What do you mean?

TOP RANI: Trees, fire, mud, and. . .

> *TOP RANI reaches for a small switch that is connected to a light bulb. He turns it on. Below the light bulb is a small cage. In it is a little girl with her head in her knees. It is AARTI.*

. . . betrayal. The four constants of this world. Betrayal is a part of nature. We are all betrayed at some point in our lives. You were betrayed by your father who drank himself to death. In turn, you will betray too.

CHANDNI: I have no intention of doing so.

TOP RANI: Can you understand why her father gambled her away?

CHANDNI: No.

TOP RANI: Trees, fire, mud, and *betrayal*. Now. Meet your new student.

CHANDNI: I will teach her nothing.

TOP RANI: Why not?

CHANDNI: She's only ten.

TOP RANI: So she will earn ten times more. *(to AARTI)* You will charge more than Chandni. Indian men believe that if they take a virgin they will be cured of all disease. Do you know how precious you are?

Pause.

Why are you silent?

CHANDNI: She doesn't speak.

TOP RANI: I forgot. Then how will she make sounds? Men love sounds.

Pause.

What if I record you and play it in the background when she is working? *(to AARTI)* Is dubbing okay with you?

We hear a phone ring. It is TOP RANI's cellphone. He answers it.

Top Rani and Company.

Pause.

Hah, jeweller *bhai*. . .

There is a pause while he listens to the jeweller's words. He snaps his fingers and sends CHANDNI away.

Which bookie are you talking about? Give me a name and I will give you his testicles. You can't just tell me that a bookie told you Matka is fixed. Tell me, how long ago did I start Matka? Ten years. Not one illegal incident. There's no cheating going on. Now give me the name of the bookie that said this. Why are you not revealing the name? I think *you* are unhappy about something. . .

The jeweller hangs up on him.

A bookie would not dare make this accusation. Our jeweller friend is unhappy. I will have to research why.

He puts the phone down. Enter CHANDNI. She looks shaken.

CHANDNI: Sudha is dead.

TOP RANI: Oh. Are you sure?

CHANDNI: She's not breathing.

TOP RANI: My daughter is dead. May she be happy in the ever after. May she never open her legs again.

   Pause.

Is that jeweller your customer?

CHANDNI: Sudha is dead. Is that all you can. . .

TOP RANI: Is the jeweller your customer or not?

CHANDNI: Yes. . .

TOP RANI: He's a very unhappy man.

CHANDNI: About what? He goes mad every time I touch him. He brings me a gift every time he comes. Last time he got me a necklace the thickness of a dog leash. So there is no problem.

TOP RANI: He's already paying you. Why the necklace?

CHANDNI: Ask him.

TOP RANI: Something tells me the answer is right here.

CHANDNI: But he's very happy with me.

TOP RANI: Then the problem lies in his happiness. What words of wisdom have you been whispering to him?

CHANDNI: I don't have any wisdom to give.

   TOP RANI goes to his wooden cupboard and removes a pack of cards. He walks back to CHANDNI.

TOP RANI: Are you sure you did not disclose anything to the jeweller?

CHANDNI: I'm sure.

TOP RANI: *(chucking cards towards her)* I would like you to use the very subtle clues I am throwing your way. Are you sure there is nothing you have revealed?

   CHANDNI tries to leave. TOP RANI throws her to the floor. He puts his foot on her chest.

Think hard. I'm not afraid to lose one more daughter. *(pointing to the cage)* Replacements are not that hard to find.

CHANDNI: I just told him. . . you do not pick cards. . . from the matka for the last bet of the year.

TOP RANI: What makes you think that?

CHANDNI: I made it up.

TOP RANI: What else did you tell him?

CHANDNI: Nothing.

He puts on more pressure with his foot.

TOP RANI: What else did you tell him?

CHANDNI: I told him that I knew how you called the closing number on that day.

TOP RANI: Why in the name of prostitution did you say that?

CHANDNI: He thought that I knew something and kept offering me the necklace if I gave him a tip. So I lied. I told him that this year you would decide the closing number based on which daughter earns the most money.

He lifts his foot off her.

TOP RANI: And that idiot believed you? The jeweller must have placed a huge bet with a bookie. Now he's calling me up to talk ill of the bookie because he doesn't want to pay up. If I intervene, then no money to pay. But his plan flopped double time. And you got a necklace on top of that. Go fetch it.

Exit CHANDNI.

(to AARTI) Now, dear one. It's time we have a little talk. Do you know what we do here? This is a *kotha* where girls rent their bodies to older men. Your own father tried to kill you. A speck of dust on his shirt sleeve that he flicked away straight into traffic. It's a small miracle that he died and you are alive, so take it that you're meant to be here. You start work tonight. It will distract you from your father's death. Chandni!

Enter CHANDNI with the chain.

I will keep the chain. As punishment, you will not step out of this brothel without my permission.

CHANDNI: I'm leaving for good.

TOP RANI digs his ear as if he did not hear correctly.

I'm buying my freedom.

TOP RANI: My dear, even gold cannot take your place.

CHANDNI: You have Aarti now. She will grow into a beautiful woman.

TOP RANI: I will watch you die in this brothel, but you will never leave.

CHANDNI: What if you die first?

TOP RANI holds his heart. He staggers back and forth, slowly moving towards CHANDNI.

TOP RANI: My own daughter. . . ooh it breaks my heart in two. . . no. . . three. . . no. . . twenty-three. . .

He suddenly grabs hold of CHANDNI's hair and pulls her to the floor. He pushes her face very close to the floor.

What do you see down there?

CHANDNI: I. . . don't know. . .

TOP RANI: Look closely and you will see the roots of your prostitution. If you leave this brothel, you will die without roots. You cannot read, you cannot write. What will you do? Hah? Maybe you can get married. Indian men love virgins. You are my daughter. Now stay at home and act like one.

He lets her go. She stays on the ground. He pats her hair lovingly as he looks at AARTI.

(to AARTI) See? Our family is very close. I just can't let her go.

CHANDNI gets up. TOP RANI looks at AARTI.

Chandni. That foreign tourist who came last night. He's staying at Hotel Baaz, round the corner. Go tell him that I have an opportunity for him—a new girl, very young, needs breaking in. But if he mentions a word to anyone, tell him that even though he came from his country in a plane, he will go back in a box.

He violently kicks the cage bars.

Even smaller than this cage!

Two

Grant Road. December 31st. Eight p.m. GANTAAL *is asleep. The white sheet covers him. The full moon shines on him. Enter* SATTA. *He is covered in blood. Shards of glass are stuck in his face.*

SATTA: I have a tip for you.

GANTAAL wakes up and looks at SATTA.

Are you listening? I have a tip.

GANTAAL: You are dead.

SATTA: That is why my tip is dead accurate.

GANTAAL: What are you talking about?

SATTA: I failed her, Gantaal. I failed my own child.

GANTAAL: Why did you have to kill yourself?

SATTA: It was either the car or Khalil Bhai's knife. I wish Aarti were dead too. Why did she have to live?

GANTAAL: It's too late now. Nothing can be done.

SATTA: They will turn my Aarti into a prostitute. . . my Aarti. . . you must do something.

GANTAAL: This has nothing to do with me.

SATTA: Here is my tip. Do something. Otherwise you will have to come home with me. *(pointing to the moon)* All bad people stay there. You know that.

The moon moves towards SATTA. SATTA *runs from it.*

It's coming for me. I have to go.

SATTA exits. A soft wind starts to blow and the white sheet flut-ters. The wind picks up momentum. GANTAAL *gets up and the sheet slowly comes off him. It floats high in the air. He looks at the sheet and deliberates.*

GANTAAL: *(to Aroramanyu)* Aroramanyu, this is your wing. Now take it to her and protect her from harm.

The wind rises to a crescendo and the sheet sails away across the stage, rising higher and higher.

Three

The brothel. Eight p.m. A wind blows through the brothel. CHANDNI *is at a clothesline. She is putting clothes into a dirty plastic bucket. There is a bedsheet on the line. It looks exactly like* GANTAAL's *sheet.*

CHANDNI: *(to AARTI)* Years ago, I was in that same cage. I was just as stubborn as you are. Until Top Rani had a man sent in.

The wind picks up momentum. The sheet rises high. AARTI *watches it.*

But you are luckier than I was. I went to Hotel Baaz, but the foreign man has left.

The sheet floats high in the air. Enter TOP RANI. *He watches as the sheet lands over the cage.* AARTI *pulls the sheet through the cage and covers herself.*

TOP RANI: Don't get too used to covering yourself. If God had intended for us to wear clothes, we would be born with them. We only wear skin, little one. Do you understand?

Pause.

Chandni, explain the rules to her.

CHANDNI *turns to leave.*

I want you to explain the rules to her.

CHANDNI: You will be given two meals a day. You will never be allowed to leave this place for the rest of your life. This is your new home. Get used to it. If you cry, you will be beaten with a cricket bat. There will be no marks on your body. But your stomach will hurt. A constant thumping of the stomach will stop babies. We do not want babies.

CHANDNI is unable to go on. She exits.

TOP RANI: She left out the best part. Once in a while, you can listen to the radio. Did you understand everything that was just said?

She does not look his way. TOP RANI fetches the cricket bat and bangs it hard against the cage. AARTI sits up, petrified. Her hands shaking, she indicates that she would like to write something.

What—you want to write?

She nods. He gets her a pencil and some scraps of paper. He gives it to her. She starts writing.

I hope it's not a letter to your father. Postage will be expensive.

She hands him the paper. He reads from it.

"My mother's sister will give money." I did not know this. Chandni is slacking in research. Where was this woman when I came to the hospital to take you? Hah? You were alone there. Your father was inside dying. No one will help you now. What does she do?

AARTI starts writing again. She gives him the paper. He reads.

"Sweeper. Jeweller's shop. Grant Road."

(reading again) Jeweller's shop. At Grant Road.

TOP RANI smiles as though his mind has just solved an equation.

(shouting) Chandni!

Enter CHANDNI.

Ask her where her mother's sister works. Ask her. You will understand why.

CHANDNI: Where does your mother's sister work?

TOP RANI: In a jeweller's shop at Grant Road.

CHANDNI: The same jeweller who. . .

TOP RANI: Word of mouth is wonderful, isn't it? I was wondering why that stupid father of hers was so sure that he would win. From prostitute to jeweller to sweeper to gambler. The Matka tip chain! And who pays in the end? A ten-year-old girl!

CHANDNI: What have I done?

TOP RANI: It is destiny. God willing, I will help her fulfill it tonight.

CHANDNI: But the foreign man has left.

TOP RANI: Are you sure?

CHANDNI: He's gone.

He studies CHANDNI'S *face for a brief moment.*

TOP RANI: *(to* AARTI*)* Sorry. No foreign university for you. But Indian education is also good. *(to* CHANDNI*)* Don't be upset. What you have done is most natural.

CHANDNI: How?

TOP RANI: One prostitute died. So you gave birth to another.

CHANDNI *turns around to leave.*

Where are you going?

CHANDNI: To make preparations for Sudha's cremation.

TOP RANI: Be careful that *you* don't get burned.

She exits.

(to AARTI*)* Chandni was my first prostitute. She was the same age as you when I had her broken in. God works in strange ways. He breaks you suddenly, when you least expect it. He takes every drop of life from you. Then one day you wake up stronger than before. . . like a tiger. No one can touch you then.

She gives him a piece of paper again.

"Chance to win freedom." Freedom? No one is *free.* Look at me. I have money. I have long, strong muscles. But when I step into the street, even a stray dog gets more love than I do. No one is free.

She asks him to turn the paper around. He does. He reads.

"Let us bet." This is turning into a very bad scene from a Hindi movie. But. . . if God wants you to be free, you will. Chandni!

CHANDNI enters with a sari in her hand. She stares at TOP RANI.

CHANDNI: Take this.

She holds the sari out for TOP RANI.

TOP RANI: What is it?

CHANDNI: It's what Sudha died in. Perhaps you'd like to wear it.

She thrusts the sari into his hands. TOP RANI *caresses it.*

TOP RANI: I'll keep it. I'll save it for Aarti.

CHANDNI tries to take the sari back from him, but TOP RANI *holds on.*

Do you remember yesterday's opening and closing numbers?

CHANDNI is still trying to tug the sari from his hands.

CHANDNI: Yes.

TOP RANI lets go. CHANDNI jerks back a little. He walks to the cupboard. He removes two blank cards from the cupboard, and a pencil. He hands the blank cards and pencil to CHANDNI but she does not take them.

TOP RANI: Now put that dead sari down and hold these cards. Write down the opening number on one card, and the closing number on the other.

She does.

Now show me.

She shows the cards to TOP RANI.

Now show her.

CHANDNI shows the cards to AARTI.

Now show Him.

CHANDNI: Who?

TOP RANI: God. *(looking up)* Pay attention. A little girl is at stake.

He puts the cards in the matka.

(to AARTI) The cards will decide your fate. If you pick the opening number, you will stay here and open your legs for the rest of your life. If you pick

the closing number, your legs can remain closed. You will be free to go. Is it agreed?

She nods yes.

Then let us proceed. But I'm afraid I know how this is going to turn out.

He takes the matka to AARTI. AARTI *closes her eyes. She collects her thoughts in her fist. She tries to throw them to the moon—to Aroramanyu. But* TOP RANI *prevents her from doing so.*

What are you doing? Just put your hand in and pull. Like Chandni.

AARTI *puts one hand over her eyes and puts the other hand in the matka and removes a card. She looks at it in horror.*

What did you pull?

TOP RANI *snatches the card from her hand.*

I knew it! These Hindi movies are misleading the public. They think some-day they will be rescued.

He takes the card from her hand throws it back in the matka.

Now for the victory dance!

TOP RANI *claps his hands twice—the loud, shrill clap of a hijra. Just as he is about to launch into a garish dance,* GANTAAL's *voice can be heard from outside.*

GANTAAL: Ten rupees only! Ten rupees only!

TOP RANI *goes to the window.*

Show me your palm and you will come to no harm!

TOP RANI: A fortune teller.

CHANDNI: What an idiot. Coming to the red-light district to tell people's fortunes.

TOP RANI: He's looking here. This is a good sign. Today is a special day.

CHANDNI: Why do you keep saying that?

TOP RANI: You have a new sister. What could be more special?

GANTAAL: Ten rupees only.

TOP RANI: *(to CHANDNI)* You are also ten rupees only. Would you like to know your fortune?

CHANDNI shakes her head.

(to AARTI) What about you?

AARTI does not respond. She just looks down at her feet. He claps his hands and calls GANTAAL up.

Will the two of you stop behaving as if somebody just died?

Enter GANTAAL.

GANTAAL: Thank you for inviting me.

The moment AARTI hears GANTAAL's voice she looks up. He catches her eye for a second and then ignores her.

TOP RANI: This flower here is very interested in knowing her fortune.

GANTAAL: Which flower?

TOP RANI: This one. Here.

GANTAAL: And what is the flower's name?

CHANDNI does not respond.

TOP RANI: Chandni.

TOP RANI goes to her and gently holds her by the hair.

Chandni would like to ask you something.

CHANDNI: What is the future like for me?

TOP RANI: Wide open.

GANTAAL: Show me your hand, Chandni. Don't be shy.

GANTAAL takes CHANDNI's hand. He smiles.

You have a very long lifeline.

TOP RANI: That is *exactly* what she wants to hear. "Hello, my name is Chandni. I am a prostitute of ninety years. Now you take off your pants while I take out my teeth."

GANTAAL: You see this lump here? That is your good-deed pocket. The mound is very high. It means you are a good person.

TOP RANI slaps CHANDNI's hand out of the way.

TOP RANI: My turn.

GANTAAL: Money first.

TOP RANI gives GANTAAL the money. Then he extends his hand. GANTAAL takes it.

Your good-deed pocket is empty. But there is something else. Oh, this is strange, very strange.

TOP RANI: What?

GANTAAL: Your lifeline. It stops.

TOP RANI: Everyone's lifeline stops.

GANTAAL: But there is a reversal in yours.

TOP RANI: What did you say?

GANTAAL: Your lifeline suddenly changes direction. It moves in reverse.

TOP RANI: What does that mean?

GANTAAL: It means that you will soon start a new life. Very different from the one you are leading. Perhaps a reversal of fortunes. Or a change of heart.

TOP RANI: How do you know this?

GANTAAL: Your hand speaks to me.

TOP RANI: Then ask my hand this: Will my cock grow back?

GANTAAL looks at TOP RANI in surprise.

I'm serious.

GANTAAL: Why would it?

TOP RANI: The Myth of Merit. It is a time-honoured custom.

GANTAAL: We have many stupid customs.

TOP RANI: I know. A eunuch is one of them.

GANTAAL nods towards the cage.

GANTAAL: What about her? She is extremely custom-made.

TOP RANI: Are you here to tell my fortune or to get lucky?

GANTAAL: I wish to buy her from you.

TOP RANI: What makes you think she is for sale?

GANTAAL: If she is in a cage, it means she has not been tamed. Has she?

TOP RANI: What are you willing to pay?

GANTAAL: Nothing.

TOP RANI: Good answer. Good answer. But what does it mean?

GANTAAL: If I help you become a man again, you help me become a man again.

TOP RANI: I don't need your help.

GANTAAL: Then why are you still in a sari?

TOP RANI goes towards him in a threatening manner.

I mean the Myth of Merit.

TOP RANI: What about it?

GANTAAL: It is not a myth.

He exits. AARTI lifts her head from the sheet and watches him leave.

TOP RANI: Today is a special day indeed.

CHANDNI: What do you mean?

TOP RANI: The Myth of Merit.

CHANDNI: Surely you don't believe in that rubbish. They are called myths because they're not true.

TOP RANI: A myth is a forgotten truth. In my village there lived a girl just like Aarti—no voice, no parents, nothing. All day she would sit in a little clearing just outside the forest with her head in her knees. One day a tiger came into the clearing. Everyone ran. Except the little girl. She held up her hand and said something to the tiger—no words, but she said something. The great beast roared and roared, but it never touched her. It walked back into the forest.

CHANDNI: What does that have to do with Aarti?

TOP RANI: Has anyone touched her so far?

CHANDNI: No.

TOP RANI: Then she has proved that myths *can* be true. The myth goes that children who have no voice. . . have God speaking for them.

CHANDNI: But you are a eunuch. That will never change.

TOP RANI: Don't be so sure.

He walks to the cupboard. From a secret compartment he takes out a glass jar covered with a black cloth.

CHANDNI: What's that?

TOP RANI: My graduation present.

CHANDNI puts her hand out to see what lies beneath the black cloth. TOP RANI grabs her hand.

When I was ten years old, my father sent me to the city to work as a servant boy. My master sold this little servant boy to a band of eunuchs, even though I was not *his* to sell. The coward had gambling debts to pay. One night, they castrated me in my master's kitchen. From then on, I dressed like *hijras* do and learnt their ways. I made money for them by begging at traffic lights, singing at weddings, and by being a prostitute myself. At age twenty, I had completed all the requirements and training of being a eunuch. I was allowed to branch out on my own. In this glass jar, they kept what they had cut off.

CHANDNI looks down at her feet.

Go ahead. Take a look. I'm proud of it. It's my letter of recommendation. It is also why I believe I can still become whole.

Four

Grant Road. Eight forty-five p.m. GANTAAL is sleeping. SATTA enters. He is trapped inside the moon. He wakes GANTAAL up.

SATTA: You must be a good father to her. There are certain things she likes. When her hair is wet, you must comb it back immediately. The knots are hard to remove once her hair dries. At night, she sometimes cries in her sleep. She dreams about her mother. Don't wake her up. One night I swear I heard her speak in her sleep. She actually spoke. She loves to watch movies, Gantaal. Take her to the movies. And let her know that I love her. Tell her how sorry I am. Tell her that her mother and I are together again. It may not be true, but it will make her happy.

GANTAAL: Where will I keep her? The streets are no place for a child. I cannot be responsible for her.

SATTA: You have no choice. She likes you too much. She will be a good daughter to you. She will look after you when you are old.

GANTAAL: I am already old.

SATTA: As long as there is breath in you, you are young. Remember that.

GANTAAL: How the hell do I save her?

SATTA: I have to go now. I place Aarti in your hands. Goodbye, my friend.

GANTAAL: Wait!

SATTA and the moon disappear. Everything is quiet.

How the hell do I save her?

He opens the trunk.

Maybe I should ask Polly. Hah? Why don't you speak? Say something. What can a poor fortune teller do? All my life I have tricked people. What trick can I pull this time? Maybe I am asking the wrong person. But who to ask then? Who to ask?

Enter CHANDNI. GANTAAL stands up. They face each other.

Five

The brothel. Close to midnight.

TOP RANI: After they cut me, the pain took me in and out of this world. The mud was washed away and replaced by oil to clean the wound. They made me go without food or water for three days so I would not urinate. On the fourth day, they fed me milk, and it left my body through a thin tube that was placed in a hole. That was all they left me: a hole. I used to wake up in the middle of the night groping. I'd feel my groin again and again in the hope that I might find something. In the bazaar, when no one was looking, I'd feel. In the kitchen when no one was cooking, I'd feel. I'd feel *nothing*. But then I realized that suffering can be a beautiful thing. If I welcomed it, it would make me worthy of being whole.

He holds his crotch.

For true works of art are born only from great suffering.

He lights a match.

Fire. When we are cremated, fire is what takes us from this world to the next. It is New Year's Eve. Each year, at this time, I light a match. As I watch the flame burn, I can hear Surya scream.

He listens.

Can you hear anything?

Silence.

Surya has *never* been silent. It means his passage to the spirit world is complete. And I will pull a king.

GANTAAL enters. TOP RANI blows out the match.

Who let you in?

GANTAAL: You did.

TOP RANI: I'm in no mood for deeper meanings.

GANTAAL: I'm talking about the Myth of Merit.

Pause.

What is the purpose of being a man? Of enabling a woman to have a child? So the cycle of birth can continue. If you do not have a cock, is it possible to have a child?

TOP RANI: No.

GANTAAL: Now what if you had a child?

TOP RANI: So what if I had one?

GANTAAL: It would mean you have a cock.

TOP RANI: Yes.

GANTAAL: But you *do* have a child.

TOP RANI: I do?

GANTAAL looks towards the cage.

Yes, she is my daughter. Even Chandni is my daughter. I have many daughters. I should have many cocks. What are you getting at?

GANTAAL: The Myth of Merit works *backwards*. If you have a daughter, it means you are *already* worthy.

TOP RANI: So if I am already worthy, I should be whole. Do I wait for my cock to grow back?

GANTAAL: Nothing will *grow*. Your part can only be reattached. But it would be cruel of me to even hope that you still have your part.

TOP RANI walks to the cupboard and takes out the glass jar. He holds it like a prize.

What is that?

TOP RANI: Top Rani. Part Two.

GANTAAL lifts the cloth and takes a look.

GANTAAL: Oh my God. . .

TOP RANI: Horrible, no?

GANTAAL: No. . .

TOP RANI: Horrible. . .

GANTAAL: There is a chance then. A very *small* chance.

TOP RANI: I will take it.

GANTAAL: Then fulfill this condition: the little girl must truly accept you as her father. If she does not accept you, nothing can be done.

TOP RANI: Why?

GANTAAL: The bond must be real. She must be attached to you.

TOP RANI: So *this* can be attached to me?

GANTAAL nods.

If we were in any other country, I would laugh in your face. But here, with a thousand gods, at least one will be in charge of cocks.

GANTAAL: Be good to the girl and she will accept you.

CHANDNI enters.

TOP RANI: *(to CHANDNI)* I told you not to leave this brothel without my permission.

CHANDNI: I was at the cremation site. It will be a few hours before we can begin.

TOP RANI: I shall attend. I will need a white pant and shirt.

CHANDNI: Men's clothing?

TOP RANI: I told you today is special. Let Aarti out.

He gives her the key to the cage, which is around his neck.

CHANDNI: What?

TOP RANI: I said let her out. She will eat with me.

CHANDNI opens the cage door. But AARTI does not come out.

CHANDNI: She's not coming out.

TOP RANI: Aarti, come out. I will not hurt you. I promise.

He walks over to the cage.

Aarti, your father is here. Don't you want to see your own father?

CHANDNI: What are you doing?

TOP RANI raises his hand to silence her. He takes the key back from CHANDNI. He bends down to talk to AARTI. AARTI leans forward, eager to see her father.

TOP RANI: *I* am your father.

In anger, AARTI hits TOP RANI's hand, which holds the glass jar. The jar falls to the floor. There is a resounding smash as the jar breaks.

No!

TOP RANI scrambles to retrieve the remains on the floor. CHANDNI quickly shuts the cage door, fearing that TOP RANI will harm AARTI.

It is destiny! You are meant to be a prostitute!

CHANDNI: It was an accident.

TOP RANI: She destroyed it! Now I will destroy her!

GANTAAL: But there are other ways.

TOP RANI: You're only interested in the girl!

GANTAAL: True.

TOP RANI: Then break her in right now. I don't want money. I want her to suffer.

GANTAAL: I. . .

TOP RANI: Either you agree or I will give her to any one of the taxi drivers downstairs.

GANTAAL: I will do it. But you must leave this place for half an hour.

TOP RANI: What for?

GANTAAL: I want to be alone with the girl.

TOP RANI: I will grant you the request. If I stay on, I will kill the girl. You have ten minutes. It will be midnight soon. *(to CHANDNI)* She's quite young, isn't she?

CHANDNI: I'm so glad you can count.

TOP RANI: You're not saying much. A little girl will be raped and you're not taking it to heart?

CHANDNI: It was done to me as well. Let's go.

TOP RANI: You're not going to stop me?

CHANDNI: Are you testing me?

TOP RANI: Should I be testing you?

CHANDNI: No.

He takes a hard look at CHANDNI to see if she is up to anything. He throws some money into the cage.

TOP RANI: Never work for free.

They exit. TOP RANI remains in the shadows. GANTAAL rushes to the cage. AARTI reaches for GANTAAL through the cage bars.

GANTAAL: Don't be afraid, my angel.

He tries to open the cage.

It's locked!

TOP RANI steps forward holding the key.

TOP RANI: She's a burning flower, isn't she?

GANTAAL: Yes, I cannot wait.

TOP RANI gives GANTAAL the key. GANTAAL turns the key to unlock the cage. TOP RANI picks up the stone phallus and strikes GANTAAL on the back of the head. GANTAAL falls to the floor. TOP RANI ties him to the cage with a rope.

TOP RANI: From the beginning, it's all about betting. From the time of birth. Will it be a boy or will it be a girl? If you start betting with the unborn, then naturally the rest of your life will also be a gamble. But every once in a while God throws us a googly: a eunuch is born. And God, the greatest bookie of them all, looks down and laughs: "It's a sin to gamble," he says. But it's not a sin to take that which is rightfully mine. At midnight when I put my hand in the matka, I am *meant* to pull a king. For I was not born a eunuch. I must honour God's wishes and live in the form he chose for me.

He holds the matka in his hands.

Ten minutes to Pull the King.

He caresses the matka. He sees that it is dirty.

Why has it not been washed? Chandni!

He goes to the inside of the brothel with the matka. GANTAAL slowly regains consciousness. TOP RANI comes back without the matka.

(to AARTI) You've already seen one father die. How do you wish to see this one go?

AARTI stares at him.

How do you wish to see this one go?

GANTAAL: Same way the first one did.

TOP RANI: Should I throw you in traffic?

GANTAAL: Matka. Let us make a bet. If I guess the closing number, she goes free.

TOP RANI: We are betting on how you die. Plus, tonight, no closing number. We play Pull the King.

GANTAAL: That is a stupid game.

TOP RANI: What did you say?

GANTAAL: Pull the King is a stupid game. No one ever wins because you are cheating.

TOP RANI: I am *not* cheating! I *want* to pull a king!

> *TOP RANI regrets uttering these words. GANTAAL notices.*

GANTAAL: I believe you. I know that you are not cheating.

TOP RANI: And who told you that?

GANTAAL: Polly the Punter.

TOP RANI: Polly the Punter?

GANTAAL: He is capable of guessing the opening and closing numbers of Matka.

TOP RANI: If that were the case, why are you so poor? You should have been rich knowing the Matka numbers in advance.

GANTAAL: Polly only helps those in *real* need. If he predicts the numbers for financial gain, he will lose his powers.

TOP RANI: *(dismissing him)* Cha!

GANTAAL: Polly the Punter said that you will *never* pull a king.

TOP RANI: You're lying.

GANTAAL: Bring him to me and I shall prove to you that I am not.

TOP RANI: Where does this Polly the Punter live?

GANTAAL: In my trunk.

TOP RANI: In your trunk?

GANTAAL: Polly is my parrot.

TOP RANI: A parrot? Why would I listen to a worthless parrot?

GANTAAL: Because the two of you have something in common.

TOP RANI: And what would that be?

GANTAAL: Your name. Because of his gift, Polly the Punter is also known as the Matka King.

TOP RANI: What?

GANTAAL: That's what the gamblers of this city call him.

TOP RANI: And he said I will *never* pull a king?

GANTAAL: Correct.

TOP RANI: Why?

GANTAAL: Ask him yourself.

TOP RANI: Where is your trunk?

GANTAAL: Just outside.

TOP RANI: Chandni!

She enters.

You must get Polly.

CHANDNI: Polly?

TOP RANI: His parrot.

GANTAAL: It's in my trunk, just outside. When you get there, keep the trunk open, just a little, for a minute, and let the smell of the city seep in. Only then will my parrot sleep. Otherwise it will escape.

CHANDNI exits.

TOP RANI: Hurry up! It's almost midnight! *(to himself)* If he is a king I must listen. Polly will tell me what I am doing wrong. I cannot wait another year.

CHANDNI enters with a small bag slung around her shoulder.

Where is my king? Let me see him.

She takes Polly out from the bag.

No. . . he's not even a real parrot. . .

He grabs Polly and flings him against the cage bars. He moves towards the cage. CHANDNI steps in his way.

CHANDNI: It's midnight.

He stops. He looks for the matka.

TOP RANI: Where is the matka? Get it right now.

CHANDNI exits. TOP RANI goes to the cupboard to get the pack of cards. He opens a new pack of cards and takes out his customary blindfold as well. He blindfolds himself and kneels on the floor.

I shall no longer be called Top Rani. I shall go by the name my father gave me. Vijay. Victory.

CHANDNI enters and puts the matka in front of him. TOP RANI throws the cards into the matka. As he does so, we hear the hiss of a cobra. TOP RANI freezes. He takes his blindfold off and looks into the matka. He cannot take his eyes off of it. Eyes still on the matka, he hands the cage key to CHANDNI.

Free them.

CHANDNI: What?

TOP RANI: If you ever set foot in this brothel again, I'll kill you.

CHANDNI: You're just letting us go?

TOP RANI: Trees, fire, mud, and *betrayal.* Now get out.

CHANDNI goes to the cage to free GANTAAL and AARTI. They exit.

Surya was right. What is a cobra if not a king?

He lets his long hair loose. He takes his bangles off. He rubs off his makeup. He slowly puts his hand into the matka. The cobra strikes. But he still keeps his hand in. The cobra strikes again. He slowly falls to the floor.

When you die. . . everybody is the same. . . neither man nor woman. . . neither woman nor man. . .

He waits for death to come. There is the sound of fire. The dark shadow of Surya looms behind him. Surya has come to take TOP RANI to the spirit world.

Epilogue

The sound of people speaking in different Indian languages—bits of Hindi, Marathi, Gujarati, and so on. The tone is forceful and congested, as if a heated debate is taking place. SATTA *stands alone on stage.*

SATTA: The moment I came to the spirit world, I looked for my wife everywhere. I called her name a thousand times—Shanti, Shanti. . . but there was no response. I understand why. She's in a different place. When you die, your own conscience takes you to the place you deserve to go to. A man who gambles his own daughter away isn't a man. He's a eunuch. Testicles notwithstanding. If you gave such a person a moral compass, it would point straight to his heart and his heart would tell him what a coward he's been.

Pause.

Right now, I'm part of a reception committee. Half of Bombay is here—gamblers, bookies, prostitutes. Even Sudha. There are scores to settle, questions to ask. So you'll have to excuse us. We're awaiting the arrival of a very important guest. We have lots to talk about.

The voices rise again to a frenzied crescendo.

End of play.

THE DISHWASHERS
BY MORRIS PANYCH

Author's Note

So often with plays that have—for lack of a better description—an absurdist bent, theatre artists can and will take liberties with both their dialogue and their stage directions that they might not otherwise attempt. Absurd and comic situations such as those often found in my plays should not give licence to producers, actors, and directors to bend reality all out of shape with overacting and silly direction. In my mind, the absurdities of the situations I have created are real, the people involved in them are real, and the outcome has high stakes for the characters involved in the world the drama creates. In *The Dishwashers*, I have created a situation that cannot play without the complete believability and integrity of all of the elements of the production: acting, directing, design. Sometimes, with the set for example, Ken MacDonald and I will try to convey a dreamlike sense of reality that should not be confused with non-reality. A dream, when you are in it, is real; sometimes frightening, sometimes alarming, sometimes funny, but the stakes for you in its "reality" are always high, and the existential outcome of its events is always vital. If you have ever woken from a nightmare, screaming, or ever found yourself laughing out loud in your sleep, you will know how deeply real and truthful a dream can appear to be. So it should be with any production of this play.

The Dishwashers is dedicated to my father, Peter Panych; a hard-working and decent man—one of millions, quietly, unobtrusively, keeping the wheels turning.

Morris Panych
August 2005

INTRODUCTION TO *THE DISHWASHERS*

This kind of thing NEVER happens, but it did.

Announcing the next season's plays is a much-anticipated event. Audience members, artists, the media all start trying to tease the information out of you before the official launch. Our marketing department readies the brochure in relative secrecy, staff getting peeks on a need-to-know basis only. In 2002 we announced Panych's *The Dishwashers* as part of our next season. Big news—a new play by an accomplished, beloved playwright. The poster image was brilliant and plastered everywhere. Word was out.

And then Morris pulled the show. Cancelled it.

He said the play wasn't ready. This never happens, not on a scale this large. You muscle through the work and pray for the best. You don't cancel. But I'm so proud we did. It's a testament to the trust and respect that Bill Millerd has for Morris both in programming the premiere and in cancelling it, and then. . . replacing it with another new play that Morris felt was production-ready, one that would win him the 2004 Governor General's Literary Award for Drama: *Girl in the Goldfish Bowl*. It was a beautiful premiere and a brilliant script. And so was *The Dishwashers*, which finally premiered with us—when it was solidly stage-worthy—in 2005.

I love this play. I loved this production. It was stunning. The performances were outstanding, Stevie Miller was spellbinding, and Shawn Macdonald's Emmet was excruciating in the best possible way. And the detailed design, the grime, the density of it, the layers of colour blending into a unique shade of brown grit was exceptional even for Ken MacDonald, whose sense of style and detail is always memorable. In the foreword to the first publication of this play Morris gives advice about how to act the show "right" based on the number of productions he felt got it wrong.

RACHEL DITOR: For future productions, is there a trick or insight you have about getting this play "right"?

Morris Panych: One thing I would add is that the play is about dish-washers, and if they're not washing dishes, there's no play. There have been productions where not much was done in the way of that, and the script doesn't work because it's like a complement to the action.

RD: Do you have a particularly memorable moment from the production?

MP: I think just to witness the water fight every night was a thrill to me; I always knew it would work dramatically, but to see it play out was very satisfying, especially as it's largely unscripted and action is important to me. It was, however, a very tricky thing, because water has a mind of its own; in fact, on opening night in Toronto the actors changed a bit of the blocking by mistake and Jonathan Crombie nearly slipped and fell—of course it was mentioned by one of these tiresome critics, who often long for action and excitement but when it happens find something to complain about.

RD: Did you learn something from working on this play? Did it teach you something about your craft?

MP: It taught me, above all things, to follow my writing instincts. Initially, I knew it was a play about three dishwashers struggling together and against each other, and that they were all a generation apart; during its long development (I think maybe five years) I was convinced to add other characters, from upstairs, et cetera, and I talked myself into following that advice. Then I dropped the whole project for a while out of frustration and when I came back to it, it was more obvious than ever that my initial impulse was the right one. Advice in playwriting is good and often useful, but a playwright must stick with his impulse, because that is the true engine of the play.

RD: What was the genesis of the play?

MP: Generally I don't start with a passion; I start with a sense that becomes a passion, but the sense is fleeting and indescribable, like an image from a passing train; you see it for a flash and spend the rest of your time trying to figure out what it was.

The Dishwashers premiered on February 17, 2005, at the Arts Club Theatre in Vancouver, British Columbia, with the following cast and creative team:

Dressler: Stephen E. Miller
Emmett: Ted Cole
Moss: Shawn Macdonald
Burroughs: Toby Berner

Director: Morris Panych
Set design: Ken MacDonald
Lighting design: Gerald King
Costume design: Nancy Bryant
Sound design: Darren W. Hales
Stage manager: Caryn Fehr
Assistant stage manager: Anne Taylor

Characters

Dressler
Emmett
Moss
Burroughs

ACT ONE

Scene One

In the cellar of a restaurant; piles of dishes impressively high; to one side a dumbwaiter, bringing more dishes. Other washing equipment; sprayers, scrub brushes, etc. Two men are standing more or less in the middle of the room. DRESSLER, the older and heftier of the two, arm around the younger man's shoulder, shows EMMETT the ropes.

DRESSLER: I just hope you got the right stuff for this.

EMMETT: Why—why do you say that?

DRESSLER: I don't know. I just hope you do. I look at your hands and I wonder. That's all.

EMMETT considers his hands.

EMMETT: Manual labour isn't really my—

DRESSLER: You look more like—your what?

EMMETT: —thing.

DRESSLER: —more like busboy material to me. Why'd they send you down here, I have to ask myself.

EMMETT: I prefer this, actually.

DRESSLER: You don't say.

EMMETT: There's a—certain degree of—what's the word?—

DRESSLER: I don't know.

EMMETT: —anonymity.

DRESSLER: You got that right. We had a guy down here once, went completely out of his mind. You know what he was doing—he was hiding from the truth.

Beat. They study one another.

EMMETT: R-ight.

DRESSLER: Know what this is?

EMMETT: A hose?

DRESSLER: That's your hot sprayer. See? That's for spackle. Know what I'm talking about? Stuff that hardens on the plate. Tomato coulis, béchamel, pesto—you get the picture. That's your Achilles tendon of dishwashing, that. Look at that. I don't give a damn about your modern technology; that isn't coming off in *any* machine. No way. Feel that. Don't be afraid of it—feel it. Go on.

EMMETT: Mm.

DRESSLER: Parmesan. Get to know your enemy.

Another beat as they eye each other.

It's teamwork down here.

EMMETT: Gotcha.

DRESSLER: Is that a tattoo?

EMMETT: No.

DRESSLER: Looks like a tattoo.

EMMETT: Just the address. I didn't have a—

DRESSLER: Uh-huh.

EMMETT: —piece of paper.

DRESSLER: Is there a story?

EMMETT: Not—that I can—think of.

DRESSLER: I'd like to talk for a moment about trust, if I may. I'm going to roll up my sleeves here. What's your name again?

EMMETT: Emmett.

DRESSLER: Wrong. It's "new guy." Got that?

EMMETT: Okay.

DRESSLER: You'll know you've gained my trust, finally, when I start using your real name. That'll be a moment, between us. You know? A rite of passage.

EMMETT: I see.

DRESSLER: I'll look over at you one day, and I'll just—right out of the blue—I'll say "hey"—uh—what's the name, sorry?

EMMETT: Emmett.

DRESSLER: That's it. I'll look over at you, with a little half-smile, and I'll say "Hey, Emmett."

Beat.

That'll be a moment.

EMMETT: Right.

DRESSLER: But you have to earn that.

EMMETT: Right.

Beat.

How?

DRESSLER: Eh?

EMMETT: How do I earn that?

DRESSLER: Trust.

EMMETT: Okay.

DRESSLER: What do you see all around you?

EMMETT: Dishes?

DRESSLER: Try to look at the bigger picture.

Beat.

EMMETT: Endless dishes.

DRESSLER: I'll tell you what I see. Responsibility. Got that? You know what happens if one dirty dish gets through, new guy? We all go down. You think Mr. and Mrs. Fancy Pants, in all their best finery, sitting up there—you think when they tuck into that rocket salad, with the lemon-sage dressing and those little herbed croutons, and they look down to encounter an encrusted speck of *basil* on the rim of the plate—you think they care if it's you or me who let that happen? We're the people they don't ever want to know about. Ever. We're like the foundations of this very building. *Unseen reliability.* Got that? What?

EMMETT: Huh?

DRESSLER: Good. You only think about us when the whole operation starts to fall apart. And we don't want that to happen. We work together as a team, here, to make sure it doesn't. You like your anonymity? You got it. What's wrong? What is it?

EMMETT: These pants look kind of—

DRESSLER: Do they?

EMMETT: Do you have another—?

DRESSLER: No.

> *Beat.*

The guy before was a—I guess the technical term is dwarf.

EMMETT: What happened to him?

DRESSLER: He never grew?

EMMETT: *Here,* I mean.

DRESSLER: What do you think? He was a fuck-up.

EMMETT: You have higher standards?

DRESSLER: We don't talk about it.

EMMETT: Okay.

DRESSLER: Maybe you could take down the hem a little.

EMMETT: If there *was* any, that would be—yeah.

DRESSLER: There's always a solution. If the pants don't fit you, then maybe you have to fit the pants. Know what I mean?

EMMETT: No.

DRESSLER: Good. What?

EMMETT: Huh?

DRESSLER: My name is Dressler. That's all you need to know about me for the time being. I don't like to divulge too much at once.

EMMETT: No.

DRESSLER: I had a testicle removed. For example. That might be something I don't want out in the open.

EMMETT: Not a testicle, no.

DRESSLER: It was a clerical error.

EMMETT: Ouch.

DRESSLER: These things happen.

EMMETT: They do?

DRESSLER: Where are *you* from? Don't answer that. It's a rhetorical question. Rhetorical? Know what that is? Hospitals. You don't know what goes on.

EMMETT: Gee.

DRESSLER: Things happen. You go in with a hernia—it's anybody's guess. But you make it work. You know where a guy's nuts are?

Beat.

EMMETT: You want me to answer that?

DRESSLER: *(indicating)* They're up here.

EMMETT: Sure.

DRESSLER: Wait a minute. You're not patronizing me, are you? Just curious.

EMMETT: No.

DRESSLER: Okay. Just curious. Because, listen. I'm twice the man you are, and then some. Don't—overly concern yourself with my balls.

DRESSLER *shows* EMMETT *his big flabby stomach.*

Look at this, new guy. Can you believe the shape I'm in? Look.

EMMETT: I—

DRESSLER: Is that beautiful or what? Do you see any fat on me? Whatsoever?

Beat.

EMMETT: Is this a trick question?

DRESSLER: You seem a little lacking in confidence, if you don't mind my saying. Maybe it's your—I don't know—lack of a formal education. Could that be it?

EMMETT: I have a degree. Actually.

DRESSLER: That'll come in quite handy. I mean that sincerely. What was your special field of study?

EMMETT: English.

DRESSLER: English. Okay.

EMMETT: Not a whole degree.

DRESSLER: Uh-huh.

EMMETT: I decided to go out and make some money. So I—went out and made some money. A considerable amount of it.

DRESSLER: Is that so?

EMMETT: Then I—yeah, lost a considerable amount; considerable being—all of it. Do we have to talk about this?

DRESSLER: We don't have to talk about it.

EMMETT: I've had a run of bad luck.

DRESSLER: And now your luck is changing for the better.

Beat.

EMMETT: Right.

DRESSLER: You don't seem like a foreigner at all, if I may say so.

EMMETT: No?

DRESSLER: No.

EMMETT: I'm not.

DRESSLER: Interesting.

EMMETT: Is it?

DRESSLER: Not really. I'm only saying because considering how you never actually finished your English degree, per se, you speak it fairly well.

Beat.

EMMETT: Thank you.

DRESSLER: Try not to get a swelled head, though. A guy doesn't want to get too big for his britches down here.

EMMETT looks at his pants.

EMMETT: And yet—

DRESSLER: Eh?

EMMETT: Huh?

DRESSLER: What?

EMMETT: Sorry?

DRESSLER: On the other hand, you need to stay sharp and ahead of the game. You can crumble in a place like this. Crumble, and disintegrate. Like those, uh, you know, what are they called?

EMMETT: I don't—

DRESSLER: Huh?

EMMETT: What are what called?

DRESSLER: I found this potato once, in the back of my cupboard, and I guess it must have been there for months. Sure. It looked like a potato, on the outside, but when I went to pick it up, it completely fell apart in my hands. Dust. I think that's a lesson for all of us. Don't you?

EMMETT: A potato.

DRESSLER: About neglect. Atrophy. Know what that is, Mr. I-Can-Speak-English? Atrophy? My secret, of course. I work out. Look at this bicep. It's important to stay in shape. Feel that.

EMMETT: Holy—Dinah.

Beat.

DRESSLER: It's not appropriate to say "Holy Dinah" in this country. Just so you know, it makes you sound like a—you know?

EMMETT: People don't usually show me their biceps.

DRESSLER: No?

EMMETT: I have a hard time with muscles and—spontaneity.

DRESSLER: Would you say that you have a healthy sexual appetite towards women at all?

EMMETT: Uh—

DRESSLER: Just asking. It's your prerogative. Would you characterize yourself as ambiguous, then?

EMMETT: You don't need to know this. Do you need to know this?

DRESSLER: No.

EMMETT: I'm engaged. Is that—?

DRESSLER: Here or back in the old country?

EMMETT: What?

DRESSLER: I would like to draw your attention, now, to this area over here. This is your locker, of course. Belonged to your diminutive predecessor. You can take down the nudie pictures if they disturb you in any way.

EMMETT: Dwarves, are they?

DRESSLER: I beg your pardon?

EMMETT: I only figured since he was so—you said he was a dwarf.

DRESSLER: He never thought of himself in that way. As far as he was concerned, he was a large person trapped inside a small person's body. Perhaps we should all take note of that.

EMMETT: Sure.

DRESSLER: Washroom.

EMMETT: Right.

DRESSLER: Sanitation; the cornerstone of good restaurant management. Pubic hair in a lobster bisque is just the sort of thing we want to avoid.

EMMETT: Mm.

DRESSLER: This here is the time sheet. They never bother changing the names, of course. People come and go. They're much too busy up there. Much. Too. Busy. You're "Koslowski," for the purposes of the time sheet. That's you. See? I'm "Wong."

They study the sheet for a beat.

Engaged?

EMMETT: What? Yes.

DRESSLER: You don't say. This here is where notices get posted. For example, a staff meeting might get posted here.

EMMETT: How often are those?

DRESSLER: What?

EMMETT: Staff meetings?

DRESSLER: Never. But why do you ask? I find that interesting.

EMMETT: Do you?

DRESSLER: No. This is the lunch area here. Meals, as you know, are provided by the restaurant. We don't eat what the people upstairs eat, if that's what you're driving at.

EMMETT: I'm not driving at—

DRESSLER: Eh?

EMMETT: What?

A horrid fit of coughing can be heard. From the top of the stairs, a very old man makes his way down, stopping occasionally for a breather. This is MOSS, a hundred-year-old chain-smoking crab-ass.

DRESSLER: Oh, Jesus.

EMMETT: Who is it?

DRESSLER: Act natural. This here is my chair. The whole area, here, as you can see, has been carefully marked off for my newspaper. I may not actually be reading a newspaper at the time, but don't let that lead you into a false sense of space at all. At any time, without warning, I could decide to take out a newspaper and read it. On-the-spur-of-the-moment type thing. It's called *latitude*, is what it's called. Eventually, you may work your way up to this kind of latitude, but it won't be in the short term.

> *MOSS lands at the bottom of the stairs. DRESSLER makes a point of ignoring him, but EMMETT can't help looking. MOSS stands, breathing heavily. He stares hard at EMMETT for a long moment, then a look to DRESSLER.*

(to MOSS) Don't ask me.

MOSS: You must be kidding.

DRESSLER: He's engaged, apparently.

MOSS: Him?

> *MOSS shuffles over to the washroom and shuts the door, as both EMMETT and DRESSLER watch in silence.*
>
> *A beat.*

DRESSLER: That's Moss.

EMMETT: Right.

DRESSLER: The guy is riddled with cancer.

EMMETT: That's—

DRESSLER: It's one of his better qualities, but hey, he's a human being.

> *As he exits with EMMETT following.*

What's the word for "terminal" where you come from?

EMMETT: Terminal.

DRESSLER: That's handy. Those are potatoes. Follow me.

> *They go out the back way. A beat. MOSS appears in the bathroom doorway; slowly he shuts it again. Blackout. Music; a cacophony of steam and dishes.*

Scene Two

Coffee break. DRESSLER *sits at one end reading a paper, carefully turning the pages so that they fit within his parameters.* MOSS *sits at the other end, smoking and staring at the wall.*

DRESSLER: I've been thinking about crème brûlée.

He turns a page.

Why is there such a deep inner satisfaction in cracking through a hard surface? Is it the softness beneath? The touching notion that if we really search for it, we will find the good in everything; if not the good, at least the vulnerable; the underbelly of the beast. That life's hardness is only part of the story? My father was a miserable fucking bastard. Beat me senseless, on occasion. But a rousing chorus of "My Hero" from *The Chocolate Soldier* could always bring a tear to his eye. Oh, look. Toilet paper's on sale. And they say it's all bad news.

"pull through the adversity"

MOSS: Don't let go of the rope!

DRESSLER: What?

MOSS: Eh?

DRESSLER: Wake up. You're daydreaming.

MOSS: I'm not.

DRESSLER: You are.

MOSS: My mind is as sharp as a tack.

DRESSLER: Is that right.

MOSS: Just look at this concentration.

He focuses intently, putting himself into a trance.

DRESSLER: Moss.

MOSS: Eh?

DRESSLER: You dozed off there.

MOSS: I was contemplating.

DRESSLER: What do you have to contemplate?

MOSS: My own redundancy.

DRESSLER: Cheer up for fuck's sake.

MOSS: What if they let me go? It happens. A guy doesn't hold up his end.

DRESSLER: They'd never do that.   ↳ young replacing the old

MOSS: This is a two-man operation. Now there's three. You think I can't add and subtract?

DRESSLER: We've had three men before. There was the dwarf, and the Venezuelan with the temper before him, the guy with the sleepy eye who never spoke, that Vietnamese transsexual.

MOSS: She wasn't anything of the kind. Just a nice girl with muscles.

DRESSLER: Downsizing. Upsizing. They can't make up their fucking minds.

Continues reading.

Whenever he gets the slightest opportunity, the guy runs and locks himself in the john. Have you noticed?

MOSS: They come over here, and they don't like anybody, these immigrants. Haven't we got enough people in this country that don't like anybody?

DRESSLER: He's not what you'd call affable.

MOSS: Why go back to a third man? It doesn't make economic sense.

DRESSLER: How should I know? They don't appraise me of every little piss-ass detail. As with all things managerial, it has to do with "restructuring."

MOSS: And here's another thing; why haven't I been paid this week?

DRESSLER: You've been paid.

MOSS: Have I?

DRESSLER: You tend to forget these things.

MOSS: Forget what things?

DRESSLER: Sometimes, life repeats itself with such blinding regularity that events appear not to have happened at all. There's a term for it if I'm not mistaken.

MOSS: There is?

DRESSLER: I believe it's called "the fog of recognition."

MOSS: You made that up.

metaphor for things we never question.

DRESSLER: Take, for example, a fork. Does anyone question four tines? We don't have the time or the inclination, and so it all gets folded into the brown gravy of inevitability.

MOSS: Do you have any idea how full of shit you are?

DRESSLER: You've gone and bought something and don't remember. It wouldn't be the first time.

MOSS: No?

DRESSLER: Aren't you the proud owner of a tortoise?

MOSS: I had a chance to buy half this town, once.

DRESSLER: Don't go on about that property again; Christ.

MOSS: No; I bought the sedan instead. That was the beginning of the end.

DRESSLER: You had no vision.

MOSS: I thought it would get me somewhere.

DRESSLER: It got you here.

MOSS: Rusted-out heap of shit.

DRESSLER: Whatever happened to that famous old car of yours? I can't remember.

MOSS: We left it by the side of the road, George. *faulty bad memory*

DRESSLER: Who?

MOSS: Eh?

DRESSLER: Lately you've been calling me George.

MOSS: I haven't.

DRESSLER: Must've been before my time.

MOSS: What?

DRESSLER: Eh?

EMMETT comes out of the washroom in his ill-fitted whites, carrying the newspaper.

Here he is, Moss.

MOSS: Who?

DRESSLER: Moss thinks you're hiding from us on your breaks in there. Avoiding the pleasure of our company.

EMMETT: I'm not feeling well.

DRESSLER: Exactly. I told the old man, "If it's his bowels, best to keep our noses out of it."

Break bell. The break is over. MOSS goes to his station and begins scraping food off of plates. Occasionally, he picks out interesting bits of scrap and eats them. Momentarily, the other two join him at the bus pans.

Nevertheless, a discussion is underway about your attitude here. Are those the want ads?

EMMETT: Attitude?

DRESSLER: There's an opinion going around that you think of yourself as superior.

EMMETT: It's inadvertent.

hard the adjury

DRESSLER: I hope you don't consider yourself too grand for this line of work.

EMMETT: I'm getting used to it. The dishes part is a little hard to take, but other than that—

DRESSLER: You think of this as manual labour. That's your problem, new guy. Don't think of it as manual labour.

EMMETT: It's just that it's—so much *like* manual labour.

DRESSLER: It is, isn't it? When you look at it from a certain angle, it is. Just an interminable stack of mind-numbing drudgery.

MOSS: Try bricklaying.

EMMETT: No thank you.

MOSS: Brick, mortar, brick, mortar, brick, mortar, brick, lunch, mortar, brick, mortar—

DRESSLER: I think we get the picture, Moss. A man of your imagination and intellect, new guy, ought to be able to adapt his thinking. You know what I'd do in this situation?

EMMETT: You are in this situation.

DRESSLER: Mind over matter. I don't see a stack of plates in front of me. I see an Olympic stadium with a hundred thousand spectators; I see judges waiting with their scores; one set of scores for cleanliness, the other for sheer style of execution. Don't see what's in front of you. If people saw what was in front of them, they'd self-annihilate.

EMMETT: All the positive thinking in the world won't make a dirty dish clean.

DRESSLER: Set goals for yourself.

achievable goals yet visions for kitchen as stadium; contradictory?

EMMETT: I have is the problem.

DRESSLER: When I say goals, I don't necessarily mean unachievable ones. Look at Moss. Sets his heights too high; always has.

MOSS: I'd like to see the world from outer space before I die; is that so much to ask?

DRESSLER: Not if you were a cosmonaut monkey.

MOSS: I'm not.

DRESSLER: Only by the slimmest of margins. One dish at a time, new guy; that's the way to do it. You can't go wrong. Dump this, while you're up.

Beat.

EMMETT: I need the dumpster key.

DRESSLER: Just leave it on top.

no responsibility for what he's not paid to do?

EMMETT: It's meat; the rats get it.

DRESSLER: On top.

EMMETT grabs a large green garbage bag and exits around the corner. They watch him go.

Try to remember; we were young once.

MOSS: Working our way up.

Beat.

Except for the "up" part.

DRESSLER: We wanted things. We dreamed. And then we found out.

MOSS: Right. What?

DRESSLER: Eh?

MOSS: What did we find out?

DRESSLER: You know. The pointlessness of it all. The mad dash to the finish line.

MOSS: Why can't I win the lottery before I die? I've been so loyal to those numbers.

DRESSLER: What would you do with all that money? Think if you were a millionaire, Moss. You might never want your life to end. As it is now, you have so little to relinquish. I figure the happiest creature on earth is some cockroach; crawling around in dark filthy corners; unattractive and unwanted. When he's finally stepped on, imagine how relieved he must be to no longer exist.

death grants happiness

They think.

MOSS: I'd buy this restaurant and burn it to the ground.

EMMETT returns.

EMMETT: That meat was perfectly good.

DRESSLER: Depends what you mean by perfectly good. Before you resume, I'd like to raise the issue of loading, if I may.

EMMETT: It's an issue?

DRESSLER: It certainly can be. We can't be redoing your work here because of incorrect loading procedures.

MOSS: Keep up your end, pal.

DRESSLER: We run out of salad plates, finished, game's up.

MOSS: It's over.

DRESSLER: Timing is all that matters up there. You think it's just a question of bringing people their food? Think again. Up there, new guy, up there, is a subtle arrangement of chaos. You've got an oasis of calm surrounded by a sandstorm, is what you've got. At the centre, of course, sits the diner. He or she, like a sultan, if I may carry the desert metaphor a little further, relaxed and undisturbed by what engulfs them. Nothing must interfere with that. Nothing. For them, time evaporates, conversations flow, ideas meld like candle wax into one another, agreements are made, marriages proposed; you can't have one of these people looking at their watch, suddenly, and thinking "where the fuck's my appetizer?" It doesn't work. You can't have the customer suddenly become aware of what's really going on. That a bunch of guys in cheap tuxedos are standing around, looking at their own asses in the mirror? That, *wait a minute*, figs don't really go with organ meat of any kind? That they're drinking fifty-year-old Chateau What-Have-You like tap water? No. In the truest sense, you want the customer to leave here not even realizing they've been; to float out that revolving door, and into the street, like the whole thing was a beautiful epicurean dream.

MOSS: A mirage.

DRESSLER: At least a width of a finger separates the plates at all times. Got that? If a plate touches another plate, forget it. Glassware is washed in a separate load; that goes without saying. To prevent filminess, we use a different soap-to-water ratio. But don't let modern mechanization lull you into a false sense of security. You've got to remain vigilant about it. Always. Jesus; I've seen a brandy snifter come out of here that would drain the blood from your neck.

MOSS: I've seen worse.

DRESSLER: What we do down here has wider implications.

MOSS: Affects the whole operation.

DRESSLER: I don't think integral would be an exaggeration.

EMMETT: No?

DRESSLER: Think of the look on chef's face, as he plates the food up there. The careful arrangement of ideas, set upon this dish, the balance; the presentation. It starts with us, down here, with us, new guy. We're the vanguard; the front line.

MOSS: Without us, they'd be picking fingerling potatoes off their laps, the bastards.

EMMETT: I used to be one of those bastards.

DRESSLER: You ate in this restaurant?

EMMETT: Ironic, but yes. *— reveals big △ of Circumstance!*

MOSS: Yes.

EMMETT: Seems like a lifetime ago.

DRESSLER: Then you understand only too well what's at stake here.

EMMETT: I hate to tell you, but I never noticed the dishes. Not once.

DRESSLER: Exactly.

Blackout.

Scene Three

The men are wearing little red Christmas hats; MOSS *is working at the sink.* EMMETT *watches with a mixture of awe and disdain. For a while there is nothing but the sound of dishes being scraped and stacked.*

EMMETT: Do you ever think about anything while you work, Moss? What do you think about?

MOSS continues, unfazed.

Politics?

MOSS: No.

EMMETT: Art? Pornography? Do you ever think about naked women, when you're slipping your hand around in the grease traps?

MOSS: That's obscene.

menial work requires thinky and imaginry to not only kill time, but preserve sanity.

EMMETT: Of course it's obscene. That's the point. Anything to take your mind off the work. Isn't that the idea? Or do you ponder bigger questions? Surely to God you have to ponder something. Surely to God, in the absence of any physical escape from here, the mind, at least, is an open door.

MOSS: I used to think about things all the time. Look where it got me.

EMMETT: Ever think about retiring?

MOSS: No.

EMMETT: No.

MOSS: What would I do?

EMMETT: Travel?

MOSS: Where?

EMMETT: Haven't you ever wanted to go anywhere?

MOSS: Why do you want me to go somewhere?

EMMETT: I'm only saying the time may come when you have finally petrified yourself into a hardened stump of oldness so old that archaeologists are brought in to chip the salad plate out of your hand—that you may decide, gee, maybe I've been here long enough. Maybe I should go somewhere else.

MOSS: It'll never happen. And anyway, I haven't got any money.

EMMETT: Right.

MOSS: Somebody's stealing it.

fossilized in one place

EMMETT: They are, are they.

MOSS: Dressler.

EMMETT: Dressler?

MOSS: You don't believe me.

EMMETT: I don't know.

MOSS: I had an opportunity to buy some property, once. Why didn't I? No, I was drawn to the glamour of the restaurant world.

EMMETT: Right.

MOSS: Before I washed dishes, I washed cars.

EMMETT: Fantastic.

MOSS: Those were the days, George. Sunshine, bubbles.

EMMETT: George?

MOSS: Eh?

DRESSLER enters from above.

DRESSLER: Well—I've been upstairs.

EMMETT: And?

DRESSLER: One day you should go up there. You really should. When the opportunity is right. It might reaffirm your faith in the place, to see it running like—well, I know this is a cliché, but like a Swiss ship.

EMMETT: So do we get off early?

DRESSLER: The question didn't arise. As such.

EMMETT: What do you mean the question didn't arise?

DRESSLER: As such, no.

EMMETT: Correct me if I'm wrong, but isn't that why you went up there in the first place?

DRESSLER: These aren't your everyday employers.

EMMETT: No?

DRESSLER: It needs to come up in the conversation; naturally. They're people of incredibly subtle style. They can get a hundred dollars out of you for a chicken dinner.

EMMETT: It's Christmas Eve. I have plans.

DRESSLER: What sort of plans?

EMMETT: I have a date, if you must know. A date.

DRESSLER: The fiancée?

EMMETT: Maybe.

MOSS: She still around?

EMMETT: Yes, she's still around.

DRESSLER: Don't worry. We can cover for you.

EMMETT: Thank you.

DRESSLER: But you're wasting your time. Women don't like dishwashers.

EMMETT: No?

DRESSLER: Generally speaking, they have bigger plans for us.

EMMETT: I've had no complaints, so far.

DRESSLER: She doesn't know what you do, then, does she? She hasn't been appraised of your current social status.

EMMETT: Of course she has. No, she hasn't. Her family wouldn't approve; end of story. Would you excuse me?

DRESSLER: I'm not standing in your way.

EMMETT: You are standing in my way.

DRESSLER: Step around me.

EMMETT: Why should I?

MOSS: Why shouldn't you?

EMMETT: All right.

He steps around DRESSLER.

DRESSLER: See that, Moss. Compromises himself. Doesn't stand his ground. Is it any wonder he never made it in the corporate world?

EMMETT: On the contrary; I did make it, Dressler. I made quite a lot of it, in fact.

MOSS: Then you lost it.

DRESSLER: Tragic.

EMMETT: Why am I being confronted here? What is this?

DRESSLER: You see your job here as a failure. This is the success part. Isn't that right, Moss?

MOSS: The acme.

EMMETT: I don't see it as a failure. I see it—yes, as a failure. I see it—yes. You're right about that. I don't see this as success. Is this a success? Hm.

Let's see. I used to eat in this restaurant, and now I wash dishes in it. What would you call that?

DRESSLER: You lost everything, in your opinion.

EMMETT: That's right. I lost everything. Not in my opinion. In the bank's opinion.

DRESSLER: But what did you really have?

[handwritten: is that the only belonging he rlly had]

EMMETT: What did I *have*? I had money—*money*; I had a big, beautiful apartment, overlooking the water, Dressler. Not just a little water, a *lot* of water. What am I overlooking, now? Nothing; because the room I'm living in—did I say room?—doesn't have a window. It's one thing, Dressler, to never have had anything. But it's quite another to have had it all, and watch it slip through your fingers. *Paradise Lost*; that's what it is. Who do you think is happier in life? The blind man who used to see, or the blind man who never saw at all?

[handwritten: JK Rowling's commencement :]

MOSS: The retarded man who collects all the bottles.

EMMETT: We're not talking about a retarded man who collects bottles. Are we talking about a retarded man who collects bottles?

MOSS: He's the happiest man I've ever seen.

DRESSLER: Of course he is; he's retarded.

[handwritten: Ignorance is bliss]

EMMETT: I was talking about a blind man. I was talking about the loss of something. About how a man feels when everything he is, the very foundation of his being, is swept away. Not even swept away; that he would be able to see. No. He just wakes up one morning to find it all gone; his entire worth. Like that. Evaporated into the air like—like not a real thing, but an idea; something that existed only as a mathematical possibility. And then someone changed the equation. Numbers on a chalkboard, erased. "Oops. Sorry, Emmett. Sorry. Oh, well. It's only money." No. It isn't. It's *my* money! See. Pronoun. Missing. That's me. Missing. Gone.

DRESSLER: You're hardly gone. You're here.

[handwritten: just a statistics and not a person In terms of the financial world]

A beat. EMMETT goes to change.

Just us, then.

They go back to work.

MOSS: How can I retire?

DRESSLER: Who's retiring?

MOSS: I don't know. Ask him.

DRESSLER: No one's retiring. What would you do?

MOSS: Travel, he says.

DRESSLER: Travel. Look at you.

MOSS: Look at me.

DRESSLER: You're not going anywhere.

MOSS: What would I do when I got there?

DRESSLER: You'd long to be back. I went on a holiday, once. Not so much a holiday as a train derailment. There was another time, too. Some lake, somewhere. Nearly went out of my mind. Children, dogs, nothing to do. So I constructed in my mind a brilliant novel. Well, really a novella. A mystery. It starts like this: "Elsewhere, things were quiet, but here along the water, the sound of a body washing up against the pier." I felt that beginning a story with the word "elsewhere" would have a kind of subtly unhinging effect on the reader. Not to mention the complete absence of a verb. "Where's the verb?" You see? Opening sentence, already a mystery.

MOSS: Spare time is the bane of my existence.

he surely likes to imagine a lot to escape what he deems drugery — vacation.

DRESSLER: Is it?

MOSS: Sunday is the most pointless day of the week.

DRESSLER: I can't agree.

MOSS: For one thing, the "sun" part of it is completely misleading.

DRESSLER: I think Wednesday has got it all over Sunday for pointlessness. First off, you've got that extra *d* nobody wants.

MOSS: True.

DRESSLER: And look where it is; directly between Tuesday and Thursday. Could there be a more futile situation?

EMMETT: *(popping his head around the corner)* He could enjoy the rest of his life is the point I was trying to make.

MOSS: *(as he goes off to the john)* What if I'm enjoying not enjoying it?

EMMETT: Sorry I brought it up.

DRESSLER: Don't bring it up again.

EMMETT: Look at him. He can hardly make his way across the room.

DRESSLER gets close; deliberate.

DRESSLER: You want to destroy the man?

EMMETT: He's already destroyed.

DRESSLER: There'll be no more talk about retirement. Rest of his life? A turkey at a Christmas market has better chances.

EMMETT: Fine. But he's old and he's sick.

DRESSLER: Which is why he's been replaced.

EMMETT: Is that—? Uh-huh. By who?

DRESSLER: You. Didn't I ever mention that? Oh. He's been replaced by you.

EMMETT: Wait a minute. Since when?

DRESSLER: Since the day you started. Merry Christmas.

Blackout.

Scene Four

New Year's Eve. Champagne bottles half full.

DRESSLER: What a time they're having up there.

A long silence as the revelry continues above them.

Look at this. Foie gras. When was the last time you saw this in such *proliferation*? If this isn't the economy trickling down, I don't know what is.

MOSS: I prefer the whole roasted *moulard* to this fucking Gewürztraminer-poached.

DRESSLER: Now, this is the kind of plate I like to see. A filet mignon with only one little bite out of it, and a cigar stuck into the smashed blue potatoes.

Beautiful. What an extraordinary little monument to overindulgence. These are people who know how to throw their money around.

EMMETT: It never occurred to me how disgusting this was.

DRESSLER: You're jealous, that's all.

EMMETT: Here's the thing; I'm not, actually. If that's the kind of person I was, this wasteful, gluttonous, boorish big spender—I'm glad I'm not anymore.

DRESSLER: We can't all be rich and successful. If everybody was at the top of the heap, there wouldn't be a heap. You don't like the game because you're holding a weak hand at the moment.

only the losers complain

EMMETT: I'm not holding any hand.

DRESSLER: Don't worry. As you get older, your dreams will become smaller. They won't even be dreams anymore; just little wishes. "I hope that car over there doesn't splash me," "I pray this cheese hasn't gone off." Little wishes. And some of them will even come true.

MOSS: I'm drunk.

Beat.

EMMETT: *(to DRESSLER)* Have you told him?

MOSS: Told me what?

DRESSLER: Nothing.

EMMETT: Nothing.

DRESSLER: *(to EMMETT)* The opportunity hasn't arisen.

A countdown from above. Cheers. A song. They wash in silence.

Gentlemen, I'd like to propose a toast, if I may.

They find glasses with bits of champagne in them.

To the ascendancy of time over all else.

They drink.

What's your resolution?

EMMETT: I'm dispensing with all optimism.

DRESSLER: She hasn't necessarily dumped you for good. She needs to get to know your other qualities.

EMMETT: What would those be?

DRESSLER: Moss?

MOSS: Eh?

DRESSLER: Resolution. It's New Year's.

MOSS: I resolve to hold up my end of things.

He passes out.

DRESSLER: Lovely. And as for myself, I intend to make this my best year, ever, gentlemen. I'm going to do some planting. A little garden; right over there. Grow something from a seed.

EMMETT: Like all those dead plants over there now?

DRESSLER: This year will be different.

EMMETT: How?

DRESSLER: I'm getting one of those growing lights.

EMMETT: And growing what?

DRESSLER: Carrots, I was thinking. That's what life is all about. Cultivating, growing. Gentlemen: to another year.

EMMETT: Another year.

DRESSLER: Cheer up, new guy. There are other fish in the sea.

EMMETT: Well, I'm not looking for a fish.

DRESSLER: I hate to sound trite, but if all she was interested in was your money, then she wasn't really worth it anyway.

EMMETT: I can't believe how shallow people are. Yes, I can. Anyway, she wasn't interested in my money, she has enough of her own. It's the idea that I'm actually working for a living.

DRESSLER: If it's any consolation, you're not doing that great a job here.

EMMETT: Rich people are awful. I'm glad I'm not rich anymore.

DRESSLER: Are you?

EMMETT: Not *glad*, no.

DRESSLER: It's time you stopped thinking about what you were and started thinking about what you are.

EMMETT: Why didn't you tell me about all this?

DRESSLER: All what?

EMMETT: This stuff with Moss. The situation here. I don't want to replace anyone.

DRESSLER: It's unavoidable.

EMMETT: What'll happen to him?

DRESSLER: What happens to us all.

Beat. They look at MOSS; they drink.

Just think how easy it would be to put him out of his misery right now.

EMMETT: Sorry?

DRESSLER: Right now. We could end it all for him. Right here. We could lift his head just ever so slightly towards those smashed potatoes. It would only take a minute. We could say he was drunk when we left for the night, and when we came back in the morning, we found him. Must have fallen over. A tragedy, but a merciful one.

EMMETT: We could, yes.

Beat.

Why would we?

DRESSLER: Don't you ever think about killing someone, just to put them out of their misery.

EMMETT: Only myself.

DRESSLER: What's left; poor sack of shit? No job, no hope, no friends. The rest is suffering, now. Humiliation and suffering.

EMMETT: Yeah, but why should we let him off the hook?

DRESSLER: Right.

They drink as they look at MOSS. Blackout.

Scene Five

Pipes are dripping. Rain. In the corner, a plant is growing. A coffee break. MOSS *sits at one end, smoking;* DRESSLER *sits at the other, casually looking over the paper.*

MOSS: Tell me again?

DRESSLER: They're reviewing your position I think is what I said.

MOSS: That's not what you told me yesterday.

DRESSLER: Didn't I? Well, they're reviewing your position, and once it's been reviewed, then that'll be that. Reviewed.

Flips a page.

Done.

MOSS: What's involved in this reviewing of my position?

DRESSLER: You know the routine; they look over your record and decide. A man fell into a vat of wine.

MOSS: Decide what?

DRESSLER: Eh?

MOSS: Would they fire me? Is that a possibility?

DRESSLER: After such a long, unblemished record of service?

MOSS: I've never missed a day of work.

DRESSLER: Well, exactly. Rather than fire you, they may simply remove your position from the payroll entirely.

MOSS: And then?

DRESSLER: It's not a personal thing. Don't take it personally. It's not you.

Turns another page of the paper.

It's the position.

MOSS: Right.

DRESSLER: You'll just be off the payroll is all.

MOSS: Off the payroll?

DRESSLER: Why speculate at this point?

MOSS: If I'm off the fucking payroll, I'm not employed here.

DRESSLER: One thing doesn't necessarily follow the other.

MOSS: You're full of shit, Dressler.

DRESSLER: Why don't we wait and see. How's your health?

MOSS: Rotten.

DRESSLER: There you are, then.

MOSS: What's that supposed to mean?

DRESSLER: What's what supposed to mean?

MOSS: "There you are, then"?

DRESSLER: I have no idea.

MOSS: You said it.

DRESSLER: Did I? Well, there you are, then.

MOSS: What about him? Why don't they review him?

DRESSLER: He hasn't been here long enough to warrant an assessment.

MOSS: What about you?

DRESSLER: I've had my review.

MOSS: How did it go?

DRESSLER: High marks all around.

MOSS: Congratulations.

DRESSLER: I see your numbers didn't come in again.

EMMETT enters from the bathroom. MOSS moves off, deeply mistrustful of EMMETT. He shows his strength and ability by taking a large garbage can and, with great effort, moving it off. EMMETT comes down to DRESSLER.

EMMETT: Have you told him yet?

DRESSLER: What?

EMMETT: I think you should tell him.

DRESSLER: Not right now. It's not a good time.

EMMETT: When would be a good time?

DRESSLER gives him a look.

I feel—bad for the old goat.

DRESSLER: If you feel bad for him, why would you want me to tell him? If I tell him, it'll break his heart. The trouble is, we live too long, now. People used to drop dead in the middle of their life, and now they hang on until the bitter end. Grasping at every last little opportunity; like drowning men clutching to a raft. Still looking at the want ads?

longevity extended → retirement troubles that are imminently applicable

EMMETT: No.

DRESSLER: Aren't those the want ads?

EMMETT: What? These?

DRESSLER: Ambition. That's what's holding you back.

EMMETT: Ambition is holding me back. I see.

DRESSLER: You could be a great dishwasher if you stopped trying to be something else.

EMMETT: Do you have any idea how much I owe in income tax alone, Dressler? At this rate, I'll be in debt for the rest of my life. Plus there are other people I owe money to, for other reasons. Reasons which—well, I won't go into them right now. But big people, big people with large. . . fists.

DRESSLER: Why don't you sell that car of yours?

EMMETT: That is the last vestige of sanity in my life. If I start taking the bus at this point, that'll be—public transit? Anyway, I have another date with my, I guess she would be my ex-fiancée at this point. She's agreed to take another look at the situation. I can't drive her around in a shopping cart.

DRESSLER: This woman's expectations for you are far too high.

EMMETT: They're not high at all. They're just—they're high. But I can reach them again. I can—I can—I just need an entry point. If only I could get back in, I just know I wouldn't make the same mistakes a second time.

DRESSLER: What makes you so sure?

EMMETT: Because I just know. I just—know. This was a painful lesson for me. This is—you don't forget a lesson like this. This is—anyway; there's nothing in here.

Tossing the paper.

Shit jobs. Nothing. I don't need a shit job; I already—well, this isn't a shit job, but it, it, well it doesn't really play to my strengths. You know?

DRESSLER: You're just not applying yourself.

EMMETT: Yeah, I'm not applying myself. I should apply myself. So tell me about this meat thing.

DRESSLER: Meat thing?

EMMETT: Is this something I should know about?

DRESSLER: Know about?

EMMETT: Well, there's perfectly good meat going out the back door here. I'm just—I'm curious.

DRESSLER: Don't be curious.

EMMETT: And yet I am.

DRESSLER: Don't be.

EMMETT: Is this maybe something I could get in on?

DRESSLER: It's really a one-man operation.

EMMETT: Okay. But is it maybe something you want me to keep quiet about?

Beat.

Because I can keep quiet about it, if that's the case.

DRESSLER: That's the case.

EMMETT: Okay, I was just checking. I'll just keep quiet about it. But, uh, meanwhile, there's a guy I know—and you don't have to answer this right now, but there's this guy and he's sort of a friend, in that kind of way that people sort of think they're your friend, because you did them a favour which wasn't so much a favour as it was a way of getting rid of them, at a time, of course, when you thought you had enough friends, when it turns out you didn't really have any at all, and anyway—he wants me to help him sell this *thing* he's got, and I said, "Gee, I don't think I can because I'd need some place to keep this *thing* some place safe," and then I thought of the cold storage here. Isn't that funny? I just thought of that right off the top of my head. And with the back entrance here. And, and, and, the thing is, you could be part of this, too. It wouldn't just be a one-man operation as in the case of the meat there. This would be a. . . be a joint operation.

Beat.

DRESSLER: Are you out of your fucking mind?

EMMETT: What?

DRESSLER: What is this guy? A drug dealer?

EMMETT: A wh—a wh—a—what? Did I say he was a drug dealer? Keep your voice down.

DRESSLER: This is a restaurant. A *restaurant*.

EMMETT: I know that. I'm sorry. I know that.

Beat.

I'm losing my mind, Dressler. I'm actually losing my mind down here. I'm beginning to get used to this; to my room without the window, to my short pants. This morning when I arrived at work, I was whistling. This is not good. I can't get used to this. I can't allow this to be my life. Even if I can't find another job, I think I'm going to have to leave this one.

MOSS: Don't let go of the rope!

EMMETT: What?

DRESSLER: Pay no attention. He's having one of his moments.

MOSS: Hang on, George!

EMMETT: I'm handing in my notice.

DRESSLER: To who?

EMMETT: I don't know. To you?

DRESSLER: Interesting.

EMMETT: Why is it interesting?

DRESSLER: Just when you're making your mark, here. I find that interesting.

EMMETT: Mark? You can't make a mark here. Mark?

DRESSLER: Give it another month.

EMMETT: A month?

DRESSLER: Why not?

EMMETT: It's my spirit. I'm losing that. . . irrational and inflated sense of self-worth I used to possess. I'm starting to feel I belong here. And if I belong here, what does that say, Dressler? About me? I'll tell you what it says. I'm not just washing dishes. I'm a *dishwasher*. Which is fine for some, but—it's fine for some. For some.

> *Beat.*

A month.

MOSS: *(from the sink)* Don't stand so close to the edge!

> *EMMETT sighs, sits at the table, covering his face with his hands; DRESSLER looks up from his paper, impassionate.*

> *End of Act One.*

ACT TWO

In a dim, rather moody light, the dishwashers go about their tasks. There is music underscoring the activity, and as the routine builds it becomes evident that this is a kind of dishwasher dream tango, building in speed and freneticism. The music finishes with a crescendo and the lights return to the drab patina of reality.

Scene One

DRESSLER tends to his carrots. EMMETT sits at the table, composing a letter and smoking.

EMMETT: How's this, then—?

DRESSLER: We won't be a part of it.

EMMETT: You haven't heard it.

DRESSLER: It goes against our whole philosophy here.

EMMETT: That would be the philosophy, I take it, of performing menial labour in squalid, substandard conditions? And by the way, you don't speak for Moss.

DRESSLER: It's doubtful he'll even make it through the treatment.

EMMETT: Why has he decided to have an enema?

DRESSLER: Wasn't a decision; it was a prize. Only thing he's ever won in his life, and it had to be that.

EMMETT: So you don't want to hear this, then?

DRESSLER: Do you know what you're asking these people?

EMMETT: Why do you defend them all the time?

DRESSLER: I can't help it; I believe in this place.

EMMETT: Is that right.

DRESSLER: I love my job.

EMMETT: No you don't.

DRESSLER: It's all I've ever wanted.

EMMETT: With all due respect, Dressler, and I don't mean to be rude, but this isn't a choice; it's a hole we all fell in.

DRESSLER: Every afternoon, when I cross the street, and I peer into the window of this restaurant, it fills me with incredible happiness, I want you to know; to be part of something so beautiful and so elegant. I can see my sparkling white dishes, set out over all the tables. My silverware, lined up like militiamen, to each side. I'm so proud of those goddamn little fellas; my forks, my knives, glinting in half-light; my spoons, all at attention; my glassware—those translucent chalices that preside over the tables with such gleaming authority. When people pass by, that's what they see; their very first impression—my handiwork. I was nothing but a prisoner before I came here.

not so much a "hole"

EMMETT: In what sense?

DRESSLER: Federal.

EMMETT: Wow.

Beat.

→ their job is easily disposable
↓ no skill req' anyone can do it.

DRESSLER: You know what happens when we start to make demands? When they can no longer afford our kind of craftsmanship? They go out and they get someone else; someone who doesn't care quite the way we do. And pretty soon the tables are looking a little less respectable. The glasses are cloudy. The cutlery smudged. And the clientele slowly starts to change. Not immediately, but inevitably. Before you know it, chef has quit because the customers are asking for something more *basic*; you know what most people are like. They want food to *eat*, not savour. And one thing leads to another and within a year, this place is doing takeout. Plastic, Styrofoam. That's where it's headed. Down the same path it all goes—down, down—to ordinary town.

can't afford it

→ they're the foundation of the high-class restaurant; the silverway display is like a fort barrier against those who

EMMETT: Fine. I'll get Moss to sign it. A simple majority is all you need to form a union.

DRESSLER sits to read his paper.

DRESSLER: Two weeks ago, you didn't give a shit about this place; you were ready to bolt.

EMMETT: That was two weeks ago.

DRESSLER: Besides, you build the old man's expectations too high. He's happy with the way things are.

EMMETT: He isn't being paid.

DRESSLER: He doesn't have a job.

EMMETT: There's that.

DRESSLER: He's getting a small sum; I sneak it into his pockets now and again.

EMMETT: You're giving him your own money?

DRESSLER: The restaurant is making an inadvertent donation.

Beat.

EMMETT: You're stealing.

DRESSLER: Not stealing. The spoiled meat we toss out the back—

EMMETT: You mean the meat that isn't spoiled? That spoiled meat?

DRESSLER: I sell it to a man.

EMMETT: A man.

DRESSLER: Who sells it to another man.

EMMETT: Uh-huh.

DRESSLER: He sells it back to the restaurant.

Beat.

It's not the worst crime in this place. I'm not peddling credit-card imprints; I'm not siphoning a profit from the soup service, or comping drinks in exchange for large tips. I'm simply removing a product that may or may not at one point go bad; I believe it's called anticipatory spoilage. A common practice in the trade.

EMMETT: How can you justify supporting these people and at the same time steal from them? Let me see if I can get my head around that. Oh, I can't.

DRESSLER: I'm only doing what they would do if they were better people.

EMMETT: Only, here's the thing: they're not.

DRESSLER: You can't judge them entirely by their behaviour towards us. When it comes to caring for a soufflé, you won't find more painstaking attention. They dote like parents over a blancmange.

EMMETT: You can't be serious.

DRESSLER: It's something.

EMMETT: They're fascists.

DRESSLER: I'll talk to them.

EMMETT: You've talked to them.

DRESSLER: They need a political way out.

EMMETT: These are legitimate grievances.

DRESSLER: This is just a game to you.

EMMETT: No, this is more than just—this is—two weeks ago I was a different man; I wasn't even a man. I was a lost cause. Yes, it's a game. But it's a game we can win. We control this place; you said so yourself. They can't serve food on nothing. Think bigger than yourself for a change. How do you think people succeed in the world?

DRESSLER: You don't need to tell me how people succeed. Running around like fucking jackrabbits, in their fast cars; shouting into phones. They're upstairs right now, eating off my plates. I'd like to kill them all, to be honest. I'd like to stick every one of them in the eyes with an escargot fork; stab them and stab them repeatedly until their brains gush out through the little holes in their heads. But do I? Why not? Why don't I? I'll tell you. Because my hatred has become my discipline, and my discipline has become my love. I love this job. Not because it's a good job, but because it's my job. Work. That's all there is. Work, death. The rest is a detour.

EMMETT: I'd like to declare this the most depressing conversation I've ever had.

DRESSLER: Then you haven't cradled your dying old mother in your arms as she prattles on unintelligibly about the child she brought into the world out of contempt for humanity.

EMMETT: No, I haven't.

DRESSLER: Neither have I.

Beat.

Speaking of cars: did you sell that thing yet?

EMMETT: I've put it on the market.

DRESSLER: Good.

EMMETT: Why is that? Why is that good?

DRESSLER: Doesn't suit you anymore. How was your date, anyway?

EMMETT: A total disaster. I told her the truth.

DRESSLER: She would have found out anyway.

EMMETT: She did find out anyway. That's why I told her the truth. It was here in my wrinkled-up hands. There's no mistaking this. Look at this. She took one look at my hands.

DRESSLER: Only honest work could do that.

EMMETT: What makes it honest, Dressler? The fact that we make no money at it? What is it, exactly, this honesty? Is it the filth? The sweat? You think real estate isn't dirty? You think trading in securities doesn't make you sweat? How is a man any more honest because he doesn't take chances? Because he advances not one iota? You know what I think? I think you're a communist at heart; that's what I think. No, wait; not even a communist. At least a communist believes in workers' rights. What are you, Dressler? A guy without dreams; that's all. A guy without dreams. Every man has a right, every woman, every person in this world, every single one of us, has a right to fulfill their dreams. Even you.

DRESSLER: What if they can't?

EMMETT: Can't what? Why can't they?

DRESSLER: *(reading the newspaper)* My stock is doing quite well at the moment.

EMMETT: You have stock?

DRESSLER: No. But I like to keep an eye on it. I would have done quite well.

EMMETT: Why do you put up with this? Because you think you have to. People up there, they don't know we exist. It's time they did.

DRESSLER: You just don't know your place, do you?

EMMETT: I don't have a place. I am my own place.

DRESSLER: When you've lived in this country long enough—

EMMETT: What country?

DRESSLER: —you'll come to realize that there are in fact very few upward opportunities. So you have to look at opportunity as a sideways possibility. Which one of these plates deserves to be picked first? They're all the same. If you were a dish, how would you feel?

EMMETT: A dish?

DRESSLER: Sitting there, waiting your turn.

EMMETT: I don't think a dish sits and waits its turn.

DRESSLER: No, but we do. We all sit and wait our turn, and what if our turn doesn't come? Then what? Do we say it was a waste of time, waiting? Collect our little beatitudes of condolence? It's possible we'll wait our whole lives, and then what? In the end, how do we accept what's become of us if nothing has?

EMMETT: We don't accept.

DRESSLER: Have you watched a man die? I guess not. You know what happens, new guy? He exhales. That's it. The breath goes out, and it doesn't come back in again, and everything he ever was, he isn't anymore. Every hope, every dream, every longing he ever had with every breath is breathed out of him. My father looked up at me and he said, "Dressler"—he never used my first name; I think he might have forgotten it. "Dressler," he said, "my life has come to nothing." Those were his last words. And I sat there and I thought, well, it's true, but only because he thought it might come to something. He wanted to be a dressmaker, and—well, that's a long story.

The point is: ambition is a dream that you wake up from at the very last moment of your life. I don't want to lie on my deathbed wishing, wondering. I want to die with the satisfaction of knowing I accomplished exactly what I set out to—very little, but with the greatest of skill.

DRESSLER *turns another page. Blackout.*

Scene Two

MOSS *smokes through a special device. He is rigged up to a small breathing apparatus.* DRESSLER *stands, arms folded. They listen to* EMMETT.

EMMETT: This is our finest hour, gentlemen. Our chance, should we choose—and we should, not to be too editorial about it—to show what we really are.

MOSS: What are we again?

DRESSLER: Let's just vote and get it over with.

EMMETT: No debate?

DRESSLER: My views are well known.

EMMETT: You seem awfully confident. Has there been some vote-buying? Moss?

DRESSLER: This man, what's left of him, is a man of integrity. A couple of cartons of smokes isn't going to bend his iron will. Moss knows, as we all know, that washing dishes is not an easy job, or a very glamorous one. The only way to make it easier and more glamorous is to replace us with a couple of shiny new machines. We don't want to be replaced with machines, do we, Moss?

MOSS *answers with a noisy intake of the breathing valve.*

EMMETT: This is why we need to organize.

DRESSLER: You say "we," but don't forget: you're new here.

EMMETT: New?

DRESSLER: In terms of seniority, you barely count for half a vote, let alone one. I've been here nearly three decades, and Moss has been here since the beginning of the dishwashing age.

EMMETT: How about if we just stick to the issues? Bad meals, lack of ventilation, ill-fitting uniforms, a paper-towel dispenser that doesn't so much dispense towels as *shyly introduce* them.

DRESSLER: Character, it's called.

EMMETT: Let's vote, then.

DRESSLER: Right.

EMMETT hands out the ballots. Music. They vote as the dumbwaiter shunts more dishes.

EMMETT: Right. Time to count.

DRESSLER: So count.

EMMETT: I'm counting.

He slowly unfolds the first vote.

One "no." A vote for nothing; the status quo. The I-would-rather-die-a-slave-than-change-my-way-of-thinking vote.

DRESSLER: What happens when you lose, by the way? Do you step down from politics altogether, or will you go on a speaking tour?

Another.

EMMETT: One "yes."

DRESSLER: That'll be yours. *(to MOSS)* That'll be his.

The third ballot.

EMMETT: And what's this? Another "yes."

Long beat.

DRESSLER: I'd like to see that.

EMMETT: Scrutinize to your heart's content.

DRESSLER studies the ballot for a long moment. Studies the others. Looks at MOSS.

By my count, that's two "yeses" and one "no." "Yes" takes it by, gosh, a fairly large majority.

DRESSLER: Why'd you do it, Moss?

EMMETT: It's his democratic right.

MOSS: What is?

DRESSLER: Democratic right? You don't have a democratic right. You know what democracy is? A whitewash. Once every four years, your opinion, please; pick one item from this sorry selection. What's democratic about living, I want to know? About some woman walking out on you in the middle of the night, with your entire collection of Strauss waltzes and a gold-plated service pen courtesy of the Knights of Columbus? Democracy is a lazy bitch who never did a day's work in her entire life; then complained if after a late shift you made too much noise coming home and dropping dead from exhaustion on the sofa. Fuck her! Fuck democracy!

MOSS: You give me no respect.

EMMETT: Not him, Moss.

MOSS: Eh?

EMMETT: Them.

MOSS: Who?

EMMETT: Management. Up there.

MOSS: That's right. Those bastards up there. Some busboy comes up to me the other day, says, "Are you still around?" What the hell is that supposed to mean? Why wouldn't I be around? I'm not just some little ass-scratcher working his way through college. I'm a career man. A full-time employee.

DRESSLER: Employee?

MOSS: Eh?

EMMETT: Nothing. Let's just—don't.

MOSS: I've had enough out of you, Dressler. Stealing my money. Treating me like shit.

DRESSLER: Stealing your money.

MOSS: That's right.

EMMETT: Look, we dishwashers need to stick together here.

DRESSLER: I'd just like to say one thing, Moss. In light of the situation.

MOSS: Go right ahead; say it.

EMMETT: Don't—say it, Dressler; just—

Beat.

DRESSLER: *(to MOSS)* You've done the wrong thing.

MOSS: Oh, I have?

EMMETT: He's voted to move history forward here; that's all.

MOSS: *(privately, to EMMETT)* Three cartons, remember.

DRESSLER: I'll tell you what he's done; what you've both done. You've made a crack in the very foundation of this place.

EMMETT: A couple of nights off and a clean pair of pants that fit isn't going to hurt anyone. Frankly, if this restaurant is so dependent on exploiting people, then maybe it should go under.

DRESSLER: It's what you've thought all along.

EMMETT: What's that?

DRESSLER: You'd rather bring everything down around you than admit what you are; a lowly working stiff.

EMMETT: My God, but you're a sore loser.

DRESSLER: We'll see who loses.

DRESSLER goes to wash dishes.

EMMETT: We've exercised our freedom of expression, Dressler. We're standing up for ourselves.

MOSS: Can we sit down now?

EMMETT: We can do anything we like. Who's going to stop us? We're the dishwashers! The dishwashers!

Beat.

Right.

Beat.

Back to the dishes.

MOSS sits. The lights fade.

Scene Three

MOSS washes dishes.

EMMETT: They're clever. I'll give them that. They agree to everything, and do nothing.

Beat.

You all right?

MOSS: Don't lose your grip.

EMMETT: What?

MOSS: Eh?

EMMETT: Grip?

MOSS: Who?

EMMETT: Let me have that plate. Let go of that.

They struggle with a plate.

MOSS: No!

EMMETT: Listen, Moss. How about some time off?

MOSS: No.

EMMETT: You look—

MOSS: *(grabbing at EMMETT)* Don't let them mention God!

EMMETT: Eh?

MOSS: At the funeral. Don't let anybody mention God.

EMMETT: What funeral?

MOSS: Mine.

EMMETT: Your funeral?

MOSS: That's right.

EMMETT: No God.

MOSS: Not a word.

EMMETT: Why are you talking about a funeral?

Beat.

You've got—years ahead of you. Not years, maybe, but—gosh—days and days.

Beat.

What's wrong with God?

MOSS: You tell me.

EMMETT: Things haven't been that bad.

MOSS: No?

EMMETT: How was the enema?

MOSS: What enema?

EMMETT: Dressler said you won an enema.

MOSS: Don't ever enter a door prize at a medical-supply store.

EMMETT: I'll try to remember that. Anyway, let's not talk about funerals and God and all that.

Beat.

I'll do my best.

Beat.

What if there is a God?

MOSS: He has a lot to answer for.

DRESSLER enters from above. Descends. MOSS sits in a pile of potatoes.

DRESSLER: Right. I've been upstairs.

EMMETT: And?

DRESSLER: They're very sympathetic.

EMMETT: Are they.

DRESSLER: Completely on our side.

EMMETT: So you didn't bring it up.

DRESSLER: What?

EMMETT: At all. Didn't bring it up. Anything.

DRESSLER: They're quite familiar with our demands.

EMMETT: And yet no ceiling fan. How is that?

DRESSLER: We have a new towel dispenser.

EMMETT: The front piece just fell off the old one.

DRESSLER: Just as well.

EMMETT: I'm going up there myself.

DRESSLER: There are problems.

EMMETT: What kind of problems?

DRESSLER: Things are not going well this month from a business standpoint. Customers aren't out and about as much in this weather.

EMMETT: It's spring.

DRESSLER: Is it?

EMMETT: If business isn't doing well, then why are we washing just as many dishes as before? It seems to me logical—

DRESSLER: Oh, *logical*! This from a man who studied a language he already knows. But go on.

EMMETT: It seems logical that if there is no appreciable decrease in the number of dishes, then one can *ascertain*—

DRESSLER: Did you hear that, Moss? One can *ascertain*.

EMMETT: —that they're not being completely straightforward with us.

DRESSLER: These people have loftier aims than being straightforward with us. These are restaurateurs. They can't be guided by the normal parameters of managerial conduct.

EMMETT: Apparently they aren't.

DRESSLER: Where's your understanding of the creative process, new guy? You storm in here, manning the barricades, calling for an all-out class war, without the least appreciation of the culinary—what's it called.

EMMETT: I don't know. What's it called?

DRESSLER: You talk about this place like it was a business.

EMMETT: Oh, I see. It's not a business.

DRESSLER: It isn't a question of supply and demand. Who's demanding sweetbreads en croute?

MOSS: No one.

DRESSLER: No one; exactly. People need to be led to these things; like slaves to the promised land. You don't go out in search of encrusted headcheese for fuck's sake. Take the case of the artichoke. Only a great mind could have seen its potential—the rest of us would have walked away, thinking "prickly green thing." This is art at its highest level. People don't necessarily want that. They don't really know what they want. They want what they had yesterday: "I want what I had before; that's what I want." Not what's coming tomorrow. But tomorrow, tomorrow is what these people are preparing. It'll be odd, possibly inedible, but it'll be visionary. What'll you be offering us tomorrow, new guy? More whining and complaining? More bitching about workers' rights? Where are you going?

EMMETT: I need some fresh air.

DRESSLER: You're not on a break.

EMMETT: *(rings the break bell)* Oh, look. I'm on a break.

   EMMETT heads out.

DRESSLER: You see that, Moss? This is what comes of all these independent ideas. Suddenly people are doing whatever they like. Imagine a world where everyone did whatever they like. You know what I'd like? I'd like to cook my own hands and eat them. How about that?

MOSS: I'd like to fly.

DRESSLER: Where?

MOSS: Around.

EMMETT returns for his cigarettes.

DRESSLER: This is a war. You don't have democracy in a war, new guy.

EMMETT: What war?

DRESSLER: What war, he says! What war! Did you hear that? The war of principled conduct. *Grace*, stupid. Excellence in the food services. We're fighting against the tide. The *tide*.

EMMETT: Oh. Did you hear that? That was the sound of me not caring anymore. Suddenly, something in my head went "pop"; like that. Pop. Hear it? Pop. I quit. See. I quit. Quit, quit, quit, quit. Quit. The inflated balloon of my own stupidity, burst suddenly. I've had enough. I'd be surprised if you even presented them with our list of grievances in the first place.

The possibility occurs to him. He marches over and opens DRESSLER's locker. The list falls out. Beat.

DRESSLER: You would have been out of a job.

EMMETT: Right.

DRESSLER: Besides, Moss didn't even know what he was agreeing to. Did you, Moss?

MOSS: Eh?

DRESSLER: He was acting on impulse. Being swayed by the crowd.

MOSS: I was bribed!

DRESSLER: Look at him. He would have been the first to go. I don't say he's my responsibility, but I couldn't see the poor idiot chucked out into the alley like yesterday's scraps. It's not like that here. They look after their own here.

EMMETT: Then why did they fire him?

Beat.

I don't mean fire, Moss, I mean—

MOSS: What?

EMMETT: Nothing.

MOSS: I've been fired?

DRESSLER: No.

MOSS: Why would they fire me?

DRESSLER: They wouldn't.

EMMETT: That's the trouble. They would. They did and you might as well know it. Do you think they give a shit about a decrepit, smelly old man, with one lung and a tortoise? They're impervious. How do I know? Because I was one of them. Business doesn't operate any other way.

    Beat.

MOSS: I'm a dishwasher here.

DRESSLER: You are.

MOSS: I've always held up my end of things.

DRESSLER: You have.

MOSS: When it comes to it, when it comes right down to it, they can always say that. "Moss held up his end." Can't they say that? I've held up my end here. I have.

DRESSLER: You don't, anymore. You don't, Moss.

    Beat.

The truth of it is this: if you were any slower, time itself would start moving backwards.

MOSS: I've never left a dish unwashed.

EMMETT: What does that matter to them? You're just part of the machine.

MOSS: I never let down the operation.

DRESSLER: You do, now.

EMMETT: Sorry I, uh—sorry, Moss.

    Beat.

MOSS: It's true, then.

DRESSLER: Yes.

EMMETT: It's true.

    MOSS walks away to the dishes. Starts furiously scrubbing a pan.

DRESSLER: Why did you have to tell him? Why?

EMMETT: It was an accident.

DRESSLER: You're the accident.

EMMETT: Moss?

DRESSLER: That pan is clean, Moss.

MOSS drops the pan. Stands motionless.

EMMETT: Is he all right?

DRESSLER: Moss?

MOSS: George?

DRESSLER: It's us, Moss. Us. There's no George. That's before our time.

MOSS: I have to let go, now.

DRESSLER: Don't let go.

EMMETT: What's he talking about?

DRESSLER: I have no idea. Moss. What are you talking about?

MOSS: Sorry.

MOSS walks a little towards the stairs.

Sorry.

He stops; disoriented.

EMMETT: Would you like to sit down?

MOSS: I'd like to sit down.

EMMETT goes for a chair.

DRESSLER: Take it easy, Moss.

MOSS: Eh?

DRESSLER: Nobody wants anybody dropping dead down here.

MOSS drops dead. Blackout.

Scene Four

DRESSLER finds a receptacle for the cremation ashes. EMMETT folds up the old man's apron.

DRESSLER: The sun came out this morning, did you notice?

Beat.

EMMETT: You weren't supposed to mention God, by the way.

DRESSLER: Why not?

EMMETT: I told you. He didn't want any mention of God. He was very specific about it.

DRESSLER: Who's to know? Two impatient-looking men from the crematorium, and a woman waiting for a bus.

EMMETT: It was his only request.

DRESSLER: What did you think of the rest of the eulogy?

EMMETT: Where did you get all that information?

DRESSLER: Off the top of my head.

EMMETT: He wasn't in the navy?

DRESSLER: I was.

EMMETT: Were you?

a man with no history

DRESSLER: Not the navy, no.

EMMETT: Do we even have a navy?

DRESSLER: It was actually a—more of a—ferry, really; I worked in the kitchen.

EMMETT: Do you know *anything* about Moss?

DRESSLER: Before he washed dishes he washed cars. Before he washed cars, he washed windows.

EMMETT: His life had a bit of a theme, then.

DRESSLER: Not all of us can say that.

EMMETT: Are you looking at me?

DRESSLER: Not at all.

EMMETT: What was it about washing, I wonder?

DRESSLER: Not hard to say. It's the starting over. The clean sweep of things. Whoosh.

EMMETT: Mm.

DRESSLER: Like a soul after confession.

EMMETT: Soul?

DRESSLER: If you confess your sins, your soul is wiped clean.

EMMETT: You mean if I went out and killed someone with my bare hands, and I came back and told you about it, blood all over me, my soul would be clean again?

DRESSLER: Something like that.

EMMETT: Stupidest thing I ever heard.

DRESSLER: Why?

EMMETT: A soul is not a thing. So you can't wipe it clean.

DRESSLER: How do you know it's not a thing?

EMMETT: That's a medical fact; so you can't wipe it clean. And anyway, even speaking metaphorically—

DRESSLER: Oh, metaphorically.

EMMETT: —you can't just drop your sins off at the laundry; you absorb them into your being. If you're going to compare the soul to anything—a futile exercise if ever there was one—at least compare it to a... bouillabaisse. Or tofu.

DRESSLER: Is there any champagne in the bus pans?

DRESSLER gets a couple of glasses and some leftover champagne from a bus pan. EMMETT is inconsolable. DRESSLER pours, then hands out drinks, then toasts.

He always held up his end. Until he couldn't anymore.

They both drink.

EMMETT: I'm going, by the way. I've done my time here.

DRESSLER: I thought you'd given up on that idea.

EMMETT: Why would you think that?

DRESSLER: I was under the impression—

EMMETT: Uh-huh.

DRESSLER: —that since you were still here, you had no intention of—you know—

EMMETT: Right.

DRESSLER: —leaving. After all the effort you've put into making changes. You've had an impact, I want you to know. Perhaps not an impact, so much as a—what's it called when a stone hits the—

EMMETT: Water?

DRESSLER: You can't expect a ceiling fan overnight.

EMMETT: I have a future to think of.

DRESSLER: A future.

EMMETT: You know? That thing that some people have in front of them instead of, I don't know, dishes?

DRESSLER goes back to work.

I'm not going anywhere.

DRESSLER: I thought you said you were.

EMMETT: I just saw the whole thing. Right there in front of me. Just now. Like a hopeless riddle. The present *is* the future. I'm going to be doing this for the rest of my life.

Beat.

I have nothing. All I ever had to begin with was gumption, and I don't even have that anymore.

DRESSLER: You have some dishwashing experience.

EMMETT: I have some dishwashing experience; true.

DRESSLER: Why not make the best of it?

EMMETT: Best of what? What's the best of it? Getting the burnt sugar out of a saucepan?

DRESSLER: There's more to it than that.

EMMETT: I'm sorry; you're right. There's roasted duck grease, and caramelized baby leeks. There's lime oil and balsamic reduction. There's purée and beurre monté and glaze. There's a sea of wet sludge and I'm drowning in it.

DRESSLER picks up EMMETT's gloves, walks over, and beats him with them.

DRESSLER: You have to pull yourself together here.

EMMETT returns to work.

EMMETT: I'll die in a pile of potatoes. I'm more important than this. I know I am.

DRESSLER: Are you.

EMMETT: Not hugely I don't mean, but relatively? And I don't mean to say this isn't important on some level—some very. . . unimportant—

DRESSLER: It isn't *what* you do in life.

EMMETT: Oh. Really. Is that—? Oh, good. Because I thought it was. I thought it mattered what you did. I guess I was under some false impression. You see, I thought all along that washing dishes was completely meaningless, because no matter how well you clean them, they all come back dirty again.

DRESSLER hands back a plate.

DRESSLER: You missed a spot.

EMMETT: Did I?

EMMETT scrubs, harder and harder, then smashes the plate to the ground.

There. How's that?

He smashes plates, one after another, as the lights fade to black.

Scene Five

Later. DRESSLER works, stopping once or twice to look in the direction of the washroom. In a moment, EMMETT appears from the washroom, dressed in his civvies. DRESSLER works some more, but stops when he notices EMMETT looking at him.

DRESSLER: I realize it can be discouraging down here, at times. But I want you to know that it doesn't go unnoticed. When all is said and done, they appreciate our efforts.

EMMETT: I know it's what you believe, Dressler. But has anyone ever come down here and said as much?

DRESSLER: It's what you don't understand about people. Their well-meaningness, their gratitude, sometimes, just has to be assumed. It's called "supposition of accountability."

EMMETT: Have you had a word with them at least?

DRESSLER: A what?

EMMETT: At least? A word with them?

Beat.

You can't do this job by yourself.

DRESSLER: What are you suggesting?

EMMETT: I'll go talk to them. This is—

DRESSLER: *No.*

EMMETT: I've got nothing to lose.

DRESSLER: I don't want them thinking there are problems down here. They'll find someone.

EMMETT: It could be weeks, months.

DRESSLER: I've never in my life caused a problem. Understand?

EMMETT: Why not?

DRESSLER: BECAUSE. I'M. A. PROFESSIONAL!!

Beat.

EMMETT: Of course you are.

DRESSLER: Leave it as it is. Leave it just as it is. Everything.

Beat.

How did the exam go?

EMMETT: There was a question about spoons and forks.

DRESSLER: No kidding.

EMMETT: A math question, but with spoons and forks. I thought that was interesting.

DRESSLER: Did you?

EMMETT: Not really, no.

DRESSLER: Well, let's hope she's impressed with your efforts.

EMMETT: I'm not doing it for her. Did I say I was doing it for her?

DRESSLER: You don't seem the legal type, if I may say so.

EMMETT: The law part, okay, that was her idea.

DRESSLER: I hope it all works out.

EMMETT: Thank you, Dressler.

DRESSLER: I never had a son, as you know.

EMMETT: Gee, well—you hardly think of me as a—

DRESSLER: Eh?

EMMETT: A son.

DRESSLER: Son?

EMMETT: But that's—

DRESSLER: I was talking about my testicle.

EMMETT: Ah.

DRESSLER: I find after all this time, I still miss it.

EMMETT: I'm sorry. Are you—comparing me to a testicle? I don't—

DRESSLER: No. I was talking about attachment. Things you become attached to, even when they're no longer attached.

EMMETT: Right.

DRESSLER: You may find that you miss this place is what I'm saying.

EMMETT: Uh-huh.

DRESSLER: Don't get too caught up in that. Move on. Not everybody can be a dishwasher.

EMMETT: I was a dishwasher.

DRESSLER: You were—never—you were never a dishwasher.

EMMETT: What do you mean?

DRESSLER: You couldn't hack it. *(tapping his forehead)* Up here.

EMMETT: It's not much of a challenge up here. I think that was a major part of the, uh, the, uh—

DRESSLER: Uh-huh.

EMMETT: Nothing to gain.

DRESSLER: What's there to gain, new guy? Eh? Why do people carry on at all? Do you ever wonder? People, every day, just going about their lives? Do you ever wonder?

EMMETT: I do wonder.

    Beat.

DRESSLER: I'd like to draw your attention, if I may, to this spider web, over here.

EMMETT: What spider web?

DRESSLER: Exactly. Did you know that every night for a month now, when we lock up and leave, a spider makes a web from here to here; a beautiful, perfect web? And every morning, when I come in to work, I walk right through it. But every night, she comes back again, and weaves another one. She must sit there all day, planning that web. She must spend all night making the damn thing. Is she stupid, or is she smart?

EMMETT: She's a spider.

DRESSLER: Tell her that.

EMMETT: I can't—tell her that.

DRESSLER: Excuse me.

DRESSLER goes back to his newspaper. He stops for a moment. Takes a deep breath. Continues. EMMETT starts to leave.

EMMETT: I don't feel bad about leaving here. Not one bit.

DRESSLER: Good.

EMMETT: It is good. It's very good. Goodbye, Dressler.

DRESSLER: A dog fell twelve storeys and lived.

EMMETT: It isn't really that I don't have a commitment to this place. It's more like I don't really have a commitment to any place. Is that—? Is that—?

DRESSLER: What an interesting commentary on life.

EMMETT: Do you think so?

DRESSLER: Eh?

EMMETT: You think. . . you think maybe there's something out of order in the world, now. That we have. . . that we have nothing, anymore; no ideas, no reasons, just naked self-interest and cold ambition?

DRESSLER: What are you talking about?

EMMETT: I don't know. What are you talking about?

DRESSLER: Moss's numbers here.

EMMETT: What? His lottery numbers?

DRESSLER: They came through.

EMMETT: They did?

DRESSLER: Not all of them, no. But a couple.

Beat.

Trust; you've just got to have trust, see.

EMMETT: Trust; right.

DRESSLER: And a little patience.

Beat. EMMETT escapes up the stairs; the door closes. DRESSLER looks up for a moment, then goes back to his newspaper. Blackout.

Scene Six

DRESSLER sits with his paper, daydreaming, eating a carrot. He turns the page. A young man enters from the bathroom in dirty, ill-fitting whites. This is BURROUGHS. He looks at the dishes as DRESSLER looks at him. DRESSLER stands, goes over to the boy, and puts an arm around his shoulder.

DRESSLER: Perfect fit.

BURROUGHS: Don't you think these sleeves are a little—?

DRESSLER: No. What?

BURROUGHS: —short?

DRESSLER: Are they? Now you don't have to roll them up.

BURROUGHS: Have you got another—?

DRESSLER: No. If I may, I'd like to draw your attention over here to the sink. This is where you'll be spending most of your time.

BURROUGHS: Yeah?

DRESSLER: I hope you're up for this.

BURROUGHS: I'm up for it.

DRESSLER: You know what this is?

BURROUGHS: An elevator of some kind?

DRESSLER: Not an elevator of some kind, an elevator of a very special kind. This is what brings us the dirty dishes; this is what takes the clean dishes away. What happens in between is entirely up to us. Got that?

BURROUGHS: Yeah. I got it.

DRESSLER: Do you?

BURROUGHS: Yeah.

DRESSLER: I want you to imagine for a minute this restaurant without any clean dishes. It's a frightening thought. Chaos. Right? Maybe you're young, and hey, the idea of anarchy is still attractive to you, but that'll change, over time. I'm telling you; you'll come to know what order means. You won't clean dishes because you have to anymore, you'll clean dishes because you want to. Got that?

BURROUGHS: I think so.

DRESSLER: So what's your name?

BURROUGHS: Burroughs. But you can call me Eddie.

DRESSLER: I'm not calling you anything, pal. You don't have a name down here until you earn one. Got that? We don't just hand that sort of thing out. We had a guy down here once, worked for two years almost—never once used his name. Not once. So what do you think of that?

BURROUGHS: Harsh.

DRESSLER: You bet it is. Pick that plate up.

BURROUGHS: This one?

DRESSLER: Yeah. Pick it up. Look at it.

BURROUGHS: Okay.

DRESSLER: Have a good look. What do you see?

BURROUGHS: Gunk.

DRESSLER: Look beyond the gunk.

BURROUGHS: I don't—

DRESSLER: You know what I see? Don't waste my time guessing, I'll tell you. Duty. Duty is what I see. We've all got one in life, and if we don't have one, we better get one. Am I right?

BURROUGHS: I guess.

DRESSLER: Don't guess. What are your interests? By and large.

BURROUGHS: I'm a drummer.

DRESSLER: Oh, yeah? With what?

BURROUGHS: Drums?

DRESSLER: I mean with an orchestra or what?

BURROUGHS: I'm looking for a band.

DRESSLER: Do I care? This is the hot sprayer. See what happens?

BURROUGHS: It sprays.

DRESSLER: Don't say it like that. This isn't just spraying. This is our advance work. See this? Look. Meringue! You might as well give up right now if that gets past you. That reconstitutes itself in the hot wash—you got yourself a meltdown! Look at this. Know what that is? Big wedding tonight. I hate weddings. The same goddamn dinner on every plate. This one's the bride's. Not a bite out of it. See?

BURROUGHS: What's this?

DRESSLER: Someone always loses a speech.

BURROUGHS: Should we send it back up?

DRESSLER: Don't ever tamper with fate.

The door above flies open; from the kitchen we hear EMMETT.

EMMETT: It's all right. It's okay. I know my way around.

Now EMMETT appears at the top of the stairs, dressed in a tuxedo.

Dressler! Dressler!

He descends, stopping at the bottom.

How are you, Dressler? How are you?

DRESSLER: Fine, thank you.

EMMETT: It's me, Dressler. Me! Emmett!

DRESSLER: Is that right?

EMMETT: That's right. Me.

DRESSLER: Right. I didn't see it at first.

EMMETT: Sorry about the outfit. I got married tonight. Married the woman of my dreams. Can you believe it? Anyway, it fits. Look at that! Like a glove. The pants; look—all the way down to the ankle.

DRESSLER: You're right. It fits. You look very—

EMMETT: I know.

DRESSLER: —successful.

EMMETT: I do, don't I? Things have turned around pretty quickly, I've got to tell you. I climbed those stairs, Dressler, and I haven't stopped climbing.

DRESSLER: So you married the rich girl; it all worked out.

EMMETT: Don't say it like that. Sure she's rich, but don't say it like that. It all worked out, yeah. It all worked out. She had a change of heart. A change of heart.

DRESSLER: Really?

EMMETT: Not really, no. *Really*, she doesn't have a heart. Forgive me. I've had a bit to drink. I'm not usually this—whatever the word is. But yes; congratulate me. I have now met all her husband criteria. "Not a dishwasher" was the real clincher. Yeah, what do you know. Suddenly, I'm material for advancement up the, up the—who's this? The new guy? Hello, new guy.

BURROUGHS: Sir.

EMMETT: He called me sir.

DRESSLER: If you'll excuse us, we've got a lot of work piling up here.

EMMETT: Sure. Sure; don't let me stop you. Don't let me stand in the way of—of this important—this commendable work.

DRESSLER: As a rule, we don't fraternize with the customers. It's not the policy of the restaurant to let people in, behind the scenes. There's a certain magic that we do, that's spoiled, if you know what I mean, by seeing the mechanics of the thing.

EMMETT: I just, I felt the need—

DRESSLER: Did you?

EMMETT: —to come and, yeah—

DRESSLER: Uh-huh.

EMMETT: Just—yes, tell you what a marvellous job you're doing down here. It really is beautiful, you know. The sparkling china, the glittering silverware; everything lined up so smartly. People don't know what you do. They just stuff food into their faces. They're pigs, Dressler. You were right. They'll never stop being pigs. It frightens me, frankly. If I were you, I wouldn't wash another dish for the gluttons of this world. They mock you with their appetites. And yet, here you are.

DRESSLER: Here I am.

EMMETT: I just wanted to tell you. Someone up there appreciates you. See? I wanted you to know that your faith has not been completely wasted.

DRESSLER: It wasn't necessary.

EMMETT: Make sure those plates don't touch each other, new guy.

BURROUGHS: No, sir.

EMMETT: No, sir. A finger width; is that right?

DRESSLER: Why did you choose this restaurant? I find it interesting.

EMMETT: Me? Are you kidding? She does all the choosing.

DRESSLER: Really? And knowing you used to work here.

EMMETT: Well, exactly.

EMMETT wanders over to the table and sits.

That's her subtle way, Dressler. Let's have our wedding reception in the restaurant where Emmett used to wash dishes. She likes to put things in perspective that way.

Beat.

But I'm happy, I have to say. On the whole, I'd have to say, taken altogether— everything. My life is coming back into focus; I'm getting it back together. The law thing, well, that didn't—but I'm involved in the investment side of the business. They've got a lot of holdings, the family, and it's like a fish in water for me. I breathe that stuff, you know? It's like I have gills. I think her father is very impressed. It's hard to tell, because he never smiles, but he's, he's okay. He's a prick, but he's—

DRESSLER: Maybe you should go back up and join them.

EMMETT: You're right. What am I doing down here? I don't belong here. Of course, I don't belong up there, either, but I definitely don't belong down here.

DRESSLER: Go back to your wife.

EMMETT: I'm going to—excuse me; I'm going to go back to my wife.

Beat. He stops.

This was the best job I ever had. No it wasn't; it was the worst job. But, no, it was the best.

DRESSLER: You really have had a bit to drink.

EMMETT: I have. Haven't I? Have I? I have. But in a way, I'm sober, too. Perhaps I have reached the pinnacle of my soberness. Perhaps I have realized, in this moment of nearly hallucinogenic clarity, that washing dishes is the ideal occupation; water pressure is about the only pressure down here.

Getting up, he stumbles across the room and suddenly rushes to the sink, grabbing a plate and the sprayer and spraying wildly.

I just—here! Give me that!

DRESSLER: What are you doing? Stop that. *Stop—it.*

EMMETT: I want my job back!

They fight over the hose until DRESSLER retrieves it. EMMETT has drenched himself.

DRESSLER: Get out.

EMMETT: Excuse me, gentlemen. I apologize for interrupting your work. I just wanted to say that I'm on my way, now. And I'm going places. But I'll never forget my roots. Well, no; I'll forget my roots. I'll forget. I'll move over the landscape above you, and never ever think of you again. Why? Because a person needs to forget, that there are crap jobs, and slime under every rock, and grease, grease, with no end. And—I can't remember the rest. But, but Dressler—that moment between us. What happened to that moment? When you were supposed to look over at me and say my name. Remember? "Hey, Emmett." I worked my ass off down here.

DRESSLER: And then you gave up.

EMMETT: Fuck you. Sorry.

Long beat.

Sorry.

Beat.

Fuck you. Okay. Good night. I'm on my way. Hey, new guy. What's your name?

BURROUGHS: Burroughs, sir.

EMMETT: That's right. Don't ever accept your fate, Burroughs. Don't ever accept your fate.

BURROUGHS: No, sir.

EMMETT: No. Sir.

EMMETT staggers up and out.

DRESSLER: Immigrant. Worked his way up in the world. Doesn't happen often; almost never at all. You got that?

BURROUGHS: Yeah, I got it.

DRESSLER: Do you? Good. Let it be a warning.

BURROUGHS: Okay.

Beat.

How?

DRESSLER: You think you're a big shot?

BURROUGHS: I'm not.

DRESSLER: You're not.

BURROUGHS: I know.

DRESSLER: You're not.

BURROUGHS: That's what I said.

DRESSLER: Okay. Because you see this pile of dishes here? It's bigger than both of us.

BURROUGHS: Yeah.

DRESSLER: Yeah. You know what else? Always will be.

Beat. They return to work. As the lights fade the sound of the restaurant above—dishes, patrons—grows louder and louder.

Blackout. The End.

UNLESS

ADAPTED FROM THE CAROL SHIELDS NOVEL
BY CAROL SHIELDS AND SARA CASSIDY

INTRODUCTION TO *UNLESS*

Carol Shields, the world-renowned and much-beloved Canadian writer, was also a great fan of the theatre. In 1997 Janet Wright directed a production for us of Shields's script *Thirteen Hands*, a story about a group of women bonding over games of bridge. This show remains one of the trickiest bits of card-play blocking in Canadian theatre history. We were thrilled to have the opportunity to work with Carol again on the stage adaptation of her acclaimed novel *Unless.* Sadly, this collaboration collided with her diagnosis of advanced stage-three breast cancer. Her daughter, Sara Cassidy, became an integral part of bringing this novel to the stage. As was actor Nicola Cavendish. She was the first actor to bring Reta, the central character, to full life. And witnessing her gloriously transform, word by word, a first-person novel into a theatrical event was unforgettable. Audiences were spellbound. It was like watching a gold-medal performance at the Olympics of Theatre, if such a thing existed.

In my experience, the most challenging thing about adapting a first-person novel to the stage is how to adapt the first-person *experience* the lone reader has to an equally intimate experience for the audience. When first-person storytelling is translated as direct address monologues by the protagonist, there's a pitfall of turning internal action and epiphanies in the book to exposition in the play. And exposition is not action. For example, if you are *told* about an argument (exposition) you may or may not remember the content, but if you *see* the argument (action) you'll learn the content and likely have an opinion about it, too. And to make adapting even more deliciously difficult, consider how much text a play can communicate in a non-verbal way: through a look that passes between characters, or a gesture, or business with a prop, like a scarf, for example.

RACHEL DITOR: For future productions, is there a trick or insight you have about getting this play "right"?

NICOLA CAVENDISH: My experience with the premiere production, as directed by Roy Surette, brought many clear insights, but above all the adage

LESS IS MORE kept ringing true. Based on a very dense and rich novel, the trick was to make sure we were working with the most vital and provocative information. This was very challenging as the material between the lines in the novel was just as rich, if not richer, than the lines themselves.

RD: Do you have a particularly memorable moment from the production?

NC: I will always remember Carol Shields arriving from her bed with her two daughters to attend the read-through of a revised draft. She was at the end of a long run with cancer, but her clearly exhausted being shone with a tangible spirit. Ms. Shields went home for a rest between Act One and Act Two and we did not anticipate her return, as it was taking a great deal out of her, so we were enormously surprised and felt great admiration when we saw the car drive up and watched that tiny figure step out once again, to come and hear the final act.

RD: Sara was able to provide some insights into the adaptation as well.

SARA CASSIDY: At the outset, Carol wanted *Unless* to be about four things: men and women, writers and readers, goodness, and mothers and children. While writing the novel she learned, she once said, about the primacy of the mother-child bond, about the opaque nature of goodness, about the choices observed by the novel-maker, and about "the rather vast assumptions of our gendered world."

The script was challenging because *Unless* is essentially an interior monologue—it is in the first person, which, incidentally, my mother came to favour at the end of her life: she felt that the third person led to writerly condescension and overly clever irony. That monologue needed to be broken up a bit, and so instead of Reta purely sharing an anecdote, the story now comes to life. You will see, for example, how Reta's scarf story is inhabited by other actors, and how it blossoms into dialogue.

She also loved to stitch in riddles or patterns for the close reader. In one book, a character actually gets younger with each appearance, for example. In *Unless*, there is in each chapter an image of a woman seated, which director Roy Surette carefully worked into the play.

Unless: The Play was co-produced by Toronto's Canadian Stage Company and Vancouver's Arts Club Theatre for performances in Toronto in 2004 and Vancouver in 2005 with the following cast and creative team:

Reta: Nicola Cavendish
Norah: Celine Stubel
Tom: Allan Morgan
Lois: Nicola Lipman
Christine: Tara Hughes
Ben: Matthew MacFadzean
Natalie: Elizabeth Saunders
Arthur Springer: Michael Spencer-Davis
And with Kevin MacDonald, Lisa Waines, and Eileen Barrett

Director: Roy Surette
Assistant director: Shane Snow
Set design: Brian Perchaluk
Costume design: Phillip Clarkson
Lighting design: Ereca Hassell
Video design: Tim Matheson
Sound design: Marguerite Witvoet
Stage manager: Jennifer Swan

In association with Canadian Stage and the Arts Club, Victoria's Belfry Theatre mounted the play in fall 2005. The play was also produced by the Stephen Joseph Theatre in Scarborough, England, in the spring of 2005.

Notes

The set is a structure of clear plastic tubing with various platforms: a box room, kitchen, French garden. Throughout the play, Norah sits, paces, stretches in one spot of the set representing Bathurst and Bloor, front stage left. A street soundscape—cars passing, footsteps, coins dropping—will at times accompany the scene. As the "moral centre," Norah is never offstage.

Pet, the dog, is offstage throughout the play.

Various openings frame the scenes: shutters, French doors, venetian blinds, curtains, awnings, signs such as the Orangetown Tearoom, Café St. Pierre.

When the theories about Norah's breakdown are offered, the various actors step forward or peer out from the various stage openings to give their opinion. They are not all specific characters, but rather friends, strangers, even a voice from a radio.

The play is punctuated by connector words—these words (centred on the page and underlined: Thereupon, Insofar As, Since, So) are to be projected onto the set as a kind of title for the current action. They are not to land heavily as titles for the scenes but more as thematic suggestions. Projections should be about five seconds. Images of the photo of Pet and the cheque to the Promise Hostel will also be projected.

Scenes from Reta's novel in progress, *Thyme In Bloom*, will be acted (broadly) in two small, cameo-shaped alcoves. Characters may also swarm around Reta while she is writing, acting out the scenes as she writes them. When characters from the novel come on, they are accompanied by a bright "ping" sound for women, or a more steely but no less plucky "pong" sound for men.

When Reta writes the letters, she is busily working in the kitchen or around the house, and we hear the tapping of a keyboard. The script comes up on a banner screen, word by word, as tapped out and said aloud. Her recitation of the letters emphasizes the fact that these are unsent, oral letters.

The theme of Reta's cleaning is strong: Reta is often sweeping, Swiffering, dusting, ordering, washing, etc.

During the flashback fire scene, a film of a fire will be projected over the entire set, with sounds of an ambulance and general panic.

A shower of "connector words" will be projected as light onto the set at the end of the play, like fireworks.

Characters

Actor A: Reta.

Actor B: Reta's daughter Natalie; coffee friend Annette; Linda.

Actor C: Reta's daughter Christine; coffee friend Sally; Alicia.

Actor D: Mother-in-law Lois; coffee friend Lynn Kelly; Sylvia; Sylvie; Gwen.

Actor E: Norah.

Actor F: Tom; Roman.

Actor G: Ben; Interviewer; Michael Hamish; Francis; Mr. Scribano.

Actor H: Colin; Professor; Arthur Springer.

ACT ONE

Here's

RETA is typing in her box room. The telephone rings.

RETA: Hello?

TOM: *(voice-over)* Hello, Reta. Wanted to warn you I'll be a little late to dinner tonight. Someone's just made an appointment for five thirty. Ingrown toenail, if you can believe it. How's the novel coming?

RETA: Hmmm. I'd like to say it was zipping along. But I'm only this minute getting started, it's been a busy morning; your mother needed some errands doing, and Pet needed a run, but now, finally, I've settled down to work.

TOM: *(from phone)* You've got the rest of the afternoon, or most of it.

RETA: We'll see you round six then? You'll be able to pick up the girls after swim team?

TOM: Yes, sure. Everything all right with you, Reta? You sound like you're fretting.

RETA: You mean other than the fact that Norah's gone out of her mind? And that I seem to be stalling on this manuscript? And that I'm just about to write this funny ho-ho hee-hee scene when Alicia boils too much rice and—

TOM: Rice.

RETA: Now, I know there is nothing intrinsically funny about an oversupply of rice, but I plan to. . . okay, imagine how it sort of multiplies and fills the room up, you see, and Roman tries to crack a joke and it isn't really funny— he's in that notch between absurd and stupid, and she—well, anyway, Tom, we'll see you and the girls shortly after six or thereabouts.

TOM: And what's for dinner? Rice?

RETA turns to the audience.

RETA: That was my husband, Tom, who loves me and is faithful to me and is very decent-looking as well and who will be home at ten past six. We live in a house with a paid-up mortgage in the prosperous rolling hills of Ontario, only one hour's drive north of Toronto. Two of our three daughters—Natalie, fifteen, and Christine, sixteen—live at home. They are intelligent and lively and attractive and loving, though they too have shared in the loss, as has Tom.

This is my—my workplace, though the actual work that comes out of here arrives slowly, like drops of medicine for the eye or the ear. It's the old box room—small, quiet. Thank God we put in a skylight. And *(reaching over and patting the fax with one hand and the computer with the other)* my beautiful electronic friends. My fax. My computer.

I would never call this room a studio. There are writers who do. . . use the term, use the term studio. And I could never, never refer to it as a study— what's to study? Other than my own need to escape by writing a light, light, light novel, my second. This room is a cubby, a closet, a. . . workplace. A room for forgetting in. Mine.

It happens that I am going through a period of great unhappiness and loss just now. All my life I've heard people speak of finding themselves in acute pain, bankrupt in spirit and body, but I've never understood what they meant. To lose. To have lost. I believed these visitations of darkness lasted only a few minutes or hours and that these saddened people, in between bouts, were occupied, as we all are, with the useful monotony of happiness. But happiness is not what I thought. Happiness is the lucky pane of glass you carry in your head. It takes all your cunning just to hang on to it, and once it's smashed you have to move into a different sort of life.

In this—my new life—I am attempting to "count my blessings." Everyone I know advises me to take up this repellent strategy, as though they really believe a dramatic loss can be replaced by the renewed appreciation of all one has been given.

And I have my writing!

She cries this out in a tone of false exclamation.

Ever

Downstairs, an awning has dropped, a round top covers a table, and a sign is raised: Orangetown Tearoom. RETA's friends, actors B, C, and D arrive. In the midst of setting down purses, settling into chairs, they shout up to RETA.

ANNETTE, SALLY, & LYNN KELLY: *(kindly, encouraging, reminding)* Reta, you have your writing!
You do have your writing, Reta!
But, you have your writing!

RETA: *(in agreement, glad to be cared for, but cynical)* And it's true, I do, I suppose. I've lost my. . . my kid, my darling daughter, but I do have—for consolation—a shelf full of books I've actually written myself. This writing, though, this "having written" is a very small poultice to hold up against my large, damaged self.

RETA hurries downstairs, takes a light scarf—it's June—to join her friends for coffee. While the three friends begin their conversation, RETA introduces them to the audience.

RETA: These are my coffee friends, Lynn Kelly—

LYNN KELLY: My house cleaner raised her fee—she's become a Clutter Consultant. A certified Clutter Consultant.

RETA: —she's a busy lawyer but every Tuesday morning she has two hours for coffee. And this is Annette—

ANNETTE: *(musing)* Clutter. . . What is that? Loose change?

RETA: —she's a poet and an economist. And this is Sally—

SALLY: Clutter, clatter. . . clot. It's a value judgment. Little Xavier isn't at all disturbed by the clutter he makes—tipping out pencil jars onto the floor.

RETA: Sally teaches after-school drama and has a one-year-old miracle baby.

RETA sits and joins them, listening.

SALLY: Can art be considered clutter? Herb's father has given us more of his marsh landscapes.

LYNN KELLY: She has some wonderful rules—for "clutter control": handle every piece of paper once only.

ANNETTE: *(singsongy)* When in doubt, throw it out.

LYNN KELLY: She says clutter has a kind of gravitational glue. If you're going to clean out a drawer, you've got to tip everything out, and spread it all apart, to break the bond—

ANNETTE: —the clutter conspiracy.

SALLY: For me, it's letters. I can't throw out letters. They're the closest I come to having a diary.

ANNETTE: Ugh, my old diaries. They're deep in the basement, like a secret gone sour.

RETA: I've still got my schoolgirl sonnets from the seventies: "Satin-slippered April, you glide through time / and lubricate spring days, de dum, de dum." There're also three boxes of unsold copies of *Isolation*.

    Beat.

Today would have been Danielle's eighty-sixth birthday.

SALLY: Really! It's been three months and I still can't believe she died. Alone in her apartment.

LYNN KELLY: Alone, with twenty-seven honorary doctorates. Professor Westerman. Doctor Westerman.

ANNETTE: Feminist, Holocaust survivor, writer, historian.

SALLY: What a terrible life she had!

RETA: No, she had a remarkably satisfying life. It's only. . . that she probably hoped for the big step forward. Not all those little legislative steps that hardly add up.

LYNN KELLY: We're going to France in August. Near Mâcon. *(pronounces it "Masson")*

RETA: *(pronouncing it correctly—"Mah-kon")* Mâcon.

LYNN KELLY: We'll visit the square— *(in English accent)* Place Westerman?

RETA: *(in French accent, jokily stressing the "mahn")* Place Westermahn.

RETA models her hair for her friends.

I've taken up her hairstyle: Le chignon.

SALLY: Looks wonderful.

The others murmur approval.

RETA: A tribute to her. And Simone de Beauvoir. It takes me exactly two minutes every morning to pin my hair into shape. It's one of my finest accomplishments. I really mean this. *(reminiscing) Isolation*—I remember when that came out.

ANNETTE: You were huge at the launch.

RETA: Yes! I was eight months pregnant with—

RETA & ANNETTE: *(tenderly)* Norah.

ANNETTE: *(telling the others)* A home birth.

RETA: *(giggling)* You could almost hear the guitars plinking in the background.

ANNETTE: But you didn't roast and eat the placenta like everyone else was doing at the time.

SALLY: I did it. It tastes like liver.

RETA: *(in French accent)* Sublime.

Lights down as LYNN KELLY waves for the bill.

RETA hangs up her coat and hat and organizes the girls' running shoes, which are flung here and there, and climbs the stairs to her box room. She sits at her desk, but soon wheels her chair to face the audience.

Hitherto

RETA: My French comes from my Québécoise mother and my acquaintance with Professor Westerman.

She picks up a photo of Danielle Westerman and looks at it.

Writing and translating are convivial, she said, not at all hierarchical. Of course she would say that.

RETA sits in her "freedom chair" as she studies the picture fondly. She shows the photo to the audience.

Look at that bone structure!

RETA lightly kisses the photo and replaces it, then wheels sharply to the bookshelves. She pulls out a book and holds it as though it were a tender baby.

And something of my own: a short story, "The Brightness of the Star." It appeared in *An Anthology of Young Ontario Voices*, Pink Onion Press. It's hard to believe I ever qualified as a young writer, but, in fact, I was only twenty-nine, mother of Norah, Christine, and about to give birth to Natalie—in a hospital this time. Three daughters and not even thirty. "How did you find the time?" People always ask me this, and always I hear the faint intonation of blame. Have I been neglecting my darling sprogs for my writing career? Well, no, I never thought in terms of career. Writing was my macramé, my knitting. But then I joined a local writers group for women which met every second week for two hours, where we drank coffee and deeply appreciated each other's company.

RETA flings her chair wildly across to another set of bookshelves and pulls out another book.

We threw in fifty dollars each to print this—*Incursions and Interruptions*. Copies were sold locally, mostly to family and friends. And here's the little book I did on Russian icons. *(proudly)* It took me a whole year to do it and I only got four hundred dollars. But I learned all about the saints of Suzdal and what went on in Novgorod—a lot—and how images of saints made medieval people quake with fear. And here's another, *Shakespeare and Flowers*. It turned out to be a wee giftie book. They want me to do one on Shakespeare and animals and I just might.

She whirls her chair in a circle.

And then *Alive*.

She takes a huge book off the shelf and pats it solidly.

My translation of Dr. Westerman's *Pour Vivre*. Oh, it was slammed in the *Star* by one Stanley Harold Howard, but Danielle Westerman said never mind, the man is *un maquereau,* which translates to something between a pimp and a prick.

She brings her knees up to her chin and sways slightly in the chair.

I lost a year after that, which I don't understand since all three girls had started school. I think I was too busy thinking about being writerly, whether Tom's ego was threatened, being in Danielle's shadow, and—I needed my own writing space!

That's when I had the skylight put in *(light shines down)* and bought my FREEDOM chair.

She whirls in her chair.

I wanted to write about the overheard and the glimpsed but I was embarrassed at what I was pumping into my new Apple computer.

We put Pet *(barks)* in a kennel and went to France for a month.

As she speaks, she rises from her chair, opens the door, and descends one landing, which opens onto a French garden—cobble courtyard, ancient roses, and hydrangeas. She sits in a wicker chair in this flower-filled courtyard, and slaps on a straw hat.

The girls took tennis lessons, Tom went hacking for trilobites, and I sat, reading novels day after day and thinking: I want to write a novel. About something happening. About characters moving against a "there." I understood something of the novel's architecture: the slope of predicament, the calculated curve upward into inevitability, and the gathering together of all the characters into a framed operatic circle of consolation and ecstasy, just for a moment on the second-to-last page, just for an atomic particle of time. . .

Looking back, I can scarcely believe in such innocence; I didn't think about our girls growing older and leaving home and falling away from us. Norah had been a good, docile baby and then she became a good, obedient little girl. Now, at nineteen, she's so brimming with goodness that she sits on a Toronto street corner, cross-legged with a begging bowl in her lap, and asks nothing of the world. She wears a cardboard sign on her chest, a single word printed with black marker: GOODNESS.

As RETA *speaks, light falls on the stage left corner where* NORAH *sits as though on a street corner. The sounds of traffic, the wind blowing, as a man passes by and drops coins in her basket.* RETA *stands and looks towards her.*

How did this part of the story happen? An intelligent and beautiful girl from a loving family grows up in Orangetown, Ontario, her mother's a writer, her father's a doctor, and she goes off the track. There's nothing natural about her efflorescence of goodness. It's abrupt and brutal. It's killing us. What will really kill us, though, is the day we don't find her sitting on her chosen square of pavement.

The light goes off NORAH. RETA *sits again.*

Beginning With

RETA: But I didn't know any of this when I sat in that Burgundy garden dreaming about writing a novel.

The light fades on the French garden. RETA *is setting a table—but she's setting it beautifully—that is at stage centre forward, and as she sets the table, she speaks.*

Two appealing characters had suggested themselves, a woman and a man: Alicia and Roman—

RETA *gestures upward to two cameo-shaped screens, one with the face of Alicia and one with the face of Roman. There is a small electronic ping or pong sound that repeats itself each time the cameos light up. Or, the characters of the novel may enter the box room and move around* RETA *as she conjures them.*

—who lived in Wychwood—they longed for love but selfishly strove for self-preservation. Roman—

ROMAN: *(declaring vainly)* The trombone is in rebellion against the octave's inner divisions.

RETA: —is proud to be choleric in temperament—

ROMAN: *(tries to play a tune, dramatically gives up)* This piece is confounding!

RETA: Alicia thinks of herself as being reflective, but her job as an assistant editor on a fashion magazine—

ALICIA: *(at work, frazzled, calling out)* Where's that feature on organic exfoliants??

RETA: —keeps her too occupied to reflect. My title—*My Thyme Is Up*— that's t-h-y-m-e thyme—was a pun, of course, from an old family joke, and I meant to write a jokey novel, a light novel, a novel for summertime, a book to read while seated in an IKEA wicker chair, with the sun falling on the pages, as faintly and evenly as human breath. Naturally, the novel would have a happy ending. I never doubted that I could finish this novel, and I did—in a swoop, alone, during three dark winter months when the girls were away all day at school.

The reviews were mixed. Several reviewers were archly embarrassed by my interest in the domestic. *(wryly)* Emily Helt of the *Chicago Tribune* held up my "embroidery of feeling" against Don DeLillo's *(in macho voice)* "broad canvas of society."

> *RETA is putting the finishing touches on the table, and glances at stage left where her daughter NORAH sits.*

Now, three years later, I am writing another book—a sequel—and I have no idea what will happen. Something that has popped out of the ground, like the rounded snout of a crocus on the cold lawn. The first sentence is tapped into my computer: "Alicia was not as happy as she deserved to be." I've stumbled up against this idea in my clumsy manner and now the urge to write it won't go away. This will be a story about lost children. About goodness and going home and being happy, and trying to keep the poison of the printed page in perspective. I'm desperate to know how this story will turn out.

Insofar As

A flurry of arrivals to the table set for six: mother-in-law LOIS, *daughters* CHRISTINE *and* NATALIE, TOM, *and dinner guest* COLIN.

RETA: *(to audience)* We are more than halfway through the year. It's the beginning of August; Tom's old friend Colin Glass came for the evening, driving up from Toronto.

LOIS: *(puts down her fork)* That was absolutely delicious, Reta, as always.

NATALIE: Great supper. I love those fish things.

RETA: I just have cherries for dessert, but they are beautiful cherries. The Cadillac of cherries.

CHRISTINE: *(excuses herself)* I'll pass on the cherries; there's something I want to watch on TV.

NATALIE: Yeah, me too.

RETA: Now, Colin, there's something I want to ask you. Do you think you could explain to me the theory of relativity?

LOIS: I think I'll just run along home. Don't want to miss the news.

LOIS clears some dishes and leaves. NATALIE *goes with her.*

RETA: My mother-in-law feels that she is helping Canada stay united by watching the news every night.

COLIN: Why on earth would you want to know about the theory of relativity?

RETA: I don't know. I've just always longed to understand such a big piece of knowledge. There was once a time when only one person in the world understood it—Einstein—and then two and then three and then four, now apparently most high-school students can understand it. Why can't I? How hard can it be? You're a physicist, can't you make it simple for me?

COLIN takes the napkin from his lap, stretches it taut across the top of his coffee cup, and places a cherry on top. Then he rotates the cup so the cherry rotates around the surface of the napkin.

COLIN: Well, you have to understand the speed of light is constant and that Einstein's theory is actually a set of two theories—special relativity and general relativity.

TOM: *(nodding)* Yes, yes, go on.

COLIN: The core idea of both theories is that two observers who move relative to each other will often measure different "time" and "space" intervals for the same events, but the content / of physical law will be the same for both.

> RETA *starts to daydream and clears plates as he talks.* COLIN, *in background, continues his explanation—as much as needed to fill the time under* RETA's *speech.*

Special relativity only considers observers in uniform motion—inertial reference frames—with respect to each other. For these observers, so the theory postulates, the speed of light in vacuum will be the same. This leads to redefinitions of fundamental notions of time, distance, mass and energy, and momentum, with wide-ranging consequences. Moving objects become heavier and shorter; moving clocks go slower. Light has momentum. The speed of light emerges as an upper limit for the speed of matter and information. Mass and energy are seen as equivalent. Two events judged to be simultaneous by one observer may be seen as non-simultaneous by other observers who are in motion with respect to the first one. The theory does not account for gravitational effects. The laws of general relativity are the same for all observers, even if they are accelerated with respect to each other. General relativity is a geometrical theory which postulates that the presence of mass and energy "curves" space, and this curvature affects the path of free particles—and even the path of light—an effect we interpret as a gravitational force. . .

RETA: *(to audience)* / I find these days I'm always asking questions and not listening to the answers. Right now, I'm thinking about Marietta, Colin's wife, a beautiful woman with a neck like a plant stem, who packed her bags a few months ago and moved to Calgary to be with another man. She claimed Colin was too wrapped up in his teaching and his research to be a true partner. She left behind her diary with all her unhappiness spelled out. Why would a woman do that? Why would a woman leave her personal diaries behind? To punish—to hurt—of course. Colin always had this tendency to treat her like a graduate student.

Surrealistically, COLIN, during his explanation of relativity, will have just bitten into a piece of cheese and will say to RETA, his hostess, these same words, while RETA merely mouths them as he says them.

COLIN: "Don't tell me this is processed cheese!"

RETA: He has said not one word about Marietta all evening long: I understand he is restructuring his life without her. But a daughter is something different. A daughter of nineteen cannot be erased.

RETA returns to the table as COLIN is winding down his discussion. He finishes awkwardly.

COLIN: . . . The theory can be used to build models of the evolution of the universe. Well? So? That's all I can say.

RETA: Would you say that the theory of relativity has reduced the weight of depravity in the world?

COLIN: *(staring at her)* Relativity has no moral position, Reta, none whatsoever.

TOM smiles.

RETA: But isn't it possible to think that goodness, or virtue if you like, could be a wave or particle of energy?

COLIN: No, no, it is not possible.

The three rise and embrace. The evening ends.

As

RETA crosses to a spot on the street from where she observes NORAH. RETA has two shopping bags in her hands as if she is out shopping. She puts these down at her feet while she observes NORAH.

RETA: Bloor and Bathurst. Always on the northeast corner. This is the place she's claimed, a whole world constructed on stillness. Norah embodies invisibility and goodness, or at least she's on the path—so she said the last time she spoke to us—four months ago. She was steadfast. She could not be diverted. She could not "be" with us. Has she had breakfast? Does she have nits in her hair?

RETA picks up the bags, crosses over to NORAH, and leaves the bags of food—bread, cheese, fruit, and vegetables—for her, an offering. She crosses back to her little spot.

The least little thing will gladden my heart these days: she looked not quite at me and nodded. I have allowed myself only one such glimpse a week, since she has made it clear she doesn't want to see us. It is like watching her through plate glass.

RETA moves from her spot towards SYLVIA's.

Hardly

SYLVIA, in her white uniform, rolls a bed onto the stage. RETA climbs up.

SYLVIA: *(with Hungarian accent)* You are at the age where you must protect the fine skin around the eyes.

RETA: *(getting on bed)* The delicate skin around my eyes has been demanding attention. Has Tom noticed? I don't think so light.

SYLVIA: A woman's face falls, it is inevitable, but the eyes go on and on, giving.

RETA: Sylvia's calls itself a Spirit Spa, meaning that, while Madame Sylvia swipes at my brows with a paintbrush, she murmurs and sings into my ear.

SYLVIA: You will be eighty, ninety, and your eyes will still charm.

RETA: *(to audience)* She knows nothing about my life. I've never been here before.

SYLVIA: Are you by any chance a Gemini?

RETA: No, my birthday's in September; next week in fact.

SYLVIA: I can tell, yes; I can always tell.

RETA: *(to audience)* What could she tell?

SYLVIA: Twenty-four dollars. Let me give you my card for the next time.

Madame SYLVIA holds up the mirror to RETA.

A woman's charm is with her for life, but you must pay attention.

Madame SYLVIA and her bed disappear off stage right.

RETA: No, I'm sorry, but I have no plans to be charming on a regular basis. Anyone can be charming. It's really a cheap trick, screwing up your face into sunbeams and spewing them forth. Compared to goodness, real goodness, charm is nothing but crumpled tissue paper soiled from previous use.

Notwithstanding

A restaurant: an INTERVIEWER comes into the room and sits at the table along with RETA. They shake hands, a little bit charmingly.

INTERVIEWER: *(perfunctory)* Ms. Winters. Nice to meet you.

RETA: Yes, thanks. Congratulations, I understand you are the newly appointed columnist at *Booktimes*.

INTERVIEWER: *(switches on tape recorder before asking)* Do you mind if I use the tape recorder?

RETA: Not at all.

INTERVIEWER: I understand you are working on a second novel.

RETA: Well, yes.

INTERVIEWER: It takes nerve.

RETA: Uh-huh.

INTERVIEWER: Actually, well, I have a novel on the go myself.

RETA: Really. What a surprise. *(knowingly, ironically)*

INTERVIEWER: I have two young children at home. Christ, what a responsibility, although I love the little bastards. One of them is quite, quite gifted. Well they both are in their separate ways. But the work of raising kids. I never have time to read the books I have to review.

RETA: Oh, uh-huh.

There is a suggestion of time passing; silence, two characters frozen for an instant, then moving again.

INTERVIEWER: And like all journalists, I'm underpaid. They also expect me to do features on the weekend.

RETA: I'll just put this on my Visa.

INTERVIEWER: And last week, I actually broke the Klein story.

RETA: *(to audience)* Oh, shut up. *(to INTERVIEWER)* Congratulations.

INTERVIEWER: Thanks.

RETA: I should be getting on my way—the parking meter, an appointment, and a long drive home.

INTERVIEWER: I understand you and your family live in a lovely old house near Orangetown. *(slyly)* I understand one of your daughters now lives in Toronto and—

RETA: *(derisively)* The mother of your children—is she a journalist too?

INTERVIEWER: Journalist?

RETA: Like you, I mean.

INTERVIEWER: Let me at least leave the tip.

He puts down a couple of coins. The INTERVIEWER leans over and whispers excitedly in her ear, pointing to another table where a man is seating himself.

I'm not sure, but I think that's Gore Vidal—he's here for the writers' festival, you know.

RETA rises and departs, head held high.

Thus

RETA slowly circles NORAH, walking around her where she sits; RETA stares longingly at her. NORAH does not acknowledge RETA—this scene emphasizes the gulf between them, and, in fact, the "visit" may really be only in RETA's mind.

Regarding

Light up on RETA *in front of a mirror, brushing her hair violently. As she speaks, her words are displayed on a ribbon monitor overhead. The sound of a keyboard.*

RETA: Dear Editor, I was interviewed yesterday by your new features columnist concerning the novel I am now working on. I was quite taken aback that in this morning's article he referred to my raincoat as "grubby at the cuffs" and that he mentioned me as "Mrs. Winters with her familiar overbite."

She starts raising her hair into a chignon.

Actually, I was wearing a rather lovely jade jacket lined with silk, which represented a rare splurge on my part. My hair as usual was in a chignon, not a bun as he suggests in his piece. He seemed reluctant to call for the bill, so I paid myself while he offered a tip—two thin dimes, would you believe it! I am writing to inform you that there will be no further interviews with your magazine.

RETA *jabs a pin into her chignon.*

Signed, Reta la Chignonneuse
Orange County, Ontariario

Wherein

RETA: *(to audience)* It was my friend Annette who alerted us to Norah's whereabouts last April. We hadn't heard from her for over a week. We tried to phone but we could never get through. We were worried. Worried sick. Springtime depression. The thought of suicide. Her last visit home at the end of March had been deeply disturbing.

NORAH *puts down her sign and stands.* RETA *and she reconstruct the discussion—a flashback.*

Is it Ben?

NORAH: Partly.

RETA: You don't love him the way you did?

NORAH: I do. And I don't. Don't enough.

RETA: What do you mean, enough?

NORAH glances very slightly towards RETA, *as if looking for reassurance, comfort.*

Try to explain.

NORAH: I can't love anyone enough.

RETA: Why not?

NORAH: I love the world more.

RETA: What do you mean, the world?

NORAH: All of it. Existence.

RETA: *(knowing how ridiculous it sounds)* Do you mean—like mountains and oceans and trees and things?

NORAH: All those things. But other things too.

RETA: Go on.

NORAH: There's literature. And language. Well, you know. And branches of languages and dead languages and forgotten dead languages. And Matisse. / And *Hamlet*. It's all so big, and I love all of it.

RETA: / But what—?

NORAH: And whole continents. India. Every little trail running off every hidden dirt road. The shrubbery, the footpaths. The little town squares. There must be millions of town squares.

RETA: You could spend a year travelling, you know, Norah.

NORAH: And the tides. Think of the tides. They never forget to come and go. The earth tipping in space. Hardly anyone understands them.

RETA: *(suddenly)* You've dropped out of university.

NORAH: I'm thinking about it. About not taking my exams.

RETA: You've dropped out of university. Why?

NORAH: It's just—you know—sort of pointless.

RETA: What about your scholarship?

NORAH: I don't need any money. That's what's so astonishing. I can give up my scholarship.

RETA: Will you talk to your father?

NORAH: God, no.

RETA: *(agitated)* Please, Norah. He went through some—some phases—when he was younger. Way back. Please talk to him.

NORAH: No, I can't.

RETA: You do realize this is serious. You are in a serious psychological state and you need help. It may be you have some mineral or vitamin deficiency, something as simple as that. Even depression can be treated these days.

NORAH: It's not one big thing. I know that much. It's a lot of little things. I'm trying to get past the little things.

RETA: *(shouting)* You have to talk to your father today. Today.

NORAH: All right.

RETA: Good. But you must talk to someone else as well. Someone in the counselling area. Today.

NORAH: It's Sunday.

RETA: We'll go to the hospital. Emergency will be open.

NORAH: It's not an emergency.

RETA: Oh, Norah. Norah, the world often seems to be withholding something from us. We all feel that way at times. You have to face up to it—

NORAH: But that's exactly what I want to do. I'm trying to face up to it. But it's too big.

NORAH clings to RETA and sobs.

I'm trying to find where I fit in.

RETA: She held onto me desperately then, her forehead pressed into my stomach. I would give anything to have that moment back.

A lighting change as RETA shakes out of the scene, addresses the audience.

It was April seventeenth when my friend Annette happened to go to the city and caught a glimpse of Norah sitting on the sidewalk begging.

ANNETTE: *(approaching NORAH on the street)* Norah?

> *NORAH says nothing. She firms her grip on her cardboard sign and thrusts it at ANNETTE.*

Norah, do your parents know you are here?

> *NORAH shakes her head. ANNETTE goes around the corner, fishes out her cellphone and reaches them in Orangetown.*

RETA: Luckily Tom was home. We got straight into the car and drove to Toronto. All the way my chest was convulsed with pain. The air around us was shaking like a great sail.

Otherwise

In the following scene various actors speak out of doors or windows or from the table/desk at centre stage. The unidentified characters could be Annette's husband or a voice on the radio or someone connected to the family. While the various theories are spoken, RETA begins to clean the house.

ACTOR F: *(unidentified)* Arrange to have her kidnapped. Then take her somewhere to have her deprogrammed.

ACTOR G: *(unidentified)* Have the police pick her up for questioning. They've seen lots of these cases and know how to handle them.

ACTOR F: *(unidentified)* Use a little force. If you and Tom force her into the car and drive her straight home, the shock will bring her to her senses. That's what she needs to break the spell, a shock.

ACTOR D: *(as LOIS, distraught)* It's drugs. Or a cult—

ACTOR H: *(PROFESSOR)* She was an excellent student, until she stopped coming to class. But you know, many students fall away once the good weather begins. She was always alert and inquiring.

ACTOR C: *(unidentified)* You're all worked up about nothing. This isn't such a big deal, a kid taking a season out on the street. It happens.

ACTOR D: *(as LOIS)* —those born-again Christians who don't let women wear makeup.

ACTOR H: *(PROFESSOR)* Well, yes. We did have one or two altercations; you know how things go these days. Could Flaubert possibly imagine himself into a woman's life? The class divided on that issue, it happens every year.

ACTOR B: *(unidentified)* I've always heard that people begging on the street are frauds. That they make big bucks. Some of them have cellphones. I've seen that with my own eyes. In Toronto, no less. It's true.

ACTOR D: *(as LOIS)* A temporary imbalance of the inner ear? Misalignment of the spine?

ACTOR H: *(PROFESSOR)* Norah saw Madame Bovary as a woman blandly idealized by Flaubert, and then reduced to a puff of romanticism.

ACTOR E: *(as TOM)* Post-traumatic stress. Nothing else makes sense.

ACTOR B: *(as NATALIE)* What happened? What terrible thing happened to her? There has to be a thing.

ACTOR H: *(PROFESSOR)* Your daughter's view was that Madame Bovary was forced to surrender her place as the moral centre of the novel.

ACTOR C: *(as CHRISTINE)* I don't believe it; I'll never believe it. She's gone mental.

ACTOR D: *(as LOIS)* I can't bear this. Not Norah, not Norah.

Since

RETA walks towards BEN's apartment.

RETA: Early on, we thought Norah's problem was a boyfriend problem. And Ben Abbot really is a boy. By thirty, he will have acquired a supple, sexual bulk, but now he is quickness and nerve. He and Norah saw each other two or three times and then for the next year and a half there was no separating them. They shared a student apartment in Toronto. After Norah disappeared, in those frightening days in April, after we'd found out she'd taken up daily residence at Bathurst and Bloor, I went to see Ben at his basement digs. I didn't phone ahead.

RETA rings the buzzer. BEN opens the door. They just silently look at each other. She enters and sits down. He sits next to her on the shabby sofa.

BEN: She changed. Over a few weeks, late January, February, March. She was short-tempered, then she'd go quiet. Her professor, Dr. Hamilton, she hated him for some reason. I asked her what the guy had done—if he'd come on to her or something, and she was furious that I'd think something like that, that that was what would occur to me—something sexual. She started giving me these, you know, these long, hard looks. Scrutinizing looks. She'd stopped going to lectures by March; she just hung around the apartment reading or staring off into space. She was thinking about goodness and evil, about harm to the earth, that kind of thing. Then she left one afternoon. I thought she was just going to Honest Ed's but she never came back. Most of her stuff is still here. And then I saw this girl I know and she said Norah was panhandling at Bathurst and Bloor, and I couldn't believe it. I went and looked and there she was with that sign, sitting on the sidewalk. I walked up to her and said, "What are you doing, Norah, what is this all about?"

He leans back in the cushions and starts to sob unrestrainedly. He howls long and eloquently and makes no effort to brush his tears away. His hands are spread out uselessly on his denim thighs. RETA *starts to reach out and stroke his hand but draws back. She sits straight and stares at him. The scene darkens.*

Throughout

RETA *walks up to* NORAH *and lunges at her, tries to grab her.* NORAH *screams and* RETA *retreats, ashamed.*

Once

RETA *is walking. She makes her way to the Café St. Pierre as she speaks and visibly "finds" the scarf hung high on stage; she will have to transfer this to her bag, or a scarf will already be there.*

RETA: Once, I embarked on a modest book tour, which began in Washington. Norah's birthday, the first of May, was coming up, and she longed to have a beautiful and serious scarf. Since her grade-twelve class trip to Paris, she had been talking about the scarves that every chic Frenchwoman wears as part of her wardrobe. I never have time to shop, but that day I had time, plenty of time, a wide springtime afternoon. Scarves—every shop had a good half-dozen—were knotted on dowels, and there was not one that was not pure silk with hand-rolled edges. I realized I would be able to buy Norah the perfect scarf. I took a deep breath and smiled genuinely at the anorexic saleswomen, who seemed to sense and respond to my new consumer eagerness. "That's not quite her," I quickly learned to say, and they nodded with sympathy. As I formed a very definite notion of the scarf I wanted for Norah, I began, too, to see how impossible it might be to accomplish this task. The scarf became an idea; it must be brilliant and subdued at the same time, finely made, but with a secure sense of its own shape.

And there it was, relaxed over a fat silver hook in what must have been the twentieth shop I entered. I found its shimmer dazzling and its touch icy. One hundred and ten American dollars *(very expensive)*. Was that all?

In the morning I took the train to Baltimore, where I was to give a short reading. I had time to see Gwen, my old writing friend, for lunch.

> *We see* GWEN *walking towards her meeting with* RETA. RETA *continues to narrate as they sit and finally linger over coffee.*

I hadn't seen her in years but had always kept in touch, especially if I came across an excerpt of her novel-in-progress in *Three Spoons*. I knew about that novel of Gwen's—she'd been working on it for years.

It was hard to tell precisely what she was wearing and she looked older than I had remembered.

> *Instead of a purse* GWEN *carries only a lumpy plastic bag, which she places on the table.*

It wasn't until we'd finished our salads and ordered our coffee that I realized she hadn't mentioned my book at all, nor had she congratulated me on the Offenden Prize. I hoped that by telling her about my search for the scarf I could somehow delight her.

GWEN: *(finally warming to something, looking interested)* How many boutiques did you say you went into?

RETA: Twenty. Or thereabouts.

GWEN: Incredible.

RETA: But it was worth it.

GWEN: Why?

RETA: To see if it existed, this thing I had in mind. This item.

GWEN: And it did.

RETA: Yes.

> *RETA reaches into her bag and pulls out the puffy pink boutique bag. She unrolls the pink tissue paper and shows the scarf. GWEN lifts it against her face. Tears glint in her eyes.*

GWEN: It's just that it's so beautiful. Finding it, it's almost as though you made it. You invented it, created it out of your imagination.

RETA: *(pleased GWEN understands)* Yes! Yes!

> *Then RETA watches as GWEN rolls the scarf back into the fragile paper, then slips the parcel into her plastic bag, tears spilling freely now.*

GWEN: Thank you, darling Reta, thank you. You don't know what you've given me today.

RETA: *(walking away from the café, towards home)* But I did, I did.

> *Beat.*

A scarf, half an ounce of silk, maybe less, floating free in the world, making someone happy, this person or that person, it doesn't matter. I looked at Gwen, my old friend, and I thought of my three daughters, and my mother-in-law, and my own dead mother. None of us was going to get what we wanted. I had suspected this for years, and now I believe that Norah half knows the big female secret of wanting and not getting.

Thereof

> *RETA is at home, watering plants, dusting. The telephone rings.*

RETA: Hello?

ARTHUR SPRINGER: I'd like to speak to Mrs. Reta Winters please.

RETA: This is Reta Winters speaking.

She gently unloads the dishwasher.

ARTHUR SPRINGER: Have I caught you at an awkward moment—you're not in the middle of breakfast?

RETA: No, this is a good time.

ARTHUR SPRINGER: I just phoned to introduce myself. My name is Arthur Springer, from Scribano & Lawrence, and I have the great honour, Mrs. Winters, of being your new editor.

RETA: Oh, well how nice of you to phone and introduce yourself, Mr. Springer.

ARTHUR SPRINGER: I hope you'll call me Arthur once we get to know each other.

RETA: Well, then you must call me—

ARTHUR SPRINGER: Reta. It would be a pleasure, Reta. I'm so glad you feel that way. That will get us off to a good start. I want to say right off that I know I can't replace the inestimable Mr. Scribano.

RETA: Such a tragedy—

ARTHUR SPRINGER: I can tell you, Reta, that our dear late Mr. Scribano was delighted that you were working on a sequel to *My Thyme Is Up*. He told me as much just a few days before his fall.

The sound of a person falling down the stairs—clunk, clunk, clunk— then moaning.

RETA: Did he really? He was always very kind and—

ARTHUR SPRINGER: I have nothing but respect for him as a person and as an editor. Though, of course, we represent different generations and have separate approaches. My own approach is very much dialogic. My training was at Yale, originally. Then Berkeley.

RETA: Well, yes—

ARTHUR SPRINGER: Now, can you give me an idea, Reta, of when you will next be in New York?

RETA: Well, actually—

ARTHUR SPRINGER: I think it's essential that we sit down and go over the manuscript together. I'm a bit of a point-by-point man when it comes to editing.

RETA: But there is no manuscript in a sense. That is, the manuscript is coming along, but very slowly.

ARTHUR SPRINGER: Fine, fine, just send me what you've got so far.

RETA: Oh, I don't think I can do that— You see, what's down on paper, or on disk, really, is still in the, you know, the tenuous mode—

ARTHUR SPRINGER: I assure you, Reta, that I appreciate the fact that a draft is a draft is a draft.

RETA: I don't see how I can—

ARTHUR SPRINGER: Look, Reta, I'm going to give you our UPS number. I'll make the arrangements for a pickup— You'll find I'm an appreciative editor. I like to bring out the best in a writer.

RETA: Yes, well.

ARTHUR SPRINGER: There's just one thing I want to say before we say goodbye. I love Alicia.

ALICIA comes on stage, quite pleased to be adored.

Your Alicia. I want you to know that my devotion to her is enormous. I am greatly attracted to her reflective nature. I've read *My Thyme Is Up* several times now, and each time I love her more. There's a golden quality about her. As though she were a gold autumn leaf among others less gold. I've thought and thought about what it is that draws me to your Alicia. It's not her sensuality—not that she's lacking in that department, not in the least. The way she has of sitting still in a chair. Just sitting. Her generosity, that's part of it. Her tolerance, too. But what really makes me want to take her in my arms is her goodness.

RETA: I'm sorry. I didn't quite hear what you said, Mr. Springer, Arthur. Did you say—?

ARTHUR SPRINGER: Her goodness. Her profound human goodness.

RETA: Oh. Goodness.

ARTHUR SPRINGER: Yes, goodness.

RETA: That's what I thought you said.

Blackout.

(elbows on desk in box room) What I can't believe—what I refuse to believe—is that I can go on writing a novel, a comic novel, while my darling kid is living the life of a street person.

RETA walks towards NORAH.

When Norah was a very small child, three or four, she was eating lunch at the kitchen table when she heard an airplane go overhead. She looked up at me and said, "The pilot doesn't know I'm eating an egg." She seemed shocked at this perception of loneliness, but was willing to register the shock calmly so as not to alarm me.

More than anything else it is the rhythm of typing and thinking that soothes me. Who would have thought that this old habit of mine would become a strategy for maintaining a semblance of ongoing life, an unasked-for gift. On days I don't know which foot to put in front of the other, I can type my way towards becoming a conscious being.

How old is Alicia now?

ALICIA appears and she and ROMAN may move around RETA as she writes.

This matter is critical. *(speaking in a highly expository voice)* She is an editor for a fashion magazine. She is engaged to Roman *(ROMAN may appear in other cameo)*, the wedding is just weeks away. This is her second marriage. She spends too much money on top-quality skin products *(in cameo ALICIA is applying skin cream)*. She says "shit" when she stumbles *(mimes falling, ALICIA may say "shit" instead of RETA)*, but she would never, under any circumstances, describe some person or some essence as being "shitty." She isn't stunningly beautiful—the genre of "light fiction" rules out bodily perfection. Romance novels are able to fill their pages with strikingly beautiful women and literary novels can permit a rare beauty, one only. Light fiction, being closer to real life, knows better. Some imperfection must intervene and usually this is in the nature of a slightly too long nose *(this can be exaggerated in the cameo—ALICIA exhibiting her nose)* or a smaller than average chin. Breasts may be on the small size or else more generous than normal.

RETA glances over towards NORAH, then back at her work: this is crazy, to be writing when her own daughter is on the street. She returns to work with a prim diligence—someone taking her medicine.

Now, Alicia wants children of her own. Desperately. But vaguely. Does she see herself unbuttoning her blouse and offering her breast to a baby's gaping mouth? Well, no, she's not quite there, yet.

Thirty-six. Yes. Forty lies ahead—and she is well aware of forty, but not frightened by it. Thirty-six. Old enough to understand the universe is supremely insufficient. And yet young enough to still stir ardour.

RETA has wandered through the house and is now sitting at the end of the bed beside TOM.

Whatever

RETA: Tom and I still have sex—have I mentioned this?—even though our oldest daughter is living on the street, a derelict. Once or twice a week, we actually lie on our queen-size bed together; it will be midnight, the house quiet, our faces close together, the warm, felt cave beneath Tom's jaw at my cheek, his breath. The specificity of his body keeps me still as though I'm listening for a signal. He reaches for me, I respond, sometimes slowly, lately quite slowly. Afterwards, one or the other of us will cry. Sometimes we both cry. Our ongoing need for sex lies between us like something we don't dare pick up.

The two smooch, roll around. After a moment, RETA sits up.

Do we still love each other? We must, if we're still having sex after twenty-plus years. Anyway, the question of love is not relevant in our case, not for the moment. We live in each other's shelter. We fit. We're together after all this time, that's what matters. Our habits are so familiar.

How odd.

TOM: Odd?

RETA: That we go on doing this.

TOM: I know.

RETA: The same way we keep up the garden.

TOM: And pay the bills.

RETA: Can you ever forget, Tom? Tell me. Are you ever able to forget about her?

TOM: I don't think so. Not completely. Never. Do you?

RETA: *(to audience)* I do love him. When I ask him a question, he asks back.

RETA lies back down and tussles with TOM for a moment, then sits upright.

Tom, I think I know what it is; what's wrong with Norah. I think *(pause)* that Norah has simply accepted, instead of power, complete powerlessness. Do you see what I mean? Total passivity. A kind of impotent piety. In doing nothing, she's claimed everything. It's something that happens to young women, to girls.

TOM: That sounds like the kind of theory Danielle Westerman would have had.

RETA: It was Danielle who suggested the idea.

With a flourish, she offers this aphoristic boil-down.

Ne faisant rien, elle avait revendiqué tout.

TOM shakes his head disbelievingly.

TOM: It sounds so perverse, claiming her existence by ceasing to exist. Does that make sense?

RETA: Does any of it make sense?

TOM: I still think it's post-traumatic shock of some kind. That makes sense.

RETA: Another thing, Tom; I'm worried about your mother. She never talks. She comes every night for dinner as usual, bringing one of her desserts, but she doesn't say a word, have you noticed? She used to join in.

TOM: It's essentially the same thing. Post-traumatic shock.

RETA: You can't have post-traumatic shock without a trauma. What exactly is the trauma?

TOM: I don't know. If only we knew.

RETA: *(lies down, then rises and turns to audience with this realization)* She's got my disease, Norah, only worse. As for Natalie and Chris, they seem, so far, in a state of calm, despite what's happened to their sister. There's an excellent possibility, however, that they're bluffing.

> *Meanwhile in the background, throughout this last scene, the two sisters are visiting NORAH, sitting with her and trying to engage her in conversation and handing her food and warm clothes. Now they stand up and leave, wave goodbye. But NORAH doesn't respond to them. They burst into TOM and RETA's bedroom.*

Thereupon

CHRISTINE: We got the early bus—

NATALIE: —then transferred to the subway, to Bathurst and Bloor—

RETA: You should have told us you were going.

NATALIE: She smiled at us. Just sat there and smiled and seemed glad to see us.

CHRISTINE: She stank. Kronk city. They do have showers at the hostel. You'd think she'd remember how to use a shower.

NATALIE: She doesn't stink, it's just that street smell.

CHRISTINE: She didn't really talk to us.

NATALIE: At first we sat about ten feet away from her. We didn't want to freak her out—

CHRISTINE: —as if she isn't already—

NATALIE: Then we sat right next to her. Chris sat on one side and I sat on the other.

CHRISTINE: She didn't mind. She just kept looking serene and people kept giving her money.

NATALIE: She gets more money than anyone else on that corner and there are about four other guys. People just seem to like her, people passing by.

CHRISTINE: It gets totally boring, but she seems to be used to it.

NATALIE: She's got some weird rash on her arms.

CHRISTINE: We took her a toothbrush. In case she didn't have one.

NATALIE: We took her her old peacoat. We just put it down near to her before we left.

CHRISTINE: We wrapped it in a plastic bag.

NATALIE: We told her we'd be back next Saturday—

CHRISTINE: We said we'd given up swimming, that we were sick of swimming.

NATALIE: We didn't hug or anything. It was like she didn't want us to.

CHRISTINE: But she doesn't seem to care one way or another. It's like she thinks it's our right to be there if we want to be there.

RETA stretches out her hands to her daughters. Darkness.

Following

We hear the soundscape of typing, and the banner screen runs. As *RETA reads/composes her letter, she Swiffers intently.*

RETA: Dear Sirs,

I was feeling more than usually depressed last night over personal matters and I happened to be sitting in a big armchair skimming through the latest issue of your magazine.

I couldn't help noticing that you have sold one of your very expensive advertising pages to what appears to be a faux institution of some kind. The product, in any case, is Great Minds of the Western Intellectual World: Galileo, Kant, Hegel, Bacon, Newton, Plato, Locke, and Descartes. Small but very authentic-looking engravings of these gentlemen's heads form a tight (let us say impregnable) band across the top of the page, and what is suggested is a continuum of noble thought, extracts of which are recorded in eighty-four half-hour lecture tapes, which one may listen to as he walks or jogs or commutes or does the CHORES.

The scholar will be guided in his study by the Faculty; that's Darren— skipping last names—Alan, Phillip, Jeremy, Robert, another Robert,

Kathleen, Mark, and Douglas. My question is: How did Kathleen make it to this race?

I might as well admit that I am troubled these days (and nights) by such questions. I have a nineteen-year-old daughter who is going through a sort of soak of depression—actually her condition has not yet been diagnosed—which a friend of mine suspects is brought about by such offerings as your Great Minds, pressing down insidiously and expressing a callous lack of curiosity about great women's minds, a complete unawareness, in fact.

I realize I cannot influence your advertising policy. My only hope is that my daughter—her name is Norah—will not pick up a copy of this magazine, read this page, and understand, as I have for the first time, how casually and completely she is shut out of the universe. I have two other daughters too—Christine, Natalie—and I worry about them both. All the time.

Yours, Reta
The Hermitage Orangetown, Canada

So

The word "so" is to be lightly emphasized as it peppers this scene.

RETA: So, time for coffee.

An awning drops down—the Orangetown Tearoom—and RETA's friends, LYNN KELLY, ANNETTE, and SALLY sit down.

So, Lynn Kelly thinks Norah is suffering from a hormone imbalance, Sally thinks it's a stale romance, and Annette thinks it's too much cerebral concentration. Not one of them thinks it's my fault, which of course is what I believe. *(joins them)*

LYNN KELLY: So, to me, goodness is just an abstraction. A luxury for the fortunate.

RETA: Goodness, but not greatness, so Danielle Westerman used to say.

ANNETTE: So how could Danielle go on living her life knowing that she was excluded from greatness?

LYNN KELLY: She'll never be included in the canon.

SALLY: Men aren't interested in women's lives. I've asked Herb; I've really pressed him on this. So he loves me but no, he really doesn't want to know about the motor in my brain, how I think and how—

RETA: I've only had a handful of conversations with men in my life. Other than Tom.

LYNN KELLY: I've had about two. Two conversations with men who weren't dying to win the conversation.

ANNETTE: So I've never had one. It's as though I lack the moral authority to enter the conversation. I'm outside the circle of good and evil.

RETA: What do you mean?

ANNETTE: I mean we're never interviewed on the subject of ethical choices. No one consults us. So we're not thought capable.

SALLY: So maybe we're not. Remember that woman who had a baby in the tree? In Africa? Mozambique? There was a flood—last year, wasn't it?—and so there she was, in labour, think of it! While she was up in a tree hanging onto a branch.

ANNETTE: So does that mean—?

SALLY: So all I'm saying is what did we do about that? Such a terrible thing, and so did we send money to help the flood victims in Mozambique? Did we do anything that represented the goodness of our feelings? I didn't.

RETA: No, I didn't do anything.

LYNN KELLY: Me neither. So? We can't extend acts of goodness to every case of—

ANNETTE: I remember that now. I remember waking up in the morning and hearing on the radio that a woman had given birth in a tree, and I think the baby lived—didn't it?

LYNN KELLY: Yes. The baby lived.

SALLY: And remember that woman who set herself on fire? That was right in our country, right here in Toronto.

LYNN KELLY: She was a Saudi woman, wearing one of those big black veil things. Self-immolation.

ANNETTE: So she was a Saudi? Was that established?

LYNN KELLY: A Muslim woman, anyway, in traditional dress. They never found out who she was.

RETA: A chador, isn't it, the veil? Or a burka.

ANNETTE: So she died, needless to say.

LYNN KELLY: But someone did try to help her. I read about that. Someone tried to beat out the flames.

RETA: *(half beat)* I didn't know that.

LYNN KELLY: It was in one of the papers.

SALLY: And what about that other young woman in Nigeria who was publicly flogged. So, what did we do for her?

ANNETTE: God, this is a brutal world.

LYNN KELLY: *(looks at her watch)* So. Time to go.

Next

RETA approaches NORAH, leaves her a bag of groceries, takes off her own sweater, and leaves it there.

Regarding

RETA is on the phone, talking with ANNETTE, who is also on stage.

ANNETTE: So I'll take the kids to the swim meet.

RETA: I find it ridiculously reassuring to have the kids on a swimming team. I love seeing them all sleek and wet.

ANNETTE: Like when they were really little and just out of the bath.

RETA: The smell of chlorine on them, in their hair. As if warding off infection.

ANNETTE: *(beat)* I was in Toronto yesterday.

She is saying she saw NORAH.

I, uh, left her some Alice Munro stories and a bag of almonds. I've read they're packed with calcium—the almonds! *(laughs)* Though Alice Munro's stories may be good for the old bones, too. I wouldn't be surprised.

RETA: *(beat)* I worry about the cold.

ANNETTE: Thermal underwear?

RETA: Good idea.

ANNETTE: On the other hand—

RETA: Yes?

ANNETTE: The cold may bring her home. You know how a good cold snap makes people wake up and look after themselves.

RETA: I've thought about that.

ANNETTE: I thought probably you had.

RETA hangs up. She climbs the stairs to the box room and sits at her computer.

Despite

RETA: *(sipping tea)* I've been careful to give Alicia a few friends. It's curious how friends get left out of novels, but the modernist tradition sets the individual—*(grandiose)* the conflicted self—against the world. I like to sketch in a few friends in the hope they provide a release from a profound novelistic isolation that might otherwise ring hollow. Alicia's best friend is Linda MacBeth *(LINDA appears in cameo screen, presented with her own ping),* an art consultant who toils at the same magazine where Alicia works. The two women have side-by-side cubicles, and they go together to a yoga class every Thursday night and then out for a drink.

ALICIA and LINDA appear doing yoga together.

Roman has a good friend, too; I've seen to that. Michael Hamish—a slightly menacing stockbroker and weekend rugby player—will be best man at Roman and Alicia's wedding, which is coming up soon.

The invitations have been sent out.

During this next scene, the Thyme *characters swarm around* RETA, *acted out mostly in tableau, while* RETA *composes at the computer. Meanwhile,* NORAH *grows visibly restless and at the end of the speech, she will stand.* MICHAEL *Hamish and* ROMAN *come on stage tossing a rugby ball back and forth.* ROMAN *is sweaty.*

However, Alicia has been having doubts about the wedding. She's noticed that Roman is inattentive to his personal hygiene, and has to remind herself that his odour of musk and his thick, oily hair was attractive to her in the early days.

And when he's in the presence of men who are taller than he is, he becomes faintly obsequious, and touches his mouth rather a lot. This is beginning to get on Alicia's nerves, and she's thinking of mentioning it to him. Roman has bought a dictionary since Alicia sometimes uses big words.

ROMAN: *(to* MICHAEL, *leafing through dictionary)* Is it my fault I don't understand the words she uses? Or is it her fault? I love her. Anachronism, she said. Anachronism.

RETA: *(composing on computer)* Roman has been having difficulties at work, with a pushy—and very attractive—bassoonist named Sylvia. Also, he's convinced the conductor hates him, that the trombone is overly pared down in the orchestral arrangements. Roman and Alicia have ended their breakfast ritual at the Frying Pan—they've read about trans fats. Instead they've taken up rock-climbing at one of those indoor places with cupboard knobs all over the walls. They are very silly during these excursions. . . They're also shopping for mountain bikes. There's a funny scene where the bicycle shop manager convinces them to take a spin on a tandem bicycle and they go off singing "Daisy, Daisy." But Alicia's been distracted lately, thoughtful. . .

We see the two cycling merrily, singing ludicrously, then ROMAN *interrupts:*

ROMAN: Just think! In two weeks, you will be Mrs. Boroshian!

ALICIA *is gripped with terror. She looks to* RETA *for help.* RETA *sets down her cup with a rattle.*

RETA: Yes. No! Yes! Yes, of course. Now I see it. How could I have gone so wrong? Alicia is not meant to marry Roman. She is not meant to be partnered at all. She will live an astonishing life, but it will be a single life. Her singleness in the world is her paradise, it has been all along, and she came close to sacrificing it, or, rather, I, as novelist, had been about to snatch it away from her. The wedding guests will have to be alerted and the gifts returned. All of them. Alicia, Roman, their family, their friends— stupid, stupid. The novel, if it is going to survive, must be redrafted. Alicia will advance in her self-understanding and the pages will expand. I'll start tomorrow. Tomorrow.

> *Lights on* NORAH *only, who is pacing. Her hands are jammed into her pockets, her neck bent against the cold, her sign,* GOODNESS, *hangs crookedly on a string around her neck. She may leave, disappear. Lights down.*
>
> *End of Act One.*

ACT TWO

Whether

RETA: *(cleaning)* Ordering my house calms me down. Cleaning gives me pleasure, though I'm reluctant to admit it. But dusting, waxing, and polishing offer rewards.

Those Buddhist monks I saw not long ago on a TV documentary devote two hours to morning mediation. They then go out into the world with buckets and rags to do one hour of serious cleaning. Saffron-robed and heads gleaming, they clean anything that needs cleaning, a wall or an old fence, whatever presents threat or disorder. I'm beginning to understand where this might take them.

Beat.

I wake up in the morning anxious to clean my house. I'd like to go at it with Q-tips, with toothpicks, every crack and corner scoured.

Beat.

If I commit myself to its meticulous care, if I seal it from damage, I will claim back my daughter Norah.

RETA scrubs and cleans for a minute in silence, then turns to the audience.

My heart is broken.

Whence

A second chorus.

ACTOR B: Her actions indicate that she's giving herself something. A gift of freedom, the right to be a truant in her own life.

ACTOR G: *(as FRANCIS Quinn)* Nine-tenths of the money she collects in her bowl, she distributes at the end of the day to other street people.

ACTOR D: Her mother has been working ever since she was quite young. She's merely reflecting her experience. She was abandoned, so now she abandons.

LOIS: I know why she's doing this—

ACTOR D: She's not yet twenty. Time is on her side. I've seen stubborn cases before and in the end they yield.

LOIS: I know what it is—

ACTOR F: *(as TOM)* The reactions to trauma are never predictable. One Vietnam vet drives his car incessantly.

ACTOR C: *(as ANNETTE, sheepishly)* I yelled at her. I meant just to bring her a book and some food and I ended up shouting at her, demanding to know how she could do this to her mother!

ACTOR G: Ordinarily, people are allowed to stay at the hostel just three months. But Norah's been here six. She's so quiet, so accommodating, we've just kind of ignored it, her long stay.

ACTOR B: *(earnest)* Don't think of it as a crisis. Think of it as a behavioural interlude. A transitional phase. A kind of a cleansing. A fast.

ACTOR D: We've put her on our prayer list. It's the biggest prayer list in the country.

ACTOR F: *(TOM)* Social isolation is the foremost indicator of post-traumatic disorder. The trauma victim doesn't trust anyone to understand or they just don't want to talk about it.

LOIS: It's—it's—

TOM: They shut down. They don't know what to do to get better.

CHRISTINE: I wonder if she remembers she's my sister.

Nevertheless

*RETA—to steady herself, since writing gives her some sort of order—
sits down at her desk in her box room.*

RETA: Alicia is still trying to decide how to end the engagement. She doesn't want to hurt Roman, her dear Roman, with his musky scent, like a wedge of cheese crusted over. She doesn't want to be the destroyer, the breaker of promises, hard-hearted, unkind, bringing corrosion to an existence that has been underpinned with natural goodness.

She wants out of the engagement but she also wants to live with a good conscience. Whenever Alicia thinks of goodness, the image of granite comes to mind, polished surfaces. But stone can be crushed, rather easily in fact. Alicia has visited the quarry near Straw Hill. She's seen the giant machines at work.

Does Alicia believe in God? No, despite her Presbyterian upbringing. God and his Son are metaphors, representing perhaps creation and renewal. It has been so unimportant in her life, the question of belief or disbelief—and she and Roman have never touched on the subject.

Throughout

*Towards the end of the last speech, RETA descends from her box room
to get a cup of tea; now she stops into a room where TOM is, clicking
through slides of trilobites, projected on a wall. RETA watches and
puts her hand on his arm. The two ooh at a particularly wonderful
slide—an image of the massive seventy-centimetre Hudson's Bay
trilobite.*

TOM: This is the largest one ever found—two and a half feet. *(keeps on clicking)* They hung around for a hundred million years. Rolled up, each bony section tucked into the next, protecting their soft insides. The act is called enrolment.

RETA: *(to audience)* It's my belief Tom thinks about trilobites all the time. While he's checking out a prostate gland or writing a prescription for asthma drugs, a piece of his mind holds steady to the idea of the extinct, unlovely arthropods that occupied every sea and ocean in the world. Ugly and adaptable creatures. A head with bulging eyes, a thorax, a tail of sorts. Tom loves them, and so we all love them.

TOM: And here— *(changes slide)* Most trilobites developed huge, complex eyes on the sides of their heads. But this species was blind. It's considered a step forward in evolution, since these ones lived in the muck at the bottom of a deep body of water. /

TOM continues under while RETA speaks over him to the audience. . .

It seems that nature favours getting rid of unused apparatuses. What's amazing is that the very erasure is in the fossil record. The fossil remains are clear, right down to the smallest lens. But we know that the loss of one sense strengthens others, and this is the question with this species: What sense won out, what sense increased? No one knows a thing about the trilobite brain or even how they reproduced sexually. . .

RETA: *(to audience)* / Why can't I adapt, too? All I wanted was for Norah to be happy; all I wanted was everything. Instead I've come to rest on the lake bottom, stuck there in the thick mud, squirming, and longing to have my eyes taken away /

(to TOM) Are these for the Estonia conference?

TOM: *(grinning)* Wouldn't you like to go to Estonia? *(gives her an amorous pat on the bum)* There'll be a researcher there who does digitized imaging of a trilobite enrolling. . .

RETA: Oh, I don't know, Tom, it depends on Norah.

She wanders off; it's clear there's no way she'll go to the conference. RETA begins absently unloading Christmas ornaments from a box and arranging them on surfaces.

An interviewer once asked me what was the worst thing that had ever happened to me. He must have been desperate for a question. I didn't know what to say. I told him that the worst thing hadn't happened to me yet, that I didn't know what it was but I knew somehow that it would be socketed into the lives of my children. There is this ripping sound behind my eyes and the starchy tearing of fabric end to end and the need I have to curl up my knees when I sleep. . . *(fully aware of how pathetic it sounds)* Whimpering.

This is my fantasy: In my mental movie, Norah has come home, exhausted, hitching a ride from Toronto. Every rerun is the same: She appears, suddenly, within the protection of our walls. She is slightly feverish with flu, but nothing serious, nothing a few days in bed won't fix. In a few minutes I'll take her some lemon tea. My daughter, my sick daughter. I don't want to wake her though. Waking a sleeping person seems to me a particularly violent act. This is how political prisoners were tortured in China. Or was it Argentina? With an intricate and automatic alarm system cutting in five minutes after sleep commenced. No, let her sleep. Let the fantasy go.

Downstairs, TOM *matter-of-factly turns off the slide projector.*

Punch the delete key.

Forthwith

A tour of the Promise Hostel, led by FRANCIS *Quinn.* TOM, RETA, CHRISTINE, *and* NATALIE *follow after her, travelling as a clump. Someone is practising a Christmas carol on a piano somewhere and keeps starting and stopping.*

FRANCIS: *(jolly, hearty)* We have a twenty-bed dorm for the women, forty beds for the men. You can see it's very clean. Volunteers come and sweep and swab—office workers on their lunches, even lawyers. Everyone finds a towel at the end of their bed; we like to provide a towel like that, a welcome.

RETA *wistfully puts her hand on the end of a bed.*

Lights out every night at eleven, even on holidays.

And here's our chapel, a room, really, but we give it a fresh coat of white paint every year. We have regular services, but mostly it's a place to think, you know; often, someone—well, Norah—just curls up in here with a paperback, it doesn't matter. And *(clanging of pots, running water)* here's the kitchen.

Chicken pot pies today. We just got a surprise donation of a hundred free-range chickens—that's on top of the thirty Christmas turkeys sent by

Honest Ed. We get plenty of donations from hotels and restaurants, but they're usually last-minute; our volunteer cooks get to be very creative. We know a hundred ways to dress up day-old bread. Once, we got four cases of tinned okra! Here's the dining hall, and that enormous TV—a gift from the real-estate dealer, Reg Boland, that's his name, isn't it? We always serve a hot breakfast—then everyone is supposed to be out by eight thirty. The doors open again at five in the winter months. In the summer, we open an hour later. *(more tenderly)* We try to keep it fresh, open the windows every day. Some volunteers are making a quilt for the foyer. One of them came upon some words of Julian of Norwich, some wise medieval woman, and she says she instantly saw them on a quilt.

How does it go: "All shall be well, and all shall be well, and all manner of things shall be well." Meaning, she explained it to me, all is well for the moment and for the moment that follows and the moment after the moment. *(looks at* RETA *warmly, helplessly)*

> *RETA, TOM, CHRISTINE, and NATALIE herd out and get into their car. They put on their seatbelts but don't go right away. They sit watching the rain stream down the windows. RETA puts her hand lightly on TOM's knee. He moves suddenly, covering his face with his hands. Then NATALIE begins to blub, and then they all do. Lights down.*

> *The phone rings. In the following scene, RETA wanders with a cordless phone, dusting baseboards as she speaks to ARTHUR SPRINGER. There should be a few Christmas ornaments about.*

Towards

ARTHUR SPRINGER: Hello. May I speak with Reta Winters, please?

RETA: This is Reta Winters.

ARTHUR SPRINGER: Oh, Reta, I am so sorry. I failed to recognize your voice.

RETA: I have a bit of a cold—

ARTHUR SPRINGER: I hope you had a happy Christmas. You and your family.

RETA: Well, yes, yes, we did. We are. And did you—?

ARTHUR SPRINGER: I do apologize for phoning you at home.

RETA: At home? That's quite all right. In fact, this is where I—

ARTHUR SPRINGER: And I apologize even further for phoning during this, the one time of year when we should put all business aside and make merriment our first concern. But I am so excited about your manuscript that I wanted to make immediate contact, and I thought to myself that you might have the goodness to forgive me for breaking into the holiday so unduly, and no doubt I've phoned at an ungodly hour.

RETA: Oh, no, we're actually in the same time zone as—

ARTHUR SPRINGER: Your new manuscript—where can I begin! I finished reading the partial draft last night. I hardly slept. Alicia and Roman were so much in my mind, all they endured, their personal courage, their sense of their very selves as their insight grew and grew, their interior vision, piercing like a laser. I woke up thinking, this is what life is, no one ever promised we wouldn't suffer as we make our way, our expectations are doomed to disappointment—

RETA: But, Arthur—

ARTHUR SPRINGER: And Alicia—her persevering goodness. I told you that last time we spoke, didn't I?

RETA: Yes, you did. I was so pleased. I'm trying to work out what goodness is, in fact, its essence, and—

ARTHUR SPRINGER: Such goodness of soul, of heart. It's integral, you don't even have to remark on it or put little quotes around it. And Roman. That man. Roman, Roman.

RETA: Yes?

ARTHUR SPRINGER: Indescribable. The one word a writer must never use, but for us editors, well, we can only think: what an indescribable character! His complexity, I mean. I see now why you have named him as you have: modern man condemned to roam the—

RETA: I never thought—

ARTHUR SPRINGER: Indescribable! I can't imagine how we're going to present him in the flap copy, but we'll work on it. The problem is, Reta, you were writing a sequel, but now I find that you are writing a—a—pilgrimage, an investigation, of human yearning itself.

RETA: But it is a sequel. There's Alicia and Roman and their—

ARTHUR SPRINGER: Anyway, I'm phoning to see when you can get to New York. Next week if possible.

RETA: Oh, I can't possibly do that, go to New York.

ARTHUR SPRINGER: Then I'll come to you! To Orangetown. Is this place near Montreal? I know Montreal very well.

RETA: It's near Toronto.

ARTHUR SPRINGER: Ah, Toronto, yes. I can easily manage Toronto. I'll get a cab from there to your place of residence. It will take us at least two days, Reta, to go through the manuscript. Is there a hotel in the village of Orangetown?

RETA: There's the Orangetown Inn. It's quite—

ARTHUR SPRINGER: January second, does that sound all right? I'll get the earliest plane.

RETA: Are you sure. . .

ARTHUR SPRINGER: (*in his most bumptious manner*) This is actually an excellent idea, getting away from New York into the countryside, much more profitable in every way. Tranquility, tran-quil-i-ty. And if I do say so, meeting like this will be a splendid way to launch the new year. Happy New Year, Reta.

RETA: Happy New Year. To you. Arthur? Hello? Are you there?

Any

CHRISTINE enters, removing her boots at the door.

CHRISTINE: Mom, thanks for not calling me Ophelia.

RETA: Ophelia!

CHRISTINE: We have this new girl in the swim club, a transfer from Prescott.

RETA: And her name is—

CHRISTINE: Ophelia.

RETA: Now that is. . . Unusual. As a name.

CHRISTINE: A ditz name. Most of the kids don't know. They don't connect, I mean. We don't do *Hamlet* until next year.

RETA: I don't think I've ever met anyone named—

CHRISTINE: Ophelia? So Willow Holiday asked me to look after her for a day or two, introduce her around. I've invited her over after swimming tomorrow. I wanted to warn you. *(imagining)* "Mother, this is Ophelia." Do you think you can keep a straight face?

RETA: I'll try.

CHRISTINE: So, thank you.

NATALIE arrives on the scene and joins in by thinking up something for which to thank RETA.

NATALIE: *(mock voice)* And I want to thank you, Mother, *(half-beat)* for releasing me from your loins!

RETA: *(laughing lightly)* Wherever did you get a word like loins?

NATALIE: Tom Wolfe. It means uterus. Or else womb.

RETA: You're welcome.

Beat.

It was a pleasure.

NATALIE: You don't mean that. Giving birth can't be filed under one of life's pleasures. God! Twenty hours of labour to push me out of your womb. *(pronounced womb-ah)*

RETA: Twelve hours.

NATALIE: You forget.

RETA: Shouldn't I remember? Of all people?

CHRISTINE: You have this thing about revising history. You and Your Husband want us to believe we girls arrived in the world without causing too much fuss and bother.

Beat.

Why are you smiling like that?

RETA: It's that phrase, fuss and bother. It makes me think of your grandmother. Grandma Winters. You know how she always wants to spare the world fuss and bother.

CHRISTINE: But demanding it at the same time. Ha! Anyway, thank you!

NATALIE: Thank you!

NATALIE and CHRISTINE leave; RETA addresses audience.

RETA: They are trying so hard, Natalie and Chris, to keep the noise of the household alive. It pierces my heart, their attempts to amuse or divert Tom and me, to assure us that they are still here, willing to be regulation daughters, to keep up with the daughterly routines, school, friends, family dinners, swim practice.

Tom is still delving seriously into the subject of post-traumatic shock, hoping to rescue or at least understand Norah by tracking down that "thing" that leapt out at her last spring and knocked her out of her life. He sits hunched over his computer in the evenings, deep into the Internet, webbing off darkly into trauma therapy, trauma stress, trauma case histories. Well, he is a doctor. The idea of diagnosis and healing comes naturally to him, the rhythmic arc of cause and effect has its own built-in satisfactions. How enviable, to me, this state of mind is.

I haven't told Tom what I now believe; that the world is split in two—between those who are handed power at birth, encoded with a seemingly random chromosome determinate that says yes for ever and ever, and those like Norah, like my mother-in-law, like me, like all of us who fall into the uncoded otherness in which the power to assert ourselves has been displaced by a compulsion to shut down our bodies and be as nothing against the fireworks and streaking stars and blinding light of the big bang. That's the problem.

Oh, time for coffee!

Only

RETA runs downstairs, throws on her coat, and joins the other women at the Orangeville Tearoom table.

SALLY: I'm thinking of suing my obstetrician. He wouldn't let me wear my glasses during delivery so I missed everything.

LYNN KELLY: Probably it was this matter of aesthetics. You and your eyewear disturbed the doctor's vision of what the Birth Of A Child should look like?

RETA: *(arriving)* Guess what! He's coming. Arthur Springer, the editor, is coming here. Next Friday. *(sarcastically)* A country weekend!

LYNN KELLY: A country weekend! What do you suppose he has in mind? Horses and things?

RETA: I suppose I could have a dinner party.

ANNETTE: A rustic dinner party?

SALLY: A potluck thing?

ANNETTE: You could take him to the Saturday-morning market. It's got much better lately. There's this woman who makes beads out of dried rose petals—

The next few lines are said quickly.

SALLY: Yes! And they're supposed to have everlasting fragrance. She has some way of compacting them.

LYNN KELLY: That's what the original rosaries were made of—

RETA: Really! I never put that together.

LYNN KELLY: What do you think he'll be like? Your Arthur Springer with his—

RETA: I don't know. But I'm terribly afraid he's going to be—I can't pin it down exactly, but—

ANNETTE: New Agey?

RETA: New Yorky.

LYNN KELLY: Cool type? Ivy covered?

RETA: *(shakes her head)* I'm afraid he's going to be smarmy.

SALLY: Oh, my God.

ANNETTE: Don't let him get away with it.

LYNN KELLY: Just smarm him back.

RETA: I'll have to ask him to stay to dinner. But the girls are formidable. They have this new word—kronk. It means shit or something like that. Kronk you, they say to each other. They call Tom the Kronkmeister, and he loves it. He does a little salute and clicks his heels.

LYNN KELLY: You know, you and Arthur /

RETA rises from the table and begins her next speech to the audience while the others let her say a line before they speak the next few lines under her.

RETA: / We know what we look like: Four women in early middle age, hunched over a table in a small-town coffee shop. / Two years ago when I went on my book tour, the three of them gave me a send-off gift of purple underpants in real silk. I wore these under my white wool suit, and every time I took a step this way or that, shaking hands and saying "Thank you for coming," I felt the rub of silk between my legs and thought how fortunate I was to have such fine, loving friends.

LYNN KELLY: / are definitely in a power arrangement, Reta.

SALLY: This man's your publisher.

ANNETTE: No, he's her editor, not her publisher.

LYNN KELLY: He can definitely decide how the book's going to go—

ANNETTE: At least you'll be on home turf. When did you say he's coming?

RETA: Friday.

She returns to the table.

(teasingly, winkingly) So. Did everyone get a postcard from Gwen?

LYNN KELLY: From Gwendolyn Reidman, you mean!

SALLY: What? I didn't get a postcard.

ANNETTE: Oh, you'll get one—she sent sixty-seven.

RETA: Yes, to tell everyone she changed her name, aaaand—

LYNN KELLY: She's a—

ANNETTE: Lesbian!

SALLY: No! Really?

Beat.

I suppose. . .

LYNN KELLY: Is this something we could have known, do you think?

ANNETTE: I wonder if she has always been a lesbian, or is this something she only discovered now, in middle age?

LYNN KELLY: Can lesbianism—or any sexuality for that matter—brew? You know, can it start off just a weak little current that just grows stronger over the years until it dominates?

RETA: How long has she known?

SALLY: There was always something innocent about her, something undiscovered. Naive.

RETA: And more and more disappointed.

LYNN KELLY: *(introducing new subject)* I almost got killed on my way here: I'm driving down Borden Road, slowing down to turn onto Main Street, and this guy goes into road rage and almost rams straight into me.

RETA: Road rage? In Orangetown? At this hour?

ANNETTE: Believe it, there's rage everywhere. Someone could walk into this café right this minute brandishing a sword. I read about a man who went into a church in England and started slicing up people.

LYNN KELLY: He was insane.

SALLY: We've got to trust that something like that isn't going to happen.

LYNN KELLY: Like being struck by lightning. You can't go around worrying about lightning.

RETA: Or planes crashing into your house.

ANNETTE: *(coolly)* If someone came in here with a sword, we wouldn't have a chance.

SALLY: We'd be helpless.

LYNN KELLY: We could duck under the table.

ANNETTE: No, we'd be helpless.

RETA: Trust. We've had it drilled into us since birth. *(the thought evolves)* We emerge from the womb already trusting. Trusting the hand that's about to hold us—or drop us.

> *LYNN KELLY's cellphone rings—the others put on their coats and disperse with goodbyes. Lights fade.*
>
> *NORAH is coughing. Alone.*

Whereupon

> *Lights up on RETA and ARTHUR SPRINGER in the living room. ARTHUR is self-consciously wiping at his shirt. There are muddy paw marks all over him.*

ARTHUR SPRINGER: I was, uh, taken by surprise, by your dog.

RETA: Oh dear! Pet! That's what we call him. Oh, goodness. I hope you're not allergic to dogs.

ARTHUR SPRINGER: No, no.

RETA: He's entirely harmless, with an extremely obedient nature, though it took forever to get him house-trained. *(considers ARTHUR)* I thought you'd be older somehow.

ARTHUR SPRINGER: Thirty-nine. And you're forty-four—I looked it up in the clipping file. What a heavenly house. Woodsmoke, I can smell woodsmoke. Ah, and there's the fire, the source of that heavenly aroma.

RETA: I thought we could sit—

ARTHUR SPRINGER: In New York only the fortunate few have access to— And the price of firewood! Ten dollars for four little sticks; of course that's for very, very good firewood, hickory— What a splendid room this is, Reta.

RETA: Would you like some coffee? I've just—

ARTHUR SPRINGER: Coffee, hmmm.

RETA: Or, since you've just got out of a cold taxi—maybe—it's early, but maybe you'd like a glass of red wine.

ARTHUR SPRINGER: I wouldn't want you to open a bottle just for me.

RETA: I'm sure we have one open. I'll just—

ARTHUR SPRINGER: So this is where you work.

RETA: Well, not in this actual room. This is the living room. I have a little spot on the third floor that I—

ARTHUR SPRINGER: And your family? They're here at the moment.

RETA: The girls will be home in an hour or so. They've got swimming today. And my husband, Tom, he'll be picking them up. We're hoping you can stay to dinner, just a simple—

ARTHUR SPRINGER: I'd be delighted. Honoured to be welcomed so warmly. I don't want to be a nuisance but—this view with the fading light, that hint of rose in the air behind the trees, it must be a source of calm and, well—I do hate the word inspiration, it's grown to be such a cliché, but in this case I feel I can believe in such a thing, that living here, in such peace, these oaks and maples, the pace of each day quietly asserting itself—ah, thank you so much—the seasons rolling along— Hmm—a lovely light red. Let me propose a toast to the new manuscript—to Alicia and Roman!

> *Ping, pong—ALICIA and ROMAN toast them back from their cameo screens.*

And now tell me, how is it coming?

RETA: I printed it out this morning. This is it, or rather, most of it.

ARTHUR SPRINGER: Let me see. Hmmm. The heft itself is most impressive—three hundred pages—oh my, Reta, you've added quite a bit since I read it in December. Quite a bit.

RETA: I still have a hundred things to do. Some patching and poking. And the final chapter.

ARTHUR SPRINGER: Ah, yes, the final chapter. The all-important final chapter.

RETA: The most difficult chapter in a way.

ARTHUR SPRINGER: I absolutely agree. It's critical. What is a novelist to do? Provide closure for the reader? Or open the narrative to the ether?

RETA: You mean—

ARTHUR SPRINGER: I think of the final chapter as the kiln. You've made the pot, Reta, the clay is still malleable, but the ending will harden your words into something enduring and beautiful. Or else beautiful and ethereal.

RETA: What an interesting thought. I was just thinking the other day about the way a bronze casting sometimes breaks unexpectedly in the forge. And now you mention pots in the kiln—

ARTHUR SPRINGER: I meant it as a metaphor.

RETA: So did I.

ARTHUR SPRINGER: I knew we were kindred spirits, Reta. Though I should tell you I am in favour, in your particular case, of not offering closure. There is a danger, you see, that you might trivialize Roman's search for identity, which is ongoing, a forever kind of thing.

RETA: Can I give you a little more wine?

ARTHUR SPRINGER: Lovely and dry, this red, just the thing for our first face-to-face meeting. The sort of meeting that could be difficult.

RETA: I do want you to know, Mr. Springer, that I am completely open to editing suggestions.

ARTHUR SPRINGER: Arthur, please. That's wonderful to know, that you don't object to the editorial hand. I understand Mr. Scribano did not really edit *My Thyme Is Up*. He was the editor, of course, nominally, but he did very little, my sources tell me, in the way of reshaping the work.

RETA: He did ask me to break one very long paragraph into two, and I thought that was an excellent suggestion. I was happy to—

ARTHUR SPRINGER: Reta. I want you to know that I, your editor, care deeply about literature and its paramount statement. And I believe you do, too. In fact, I know you do.

RETA: Perhaps you will let me refill that glass.

ARTHUR SPRINGER: You are an intelligent woman, Reta. And we have a chance to turn this manuscript around. That's why I've come all the way up here to the north. To tell you that your new novel is not in the same company as your first book.

RETA: But the new book is a sequel to *My Thyme Is Up.*

ARTHUR SPRINGER: That's the first thing we can turn around. I think it is exceptionally important we not present this with the title you have suggested—*Thyme In Bloom.*

Personally, I suggest *Bloom* on its own.

RETA: Just—*Bloom*?

ARTHUR SPRINGER: What a word that is suggestive but not literal, and you can see how it gestures towards the Bloom of *Ulysses*, Leopold Bloom, that great Everyman.

RETA: But my literary name is associated with—

ARTHUR SPRINGER: Associated with light fiction. This is why in my thinking over the last two weeks, I've come to favour a pseudonym. Now what was your name before you married, Reta? And do you have a middle name?

RETA: Reta Ruth Summers.

ARTHUR SPRINGER: Wonderful, I love Summers. It fits perfectly with Bloom, doesn't it? Bloomsday, et cetera. The month of June. There's a kind of preternatural blood hyphen there, if we can just pin it down. We, Scribano & Lawrence, could present you as R.R. Summers. I like it. It sounds solid. Yet fresh. A new writer, a new discovery: R.R. Summers.

RETA: Using initials, though, might sound like, you know, that I'm a male writer.

ARTHUR SPRINGER: Does it matter!

RETA: But this book— Well, Alicia is thinking quite hard about gender, at least in her own way.

ARTHUR SPRINGER: But even at this stage, we can put a kind of torque on the book and move it towards the universal. I have a number of ideas that I want to put before you, Reta. The first is—

RETA: You make it sound as though we'll be rewriting the whole book.

ARTHUR SPRINGER: Just tweaking, that's all. Everything is here, Reta.

RETA: I had thought—

ARTHUR SPRINGER: I've made a list of things. First there's the matter of Roman. His role needs enlarging. His interiority.

RETA: But Alicia is really the focus. I thought you admired her for her goodness.

ARTHUR SPRINGER: Goodness, but not greatness. Who said that?

RETA: Danielle Westerman, among others.

ARTHUR SPRINGER: I don't think Roman should be a trombonist. He should be the conductor of the orchestra. Or even a composer. And Wychwood City—

RETA: *(cottoning on)* Could be re-sited to New York.

ARTHUR SPRINGER: Or Boston. Even Toronto, though that would limit its readership—

RETA: Oh, I don't think so. Not anymore.

ARTHUR SPRINGER: He suddenly, in mid-life, wants more. He yearns for more.

RETA: Who?

ARTHUR SPRINGER: Roman.

RETA: Oh.

But I can't see Roman as a serious—

ARTHUR SPRINGER: Think of it. He got educated, became a musician. He's wonderfully attractive to women, that thick hair of his, that very physical body, and his ever active brain. And then, Alicia, who works in, of all things, the world of fashion. Everything he despises. The marriage must not happen.

RETA: I absolutely agree with that, the marriage must not happen, but—

ARTHUR SPRINGER: I'm so glad you are in accord with me there.

RETA: But, really, it is Alicia who sees that—

ARTHUR SPRINGER: I am talking about Roman being the moral centre of this book. And Alicia, for all her charms, is not capable of that role, surely you can see that. She writes fashion articles. She talks to her cat. She does yoga. She makes rice casseroles.

RETA: Oh. It's because she's a woman.

ARTHUR SPRINGER: That's not an issue at all.

RETA: But it is the issue.

ARTHUR SPRINGER: She is undisciplined. She can't focus. She changes her mind. She lacks—a reader, the serious reader that I have in mind, would never accept her as the decisive fulcrum of a serious work of art.

RETA: Because she's a woman.

ARTHUR SPRINGER: Not at all, not at all.

RETA: *(to audience)* Because she's a woman.

At this point, two things happen simultaneously. ARTHUR SPRINGER lifts his arm in protest and knocks over the bottle on the coffee table, drenching the morning newspaper with red wine. And NATALIE and CHRISTINE come in the front door. They are loud and noisy, scrambling out of their boots and throwing their books onto the floor.

Yet

CHRISTINE: Kronk car!

NATALIE: What was that smell? And how slowly can you turn a corner? I thought she was going into cardiac arrest or something.

The girls notice RETA.

Hey, what happened to the Kronkmeister?

CHRISTINE: He failed to pick us up at swimming!

NATALIE: We had to get a ride with Willow Holiday.

CHRISTINE: Dangerous!

RETA rises to introduce ARTHUR SPRINGER but the telephone is ringing. She leaves ARTHUR to mop up the spilled wine with his handkerchief.

RETA: *(picks up phone)* Hello?

TOM: Reta! It's Tom!

RETA: You were supposed to pick up the girls—where are you?

TOM: There's nothing to worry about. Everything's fine.

RETA: Mr. Springer's here from New York. You're late.

TOM: Reta, it's Norah.

RETA: What?

TOM: She's in the hospital. Has pneumonia.

RETA: Pneumonia?

TOM: She's going to be fine; she's sleeping right now—

RETA: Where is she?

TOM: Toronto General.

RETA: I'll come right away.

TOM: They're taking excellent care of her—

RETA: It'll take me an hour—

TOM: I'll be in her room. 434, south wing.

RETA: *(starts putting down phone; to girls)* Put your coats back on. Norah's at Toronto General.

TOM: Reta!

RETA puts the phone back to her ear.

Drive carefully.

RETA: *(to ARTHUR SPRINGER, hurriedly)* Something's come up. There's a casserole in the oven— More wine in the cupboard, plenty of firewood. Make yourself at home. I have no idea when we'll be back.

RETA and the girls leave. A silence. ARTHUR makes himself at home. RETA, in the car with the girls, remains on stage.

Instead

ARTHUR SPRINGER clears his throat largely and looks about the room. He makes a feeble attempt to clean up the wine, and finds another bottle in a cupboard. He looks at his watch, finds a corkscrew, opens the bottle of wine, and pours himself a glass. He puts the TV on. He settles down in a chair, with his glass of wine, stands up, looks around him, sits down again. The TV is playing—the Lehrer Newshour— he grows more relaxed, starts swinging his feet over the arm of the chair, probing an ear. Very gradually, we hear a knocking at the door. ARTHUR jumps to his feet, kind of embarrassed, dusts himself off, and opens the door to LOIS, who is carrying a large Pyrex baking dish.

ARTHUR SPRINGER: *(turning down the volume)* Sorry I had the volume turned up so loudly. You must be. . . Reta's. . . mother.

LOIS: Mother-in-law. Lois.

ARTHUR SPRINGER: Oh. Reta's gone into town, with her daughters—some emergency. The daughter who lives in Toronto has pneumonia—I think. But I'm very pleased to meet Reta's mother.

LOIS: Norah and pneumonia.

ARTHUR SPRINGER: I'm sure Norah will be fine.

LOIS: Norah's not very fine. She hasn't been fine for some time.

The sound of Pet whimpering outside. LOIS looks out.

The poor creature! Has he been fed?

ARTHUR SPRINGER: Oh, I'm so sorry! I'm not very good with animals. They seem frightened of me. I had quite frankly forgotten the dog was around.

LOIS hangs up her coat and takes charge. She puts food and water into the dog bowls and sets them outside.

LOIS: Pet's used to being fed at around six thirty.

ARTHUR SPRINGER: There was something about pasta. I didn't take in the details—everything happened in such a rush.

LOIS busies herself warming up the pasta, gesturing to ARTHUR to sit at the TV. But he lingers.

I've been watching the news and there's nothing interesting at all. Now and then, not often, there comes a day when nothing seems to happen.

LOIS: Yes, that's true.

ARTHUR SPRINGER: It's like God's decided to give us a day off.

LOIS: I can always tell from the first news item. If it's about new safety standards for hockey helmets, that is an indication nothing terrible has happened. No bombs or murders or riots or fires or plane crashes or terrorists or—

ARTHUR SPRINGER: I love those blank days.

LOIS: So do I.

ARTHUR SPRINGER: They're so rare.

> *LOIS serves up meal. ARTHUR SPRINGER pours himself another glass of wine after first pouring one for LOIS, asking her with the raise of an eyebrow if she would like one. Then they both sit down at the same instant, as though a gong has sounded.*

(with extreme solicitousness) And now, tell me all about yourself, *(beat)* Lois.

> *LOIS now turns and faces the audience. ARTHUR SPRINGER, for the most part, is not listening; he is mostly looking down at his plate. At one point, he removes the plates and carries them to the kitchen. LOIS seems to be speaking at a great distance.*

Beginning With

LOIS: I saw a play several years ago. I can't remember the name of it or even whether I enjoyed it or not. Directly in front of me in the audience sat a young couple.

The woman was exceptionally slender and beautiful, with a low voice and a smiling way of inclining her head towards her young man. He could scarcely take his eyes off her. He held her hand in his throughout the play. He kneaded it—hungrily. Several times, while the actors were shouting and dashing around the stage, he brought her hand to his lips and held it there. I had never seen such tenderness between a man and a woman. I scarcely slept that night, and a few times I even brought my curled hand up to my own mouth and pressed my lips against it. I was about forty years old at the time, a wife, the mother of a son.

Twelve years ago I was widowed—but I never use that word. Instead I say, "My husband died in 1988. I've been alone since then." I know exactly how pathetic that sounds.

I hope you like a good bread pudding. I have a list of one hundred desserts, alphabetized in a recipe box, beginning with almond apples, moving to date pudding, on to nut brittle mousse and ending with Zwieback pastry cheese-cake; I rotate this list around the year. It is no longer easy to find Zwieback biscuits, but graham crackers can be substituted. Needless to say, seasonal ingredients mean that the desserts themselves are not served alphabetically. I once overheard my granddaughter, Christine, make fun of my dessert list. I can understand this in a way, but I still think it was rather mean.

I was twenty-four hours in labour when Tom was born. When I first started having pains, I insisted that my husband drive me to the hospital straight away. "Ten minutes apart?" the receptionist said. "Didn't they tell you not to come till the pains were at five minutes?" At that point I could hear a woman screaming from another floor. "Is that woman having a baby?" I asked the receptionist.

She rolled her eyes and said, "That's an Italian woman having a baby.'"

My first granddaughter was named Norah Charlotte Winters—a beautiful baby. The Charlotte is after a friend of Reta's who died very young in a car accident. I never met this Charlotte person. I was in a car accident once, a fender-bender, really, but it was a terrible shock. So much that I gave up driving.

A woman named Crystal McGinn once lived next door to me—in this very house—with her very large family, four children at least, teenagers, boister-ous youngsters. Once, Crystal invited me over for a cup of coffee and she asked me where I had gone to university. Not if I had gone to university, but where. She had gone to Queen's and studied economics. I didn't tell Mrs. McGinn that I myself attended secretarial college for six months in Toronto, then married my husband—a young doctor—and moved to Orangetown; I felt strongly that Crystal McGinn overstepped with her question about which university. We didn't see much of each other after that, nothing more than an occasional wave. I regret this now. I realize that Mrs. McGinn's question wasn't cruel, only a little tactless.

Especially considering that I was the doctor's wife. There was a certain prestige in that role, at least in the early days. It became my habit to remind myself of this fact, standing in front of the hall mirror, sucking in my stomach and saying musically: I am the wife of a physician.

My granddaughter, my favourite—Norah—there's an enduring sweetness at the girl's core—has been going through a hard time. I myself understand about times of difficulty. When I was in my early fifties, I stopped baking and went to bed for two weeks. My husband wanted to take me to the Mayo Clinic; that was all he talked about, the Mayo Clinic. Then I got up one day and cleaned the bathroom as it had never before been cleaned. That plunge into hygiene seemed to set things right. I was better able to cope after that.

I love Oprah. I arrange my day around Oprah. I have found a new self-courage recently, as a result of watching Oprah.

Except lately. I can't talk anymore. I don't trust myself. Toads will come out of my open mouth. I'll hurt people's feelings. I have an opinion about what happened to Norah, and I don't want anyone else to know. They'd think I was crazy. Women are supposed to be strong, but they aren't really. They aren't allowed to be. They are hopelessly encumbered with fibres and membranes and pads of malleable tissue; women are easily injured; critical injuries, that's what comes to you if you open your mouth.

On the other hand, Norah should be all right. It's always just a matter of time, though the pneumonia is worrying. I do wish Reta would telephone. I'm glad, though, to have good company on a winter's night. Bread pudding with lemon sauce. A cup of tea. I've been bending your ear off. This is so unlike me. I don't know how I got started.

On the whole, I believe things work out for the best. Don't you agree, Mr. Springer?

> LOIS *says the last of her speech and looks towards a spaced out* ARTHUR SPRINGER, *satisfied.*

Hence

TOM: *(gesturing towards NORAH's hands)* They're burns. *(in doctorly voice)* A combination of severe second-degree burns.

Beat.

I drove by the corner of Bathurst and Bloor for a glimpse of her this morning. For the first time since April, she wasn't there. I rang the bell at the hostel.

RETA: And they told you she was in hospital.

TOM: She's been asleep since I got here. The burns haven't been cared for properly, there's a fair amount of scarring, but you can tell they're about six months old. That guy at the hostel remembers that Norah's hands were bandaged when she first arrived there. There's a record of a woman being treated for burns right here, at Toronto General. But she disappeared before giving her name. The story as we know it goes like this: On the tenth of April, Norah had just bought a plastic dish rack and was leaving Honest Ed's—

RETA: That's right at Bathurst and Bloor—

TOM: Yes—a Muslim woman—or so it would appear—poured gasoline over her veil and gown—

RETA: —and set herself on fire. I remember that.

TOM: Outside of Honest Ed's. They caught it all on security tape. I've seen the film twice now; Norah rushing forward to stifle the flames, the dish rack catching fire, and the plastic bag burned itself to Norah's hands.

CHRISTINE: She always had those gloves on. Even last summer when it was boiling hot, in the middle of July, she wore these old floppy gardening gloves.

NATALIE: Yeah, we thought it was weird.

TOM: The smoke, the smell must have been terrible. Two firemen pulled Norah away. And drove her to Emergency where she was given first aid.

RETA: *(half beat)* Do they still hurt? Her hands, I mean. They're so red.

TOM: That's a step in the healing process: the destruction of body tissue.

Beat.

I'm going to make a few more phone calls. I'll let Lois know where we are. Girls, let's find you some supper.

(to RETA, *touching the side of her face lightly with his hand)* You should have something to eat.

RETA: I can't. I'll just sit here. In case she wakes up.

> TOM *and the girls drift out.* RETA *simply sits. Eventually,* NORAH'S *eyes open and she reaches her hand out for* RETA. *There's a sigh-like sob from them both.*

Norah. Norah. You're awake,

NORAH: Yes. *(or simply smiles)*

> *The stage darkens. While* RETA *gives this next speech, the stage is lit by a huge projection: flames and cloth burning, people running, the sound of sirens.*

Unless

RETA: A life is full of isolated events, but these events, if they are to form a coherent narrative, require odd pieces of language to cement them together, little chips of grammar: once, nearly, so, next. The conjunction "unless" prises open the crusted world to reveal another plane of meaning. Unless you're unhealthy.

Unless you're alone. Unless you find just what you need.

Unless Tom had worked late and hadn't driven by the corner of Bathurst and Bloor for a glimpse of Nora. Unless he'd hurried home, and hadn't gone to the hostel to look for her. If Norah's lung sacs hadn't filled with fluids, if a hostel volunteer hadn't reported a night of coughing, we would never have found her. All this would be lost.

Unless—that's the little subjunctive mineral you carry along in your pocket crease. It's always there or not there. Unless you're lucky. Unless you're unlucky. Unless is the worry word of the English language. It flies like a moth around the ear; you hardly hear it. It makes us anxious, it makes us cunning. But it gives us hope, too.

Unless provides you with a trap door, a tunnel into the light, the reverse side of not enough. Unless keeps you from drowning in the presiding arrangements.

Of

RETA phones ARTHUR SPRINGER.

RETA: Arthur. It's me, Reta. I want to ask you something: How is it you managed to get my mother-in-law Lois to talk while you were here?

ARTHUR SPRINGER: Well, hmmm. It's a new technique I learned recently. At a publishing workshop on personal relationships that, hmm, Scribano & Lawrence sent me to. This was after some author went stomping off to Knopf *(emphasizing rhyme)*. Something tactless I'd apparently said. A rather large fuss over a very small nothing. But I was asked to sign up for a sensitivity weekend, Vermont, an old hunting lodge. The key I learned from the workshop director is simple. One has only to ask people—especially writers, but anyone will do—for a recital of their lives, and they fall right into it.

RETA: You didn't say it to me. You didn't ask me to tell all about myself.

ARTHUR SPRINGER: Oh, well I could. Shall I?

RETA: No, it's too late.

ARTHUR SPRINGER: I'm so sorry, Reta. Really, I mean it. I do want to know all about the real Reta Winters. One day when we have time.

RETA: *(to audience, moving up to box room as she speaks)* I have brought my novel *Thyme In Bloom (lightly emphasized)* to a whimsical conclusion. Mr. Springer withdrew his editorial reservations when my first novel, *My Thyme Is Up*, was analyzed exhaustively in The *Yale Review*. A surprise reappraisal and appreciation: The subversive insights of the novel had not been grasped, it seems, by its original reviewers three years ago. So now, in *Thyme In Bloom*, Alicia triumphs, but in her own singular and capricious way. And the book will be published in early fall.

Everything is neatly wrapped up at the end, since tidy conclusions are a convention of comic fiction, as we all know. I have bundled up each of the loose narrative strands.

But what does such fastidiousness mean? It doesn't mean that all will be well forever and ever, amen. It means that, for five minutes, a balance has been achieved at the margin of the novel's thin textual plain; make that five seconds; make that the millionth part of a nanosecond. I'm already thinking about the third book in the trilogy—*Autumn Thyme*. It will open to a wide range of formal expression. I want the story to have the low, moaning tone of an orchestral trombone and then to move upward towards a transfiguration of some kind, the nature of which has yet to be worked out. I want it to be a book that is willing to live in one room if necessary. It will be a sadder story than the others, and shorter. The word autumn taps us on the head, whispering melancholy, brevity, which are tones I know a little about now.

Next

Keyboard sounds. The letter comes up on the monitor as the words are tapped out.

RETA: Dear Peter Harding,

So! You've died. I read your obituary this morning in the *Globe and Mail* while sitting in a sunny corner of my living room; you don't even want to know what it's like outside today. It's so bad the weather report on the radio broke into poetry and called what we're experiencing "bitter cold," which sounds like a phrase from an ancient Anglo-Saxon epic. There's a bitter wind, too, meaner than a junkyard dog, as the old song has it.

I was sorry to read that you struggled so long with your cancer, but "bravely" as the report says, all the way to the end. What an interesting life you've led. I'm sure you didn't dream growing up on a hardscrabble Saskatchewan farm that you would be awarded the Douglas McGregor Scholarship and end up in Toronto, a beloved teacher at the very private Upper Canada College, and that you would always give your—quote—"utmost"—unquote—to your students. Kay, your wife, will miss you, as will your children, Gail and Ian. And your three grandchildren and your old colleagues, who visited you in hospital, sitting upright in those stiff, steel hospital chairs. You were comforted in your last days, the obituary notice concludes, by the pile of books on your bedside table. You would not be parted from them. Mark

Twain, Jack London, Sinclair Lewis, Fitzgerald, Hemingway, Faulkner, Joyce, Beckett, Eliot—that's T.S., of course, not George—their texts constituted for you an "entire universe." Another "entire universe" reached you through the earphones provided by the hospice and for which your family gives thanks: Bach, Beethoven, and Mozart; Johann, Ludwig, and Wolfgang sang you off to your death. I have been going through some bleak days, Mr. Harding. I, too, am hungry for the comfort of the "entire universe," but I don't know how to assemble it. I sense something incomplete about the whole arrangement. I'm frightened that I might be missing something.

Goodbye, rest in peace. Go well, as they say in Swaziland, where my friend Sally Bachelli spent a year making dresses with village women. Four-hour dresses, they were called; that's how long it took to make a dress without a sewing machine.

Dresses appear on the cameos.

Reta Winters
Orangetown, Ontario. Canada, the World.
PS I grieve for you, too.

Not Yet

RETA: Day by day Norah is recovering at home. Awakening, atom by atom, and shyly planning her way on a conjectural map. It is bliss to see, though Tom and I have not yet permitted ourselves wild rejoicing. Right now, she is sleeping. They are all sleeping, even Pet, sprawled out on the kitchen floor, warm in his beautiful coat of fur. It is after midnight, late in the month of March.

ALICIA and ROMAN are curled up asleep, too. The stage goes black. These words are projected all over, in light, like fireworks, multiplying: unless, here, nearly, once, since, wherein, forthwith, nevertheless, any, as, so (a shower of sos), otherwise, unless unless, instead, yet, thus, insofar as, thereof, every, regarding, hence, next, notwithstanding, thereupon, despite, throughout, hardly, only, unless unless, toward, whether, ever, whence, forthwith, as, already, hitherto.

End.

MOM'S THE WORD REMIXED: FOR CRYING OUT LOUD

BY JILL DAUM, LINDA A. CARSON, ALISON KELLY, BARBARA POLLARD, ROBIN NICHOL, AND DEBORAH WILLIAMS

Dedication

To our children, without whom we wouldn't have had anything to complain about and who have allowed us to make a living off their backs. And to our partners, husbands, and the fathers of our children. Without whom this journey would never have begun.

Acknowledgements

Thank you to Marion Allaart; Ewan Burnett; Andy Burnett; Rachel Ditor; Mary Desprez; Susan Ferley; Wayne Harrison; Pam Hawthorn; Ronaye Haynes; Jane Heyman; Jan Hodgson; Pam Johnson; Robert C. Kelly; Michael Levine; Bill Millerd; Judy Richardson; Rob Richardson; Colin Rivers; Meg Roe; Zoe Sanborn; Kim Selody; Kathryn Shaw; Michael Shamata; Allison Spearin; Kim Smith; Donna Spencer; Roy Surette; Jennifer Swan; Ken Walker; Kate Weiss; Donna Wong-Juliani; Studio 58; the Women in View Festival, Vancouver; the Arts Club Theatre, Vancouver; the Belfry Theatre, Victoria; the Grand Theatre, London, Ontario; Theatre Calgary; and Back Row Productions.

INTRODUCTION TO *MOM'S THE WORD REMIXED*

Mom's The Word Remixed incorporates the best material from *Mom's The Word* (a show about raising infants) and *Mom's The Word: Unhinged* (about raising teenagers). This condensing of two plays was tricky—it was very hard to pick the best material and cut other bits out when all of it had been successful. It was hard too to strike a balance between material that is outrageously funny and material that is heartbreaking, finding the right tone to create a coherent but varied experience for the audience. We were building an emotional roller coaster that continued to be adjusted right through previews until the opening night of its premiere production.

I went to a high-school fundraiser one night to see the moms try out some of their new material in front of an audience of parents. I thought I was at a rock concert. People cheered them on stage. The laughter was raucous and the silences only broken slightly by the sound of people sniffing back tears of recognition. The whole theatre felt electric. Anyone who thought a show about raising children would be of limited appeal, or doubted the value of the content, has been proven wrong time and again as these plays continue to travel the world, being translated into many different languages. This play creates community in the audience, just as it created a community for the talented women who created these shows.

RACHEL DITOR: For future productions, is there a trick or insight you have about getting this play "right"?

JILL DAUM: Casting is important. The moms should be very different. That's part of the beauty of the play. That we are all so vastly different yet share so many of the same struggles as mothers.

ALISON KELLY: Getting the show right is about casting mothers and about having a cast and director who can trust each other. This show brings out sharing and secrets during rehearsal. You need to know that your fellow cast members aren't going to judge when you come in and reveal that you can't stand your husband (temporarily) or that you read your daughter's diary.

RD: Do you have a particularly memorable moment from the production?

DEBORAH WILLIAMS: I remember being backstage with Alison on the first preview, horrified. Even though I'd done *MTW 1* and *2* about two thousand times, I couldn't believe we thought this was a good idea. Telling these embarrassing, revealing, intimate stories? AGAIN? "Why do we do this? I'd rather poke my eyes out with barbecue forks. No one wants to hear this anymore; the world has moved on." Then I heard the audience's laugh of self-recognition and I knew we still had something important to share.

RD: Did it teach you something about your craft? About process, about theatre, etc.?

ROBIN NICHOL: There are no rules that can't be broken and you are always stronger and more creative together than you are alone.

BARBARA POLLARD: The process of our show was organic and completely new. We tried for a long, long time to make it around a concept or idea, but eventually just scrapped all of those and just told our stories. Also, our play(s) have a very female structure. Traditional plays have a shape that leads to a very specific culmination, whereas our plays seem to have "multiple" orga— er. . . places that peak again and again and again. . . 'Nuff said.

RD: What was the genesis of this play?

JD: Moms can't be perfect, so we might as well embrace our flaws and laugh.

RN: The shock of realizing that, though motherhood is one of the common experiences in the world, it has been shrouded in secrecy. Why didn't anyone tell me?

Mom's the Word Remixed premiered on September 30, 2009, at the Arts Club Theatre's Granville Island Stage in Vancouver, BC. It featured the following cast and creative team:

Performers: Jill Daum, Alison Kelly, Barbara Pollard, Susan Bertoia, and Deborah Williams

Artistic director: Bill Millerd
Director: Wayne Harrison
Dramaturg: Rachel Ditor
Set, prop, and costume design: Pam Johnson
Lighting design: Marsha Sibthorpe
Sound design: Andrew Tugwell
Stage management: Pamela Jakobs and Allison Spearin
Technical advisor: Craig Fulker

Characters

Alison
Barbara
Deborah
Jill
Robin

ACT ONE

K-Tel Remix

Music plays: "I Want You Back" by the Jackson 5.

ANNOUNCER: *(voice-over)* Hot off the charts, it's *Mom's the Word Remixed*
A colossal double album!
Twenty fantastic hits
Twenty original stars
You'll freak out to golden oldies like
The Maternity-Five's big hit:

ALL: "Oh baby,
Give me one last push
Past your perineum. . .
Baby, baby, baby
I want you out."

ANNOUNCER: *(voice-over)* And the follow-up smash, "Nursin' Machine":

> *"Dancing Machine" by the Jackson 5 starts to play.*

ALL: "She's a nursin' nursin' nursin'
She's a nursin' machine."

ANNOUNCER: *(voice-over)* And who could forget Peter, Paul, and Weary:

> *"Where Have All the Flowers Gone" by Peter, Paul and Mary plays.*

ALISON: "Where have all my brain cells gone?"

ANNOUNCER: *(voice-over)* And the disco classic from Momma Summa's:

> *Donna Summer's "She Works Hard for the Money."*

BARBARA: "She works hard for no money
And the hours are crummy
She works hard for no money
Her vagina's no longer tight."

ANNOUNCER: *(voice-over)* And, from Rocky and Bullwinkle, the postpartum hit:

"*The Sound of Silence" by Simon & Garfunkel.*

DEBORAH & JILL: "What are these tantrums and your endless tears?
You haven't slept for twenty thousand years
I need one hour of silence."

ANNOUNCER: *(voice-over)* Or the billboard number-one from Dummy and Chore:

ROBIN and DEBORAH sing to the tune of Sonny and Cher's "I Got You Babe."

ROBIN: "She wants you, Babe"

DEBORAH: "But she's wet, Babe"

ROBIN: "She's not mine, Babe."

They hold the babe, passing the bundle back and forth as they sing.

ANNOUNCER: *(voice-over)* You'll groove to recent hits like Swedish sensation, Pabba:

ABBA's "Take a Chance on Me" plays.

ALISON & ROBIN: "So you think you're gay
Well I heard you are
If you don't tell Gran
We'll buy you a car."

ANNOUNCER: *(voice-over)* And from Swedish Meatballs to British Fruit:

Culture Club's "Karma Chameleon."

DEBORAH: "Text me text me text me text me
Text me when you stay out
I need to know
Your whereabouts."

ANNOUNCER: *(voice-over)* And who could possibly endure Burnt Cocaine's "Smells like Teen Pregnancy":

Nirvana's "Smells Like Teen Spirit."

JILL: "With the lights out, it's more dangerous
That's why you have to use protection
You could get pregnant or an infection
That's why you have to use protection."

K-Tel-like sales music plays in the background.

ANNOUNCER: *(voice-over)* It's *Mom's the Word Remixed*
Records $6.99
8-track $7.99
Piano rolls by special order
Order all three now and receive a Veg-O-Matic.
Available at playgrounds, parks, spray pools, rec centres, grocery stores,
libraries, elementary schools, high schools, grocery stores, malls, landfills. . .

*"RIP!"—the turntable needle is dragged across the album, pelting
right into contractions.*

Contractions Quickening

JILL: Contractions quickening. More intense.
Water gushing on admissions floor. We're here.
Too busy? No rooms! But we're here.
A room. A bed. A husband. A nurse? Maybe? Yes.
Ouch! Gregarious! Too loud! Too jolly! But forgiven, her heart is in the
right place.
My husband, he's quiet, this is hard for him, but he's there. . .
On and on.
Pain more excruciating pain.
Panic—pain—soft words—
Shoot the nurse!
My doctor, here, so quiet, soft, encouraging,
"Try the shower again, then we'll see." "Take each one."
My nurse, "Do you want drugs? This? That?"
My doctor, quiet, "Just give it one more."
More pain, panic, failure, heartbreak. Can't give up.
Come too far. Body won't allow to give up!

No more, please! But body has kicked in! Please be over!
Nurse's hand to squeeze. I deliberately bite my nails into it.
She is too loud, too confident, don't talk about other stuff while I hurt!
Seems a week. Only four hours.
Can I push?
No.
Can I now?
Not yet.
I want it over!
Okay, push!
It hurts! The pushing hurts!
I thought it would be better, easier, gentler!
How? I can't!
Big nurse face blasting inches from mine, yelling, scolding, instructing.
Okay!
On and on. On and on.
I can't.
I cry.
I am no good at this. . .
I see it. . .
A little head. . .
Hard to keep looking. Seems stationary.
Weak encouragement, "You're doing great."
I'm not though,
I know it.
On and on. On and on.
Until finally it starts to come.
Ooooouuuch! Skin streeeeeeetching. . .

Gentle doctor, "Pant through it."
I can—I did! It's happening!!
Great excitement in the room. Much different from the flat "doing greats."
All excited. . .
Puuuuush. The head. Eyes up!
Puuuuush. The shoulders! The body!
Such relief. Flooding relief.

Such beauty,

The baby. So gentle.
Looking at his mama, his daddy, his doctor. . . (go to acknowledge nurse but decide against it). . .
His mama.
Such relief,
So happy,
So proud.

Sam #1

ALISON: My youngest baby looked like E.T. when he was born. He arrived almost three months too early. He was very sick, very little, and needed a lot of medical intervention to keep him alive. Moments before the birth, I remember my doctor warning me that I wouldn't be able to nurse him or even hold him. But afterwards, as the medical team whisked him away, she said, "If you look quickly you'll see him," and a nurse running by held him up for me to see: a tiny two-pound bundle. And when I saw him I felt love physically enter my body—deeper, stronger than anything I'd ever known. And I knew that I would die for him.

I Used To Say

ROBIN: Now, I always used to say that I wasn't a feminist because I didn't need to be. You get what you ask for, and if I expected to be treated "equally" I would be. I also always used to say that, on the whole, I didn't particularly like women very much. I much preferred the company of men. And I hated those things about myself that were stereotypically "female"—you know, like irrational emotional reactions, the desire and ability to knit. . . stuff like that.

Then I got pregnant.

I really hated it. I couldn't escape those things about myself that were stereotypically "female." The most inescapable fact about me every minute of every day was that I was female, and my body was doing the most female job on earth. Women would come up to me in stores, on the street. . . any-where. They wanted to tell me their stories, they wanted to comment on my development. They wanted to touch me. It was like they wanted me to join this giant club.

What is the big deal about this shared experience? I mean, I'd been sharing the experience of menstruation with these same people for twenty years, but that hasn't been cause for this group hug with the sisterhood.

I'm not going to be one of those women who sit around all day gossiping and talking diapers. I'm not going to live in shopping malls, and I'm not going to watch hours and hours of daytime TV. Just because I'm going to have a child doesn't mean it's going to change who I am, and it certainly doesn't mean that I'm going to suddenly have anything in common with other women.

Then I gave birth.

And I'm a member of the giant club. I see women on the street with babies and I feel like I understand them. I see mothers with two-year-olds having tantrums in grocery stores and I catch myself smiling with my lips together and my head on one side in that "I've been there" kind of way. I pass another stroller on the sidewalk and we give each other the high sign like two Harley riders passing on the open road. . .

So I guess I'm a feminist now. And now that I am a member of this club, I move that we have more parties!

ALL: YEAH!

Mom's The Word

This piece begins with some choreography to an action-movie theme.

A music selection will be inserted here.

All except JILL *(who has left the stage) don black trench coats and perform a number of spy-like moves (hiding, looking for clues, pretending to aim guns, etc.) all set to the music. By the end of the song they are in a line mid-stage centre waiting for a bus—they have dropped the spy personas and are now just sophisticated business people.* ROBIN *is reading a book. Whenever the stage directions say that they "return to neutral," it is back to this sophisticated waiting.*

JILL enters in a rush, wearing an unflattering hat and straightening a dishevelled raincoat (similar to the ones worn by the other women but nowhere near as cool). She notices baby puke on her shoulder, sniffs it, and tries to wipe it off. She can't. She carefully covers that section of her coat with her collar and takes her place at the end of the line. She notices the audience and realizes that they've "caught" her, but they look friendly so she approaches them and tries to explain.

JILL: Oh, hi. . . I'm really just a mom. *(reveals the messy hair under her hat)* I haven't been able to fix my hair for weeks! *(puts hat back on)* Shhhh! Mom's the word!

Pause.

ROBIN: *(to JILL)* Psst. . . I'm a mom, too.

ROBIN reveals that under her paper book cover—some sophisticated bestseller—she is actually reading The Cat in the Hat. BARBARA catches them—she does not approve.

BARBARA: *(to JILL and ROBIN)* Shhhh.

Return to neutral.

Pause.

(to JILL and ROBIN) Anyone else carry one of these?

She pulls out inflatable doughnut-shaped hemorrhoid cushion. JILL laughs.

JILL: Carry one? I'm wearing one!

She flips up her coat to reveal a similar cushion attached to her backside— they all laugh. ALISON catches them. She does not approve.

Shhhh.

Neutral.

Pause.

ALISON: *(singing to herself)* The wheels on the bus go round and round. . .

JILL, ROBIN, BARBARA, & ALISON: *(singing, gradually building to rousing)* . . . round and round, round and round. The wheels on the bus go round and round, all through the town. The horn on the bus goes beep beep beep, beep beep beep, beep beep beep. . .

DEBORAH: LADIES, PLEASE!!!

They return to neutral.

Pause.

DEBORAH steps forward, lifts her shirt and bra, reveals her breast, and squirts milk. There is a moment of shock. Others then fire back and a milk fight ensues. Some with breasts, some with bottles. DEBORAH gets carried away and heads for the audience.

JILL, ROBIN, BARBARA, & ALISON: Deborah!!!

DEBORAH: *(to audience member)* Sorry:
(sings) The people on the bus say no tits here.

They all skulk back into line except DEBORAH.

EVERYONE: *(sings)* No tits here
No tits here
The people on the bus say no tits here
All around the town.

DEBORAH: *(to audience)* I saw you judging.

I Was A Woman

This directly follows from the previous line.

DEBORAH: I was a woman who raised her eyebrows at mothers who raised their voices, at children who raised their hands grasping for sugar from a cart.
I was a woman who thought disdainfully of mothers
Who plugged endless coins into motorized elephants,
Who plugged babies into video-sitters, plugged soothers into snot-glazed faces.
I was a woman who judged mothers who smacked bottoms for the last misplaced head-butt at the end of a long day.
I was a woman who internally "titched" *(sound of disapproval)* at mothers

Who had a beer while they nursed.
Who used Smarties as rewards.
Whose children looked like dirt magnets.
Who left the kids in the car while dropping the mail in the box.
Who put their child in daycare.
Who hadn't put their child in daycare.
Who lost interest in their careers,
Who couldn't put themselves together in the morning. *(asks JILL to sit down)*
Who'd really let themselves go.
I was a woman who wasn't a mother.

Diaper Soup

BARBARA: I wish I had known when I was in university that I would be spending the top earning years of my life in the laundry room cooking diaper soup. I might have diverted one of my courses to reflect the more primary requirements in a mother's life: Drama in Education, Business Administration, or a degree in Shit Management. I mean, I complain all the time about being overworked and underpaid, but last week, after a particularly nasty splash emptying the diaper pail, I finally decided to do something about it.

Actually, I lie—it wasn't the diaper pail I was emptying at all, but rather the "pre-soak pail." This is a system my husband, the environmentalist, dreamt up because he's not fond of rinsing poopy diapers in the toilet. He prefers to put them straight into the pre-soak pail where they float clean.

It was an innocent trip down to the laundry room when suddenly the pre-soak pail caught my eye and I knew it had been forgotten. With trembling hand I reached for the lid. *(lifts lid—reacts)* I deduced from the overwhelming evidence of a thick brown sludge gurgling on the top that it had been fermenting happily next to the furnace for a full ten days. I dragged the stinking cauldron across the room and managed to lift it just to the lip of the laundry sink where, with a monstrous impetus of its own, it flew forth.

She tracks the journey of the slop from bucket into sink, back out, and straight into her face.

And I found myself facing an angry brown tidal wave. Luckily I had my glasses on that day, because I remember this tiny brown meatball trickling slowly down one lens.

I did what I had to do. I marched straight upstairs, got on the phone, and phoned the sewer department. I wanted to find out what they earn, what my efforts were worth in the real world.

So next Earth Day I want you to think of me marching with pride at the front of the parade and remember that while sewage workers are earning $37.50 an hour, me? the one covered in shit? I am a volunteer!

Letter #1

ROBIN: Dear Partner,

I didn't want to have to write this letter but since we seem to be having a communication issue, I thought I'd try another approach. It feels like we live in different countries. Before we became parents we were both pretty damn interesting people. Now you come home and say, "How was your day?" and I say, "Well, I fed her and I changed her and I dressed her, then I fed her and I changed her and I dressed her. . . And we went for a walk but she cried so I had to carry her and push the stroller. . ." and I realize that you're not listening. You're reading the paper. I know how boring and trivial this all sounds to you but, strangely enough, it's incredibly significant to me. I know you don't live in this country all the time, but you visit regularly and it would really impress the locals if you learned the language.

Love, Robin.

Sam #2

ALISON: In the three-and-a-half months that my son lived in the hospital, our daily routine consisted of waking up, phoning the hospital, eating breakfast, getting the little one to the sitter, and heading off to the hospital in time to catch doctors as they came off their morning rounds. One day my husband and I arrived to get the wonderful news that Sam's ventilator pressures had been dropped in the night. This meant three things: his lungs were getting stronger, he was doing more breathing on his own, and there was less chance of his lungs collapsing.

We were elated—we were one step closer to having our baby home. I floated off to the pump room to express my breast milk, but upon returning to the nursery was told I couldn't go in. Now, this was no cause for alarm. It could have meant one of many things: a nurse changing an IV, doctors consulting with parents or doing more rounds. But I explained to the receptionist that I didn't want to visit with my baby, I just wanted to get my breast milk into the fridge, so she waved me on through.

Now, to get to the nursery where the fridge was I had to cross through the nursery my son was in, and as I did I glanced down towards his incubator to wave at our favourite nurse.

There was a team of surgeons standing around his incubator: six doctors and nurses operating on a two-pound baby. The voice in my head told me I wasn't supposed to be seeing this. This is why they told me not to come in. MOVE. But I couldn't. An intern observing the procedure came over and explained that both of Sam's lungs had collapsed; they would let us know something as soon as they could. I got my breast milk into the fridge, walked back through his nursery without looking at his incubator, went into the parent lounge, curled up with my husband, and cried.

The Life

DEBORAH: It always happens when child care cancels at a quarter to. And I have to be somewhere on time, and looking good. And I'm not and I don't. And on the way home from the job interview, one of them gets a nosebleed while the other one sucks on the germ-encrusted handrails of the eastbound SkyTrain. And the connecting bus is late because of some fucking accident. And I have to walk across the bridge; in rush hour; with one baby strapped to my body; the other one in some goddamned $15.95 stroller with one wheel that goes g-flap, g-flap, g-g-g-g-g-g-g-g-g-g-g-g-g-g-g-g-g-g-g-flap; twenty-five pounds of wet diapers on my back; while the two-and-a-half-year-old whines "Mom Mom Mom Mom Mom Mom, Mooooom. Mooom. Mooooooooooooooooom."

She holds this pathetic whine for as long and painfully realistically as possible.

She regains her control.

So we're at home and it's dinner. Where he picks out every shred of grated zucchini and flicks it on the fridge. And I remember he's probably not hungry because he had a tube of toothpaste earlier in the day.

And the phone rings and I didn't get the job.

She regains her control.

So it's bath time. Where they wait for all the water to run out *before* they get soaped up. And I'm naked by now because I refuse to get changed for a fourth time. Just to have my clothes soaked in bathwater, food, spit, snot, blood, urine, vomit, or feces. And they find a four-day-old cup of wildberry yogourt and dump it in my lap.

Pause.

(rigidly controlled, very quietly) Jeremiah. . . Georgia. . . Mommy is angry. . . and it's not at you. . . GO OUTSIIIIIIIIIIIIIIIIIIIDE!

Every day I start out Mary Poppins but I end up Cruella de Vil.

Hose

BARBARA: It was spring. The first evening we could be outside without our coats on. I started puttering around in the garden. Then I got out the hose and right away the kids wanted to get involved. That was fine. The little guy was too small to squeeze the nozzle and get any water out of it but his big sister was going to help him and that was great, but I was cautious. *(crouching, talking to child)* "Now, Emma, you're just getting over your cold and your little brother still has his, so you can play with the hose, just. . . don't get wet." Well, I had just turned my back when I heard "WAAAAAAAAAA!!!" I looked and there was a stream of ice-cold water blasting into my son's ear and my daughter was standing there with the hose in her hand and this maniacal little smirk on her face.

Well I lost it. I grabbed the hose out of her hand and pointed it right in her face. "EMMA! HOW WOULD YOU LIKE IT IF SOMEONE BLASTED ICE-COLD WATER IN YOUR FACE?" and she said, "YOU DON'T LOVE ME ANYMORE. I WISH I'D NEVER BEEN BORN," and she ran screaming into the front yard. And that's when I saw them. The neighbours. They were sitting on their deck. . . with candles. . . and wine. . . and company. *(waves)*

Five minutes later my daughter and I were wrapped up together in forgiveness and I thought, "Why can't they see this?" Anger is so loud and love is so quiet.

Advice

JILL: You guys, what do you think of this advice? I got it from my girlfriend: I was telling her about what happened with my three-year-old son and myself. He and I were having a day from hell. I just couldn't take it anymore and I burst into tears. Well it was incredible what happened. He instantly transformed. He stopped fingerpainting with his lunch and he came over, very concerned. He put his arm around me, he started to pat my back, and for the rest of the day he was an absolute pleasure. So I was confessing to my friend that if things get really out of hand again, I just might use tears. And she said, "Oh yeah, I used to do that too. But you know what I found works even better? Pretending you're dead."

Shit

ROBIN: So, the other day we're in the backyard looking at a tree being decimated by tent caterpillars and my daughter, two years old, points to the tree, big smile, "Looks like shit." Now, we all know whose fault this is. We all know how big this is going to go over with the in-laws, to whom it's already had to be explained, "She's talking about the truck; she just pronounces it with an "F.""

You know, I quit smoking four months before I got pregnant. I eat healthier, I go to bed earlier, I even wear my seat belt, for Chrissakes. . . !

Just how much more am I going to have to. . . trucking give up?

JILL, DEBORAH, BARBARA, & ALISON: Shhhh.

DEBORAH leaves to get a box.

Dresses

Five dresses, representing the pre-child lives of the five women, are brought out. Maybe from the fridge. After each actress speaks she puts her dress into a box that will go to charity.

JILL: I bought this dress in Venice with my fiancé, after a lunch of Chianti Classico on our way to an art exhibition.

BARBARA: I used to wear this little dress. I wore it opening night at the Stratford Festival: hundreds of guests, champagne, a live orchestra, and at one point everyone stopped and watched us dance.

ALISON: With my hair up and in fuck-me pumps, I used to party all night in this dress. Now I just look ridiculous in it. Besides, my bedtime is nine o'clock.

DEBORAH: Oh, get over it! It was the '80s. I primped. I fussed. I worried. Oh hell, I'm comfortable now.

ROBIN: I made this for my brother's wedding. When he told me he was engaged I cried. . . Oh I'll wear it again.

ROBIN returns her dress to hanger.

They all talk over one another while they put the stage back together.

ALISON: You missed the point of the exercise. Put it in the box.

JILL: You can't wear puffed sleeves. That is sooo not you.

BARBARA: That's a terrible colour on you. No, that's cheating.

DEBORAH: Your brother never liked that outfit. Makes you look like a drag queen.

Home

JILL: I wish I had understood when I was younger what amazing things my body was going to do. Maybe I would have criticized and mistreated it less and appreciated it more. The other night my husband and I made love and as we were lying together, I had this incredible feeling that he was home. That we were meant to be this close and he had returned home. And then I thought about our two children and how they had lived and grown inside me, and I had this sense that. . . I am my family's home. I am home.

ROBIN, DEBORAH, BARBARA, & ALISON: You had SEX!!!

JILL's taken aback—weren't they listening?

BARBARA: I haven't had sex in two months.

ROBIN: I might have had sex. I can't remember.

DEBORAH: I haven't had sex in eight months.

JILL: How can you not have sex for eight months?

ROBIN, DEBORAH, BARBARA, & JILL: WELLLL.

Mop

ALISON is mopping the floor. The mop handle ends up under her shirt at eye level, with the head of the mop between her feet. She talks to the handle, which represents her husband.

ALISON: Whoa! Sweetheart!
A surprise attack!
That was fast.
How are you?
Well, I can see how you are. . . but I meant on a bigger scale, how are you?
You want to now—yes I can see that.
Look, could we just talk?
We never get to talk anymore.
When was the last time you and I had a conversation about anything?
You don't want to have sex with a stranger, do you?

The mop handle rises, becoming more "erect."

Look. . . it's not you. . . it's me. I'm in demand all day with the kids and then sex just becomes another demand. So when you say you. . .

She steps forward as she talks and the mop falls forward—this explanation has put out his fire.

I'm sorry.

She's not.

Yes!

A quiet celebration.

Penis Puppet

BARBARA is bending from the waist multiple times to pick up laundry and then throwing it into a basket. She puts her hand in the foot of a baby sleeper and it becomes the mouthpiece for her husband.

BARBARA: Why am I the only one who ever picks up anything in this house? I swear to God if I went away for a week, we'd lose the baby!

PUPPET: Honey. I'm home!

BARBARA: What are you doing home so early?

PUPPET: I thought you might want to have sex!

BARBARA: I am doing housework! What put that idea into your head?

PUPPET: It's not my fault. You bent over.

BARBARA: Why didn't I listen to my mother? Bend at the knees. Bend at the knees.

PUPPET: And sexy knees they are too. I'm seriously horny.

BARBARA: This house is a pigsty and all you can think about is—

PUPPET: Your bodacious bum! You little sex monkey!

The puppet makes jungle sounds and she clamps his mouth. She lets go.

Here, honey, let me help you. . .

BARBARA: I'll admit that the thought of you doing housework is about the only thing that could even remotely turn me on *(this excites him)*, but right now I'm exhausted and I need my sleep!

PUPPET: Honey. . .

He thinks.

. . . I'm just gonna go dust the bathroom and I'll be right back!

The puppet exits behind her back.

BARBARA: *(to audience)* He's right. It's my own fault. Twenty extra pounds of flesh, saggy tits, greasy hair, big black circles under my eyes. . . I'm just too damn attractive!

ROBIN, DEBORAH, JILL, & ALISON: SHHHHHHHHH.

Shh Shh Shh

ALISON is beyond exhausted. She enters with a baby carrier, bouncing it rhythmically until she notices the mess on the floor.

ALISON: Shhhh shhhh shh sh sh. I'm trying to get her to sleep. She's almost there—I just have to keep doing this and talking quietly. I'm obsessed with sleep these days—her sleep, or lack thereof, and my sleep and very much lack thereof. I have told her over and over again that she's a big girl now, so five thirty in the morning is a really BAD time to wake up. Bad is too strong a word isn't it? I worry about using words like that and how they'll affect her, and how much therapy she'll need if I do use them. Where was I? Oh yeah, I feel like shit. Well, look at me. A shower would be a luxury right now. And I think I'm losing my mind. I went to the door the other day, and I wondered why the postie gave me such a weird look, and then I realized I had no skirt on!

And how am I supposed to resume a sex life when I wear a nursing bra? Of course, it comes off, but then I'm a walking milk fountain with no shut-off valve.

(sudden realization) There! She's asleep! Isn't she beautiful? And smart. And I tell her that too.

> *She drops her diaper bag and moves off to the side of the stage to put the carrier down. She continues to bounce as she puts the carrier down very carefully.*

I know it's important that she knows she is valued for something other than her looks.

> *The carrier is down. She keeps bouncing. She straightens up. She keeps bouncing. She moves away from the baby and searches through her bag, looking for a soft toy for the baby. She hurls things out of the diaper bag, finally finds a toy, moves back, and puts it in the carrier with the baby, still bouncing. All is under control! She looks back and sees the mess created by the search through the diaper bag. She slowly stops bouncing.*

You know, I've never thought of myself as a particularly anal person, but now that I'm a mother I long for order and routine in my life. I know I would be a better person if I were more organized. A better mother if I had lists of craft ideas I could resort to happily and promptly on rainy days. My children would grow to be well-adjusted adults if they had days filled with routine, balanced with a healthy amount of free play. If I were more organized, I'd never run out of diapers because laundry would be done on a schedule. I'd never be caught with food goo on my shirt because I'd always have a spare one tucked neatly in my bag. I'd never ever forget the diaper bag, always have the right things on hand to whip up nutritious meals because groceries would be done on a schedule too.

> *Becoming excited by the ideas.*

My children would be perfect; I'd be witty, forget nothing, be able to have a career and a clean home, sew a new wardrobe with every passing season, plan perfect parties, attend perfect parties, have a perfect marriage, *(becoming mildly aggressive)* be able to speak my mind in a non-threatening, non-confrontational manner, *(impassioned)* stop wars, feed the hungry, and no child would ever be mistreated again—EVER.

> *Returning to her normal state.*

Okay, so maybe I am expecting too much. But those last three things, I want them. I feel sort of responsible for all kids now that I have my own. I'm sorry. I'm becoming maudlin. I cry at the drop of a hat and please don't tell me its hormones. *(bursting into tears)* Oh shit, she's awake again!

She automatically resumes bouncing, packing up, and picking up the carrier.

Shhhh shh sh sh. . . At least I've got my skirt on.

I've Made A Mistake

DEBORAH: You know, it may be time to acknowledge the passing of post-birth bliss when you look at them and the word "asshole" flashes across your mind.
I'm tired of being selfless.
Of giving my meal away. One bite at a time.
Of reasoning when I want to scream.
Of understanding when I want to hit.
Of being ruled by erosion.
They're breaking my heirlooms and sucking me dry.

I want my life back. All of it. Me. Myself. Mine.
I hate this. I hate them.
I'm tired of being a nag. A bag. A rag. A snag.
For loathing every second I am stuck in this tar pit with them.

I've made a mistake.
Those wonderful gifts of life,
Those pink and blue snuggly packages, have turned into writhing, squirming, kicking, biting, pinching, puking vermin.
This is bad.
Oh my Lord! This is permanent.

Aquatic Centre

BARBARA enters from the wings, coming from a pool and holding a towel to represent a swaddled child.

BARBARA: Whoooo! *(to kid)* That was fun, wasn't it? We went swimming, didn't we? Yeeesss!

She goes behind a screen, sheet, or towel and then faces out. She is only visible from the shoulders up and the child is no longer seen.

Okay, here's our locker, I'll just get my key. . .

She fumbles with her free hand trying to unpin the key from her bathing suit strap. She fails.

Uhhh, have to put you down for a sec. . .

The baby starts to run.

Oh! Stay here, please! Stay here. . .

She frees the key from her strap.

There we go!

She yanks a towel from the locker.

Ooooo, chilly willy! Let's dry you off. *(bends, cheery)* Step out of your bathing suit, please. . . *(insistent)* Step out. . . *(barks) Step out!* There we go. Now let's dry your bum, your tiny, tiny, tiny little bum! *(rubbing)* Now a diaper. *(rummaging in diaper bag)* Diaper, diaper, diaper. . . *(pops up)* Where is Mr. Diaper?

He is also rummaging, in another bag, away from theirs.

Oh! don't touch that! That's not our stuff. You come here and help Mommy find Mr. Diaper. *(turning it into a game)* Where is he hiding?? *(pokes her head down, finds it, pops up)* There he is. Naughty Mr. Diaper! Okay, let's get him on. You lie down.

She bends over to help him down onto bench, but pops back up.

Now what have we here? *(mock serious)* Is this a tummy? *(bends rapidly and does a tummy blast)* Ha! Gotcha! *(back to business)* Okay, let's do that up and get your shirt on. . . *(bending and wriggling him into clothes)* And some. . . *(struggle)* pants. . . There we go!

He grabs the shampoo, opens it to taste.

Oh! don't drink that. That's shampoo.

She snatches it away.

Shampoo is yucky! *(pulling face)* let's put the lid back on. . . We'll wash your hair tonight in the bath. Right now, *(glances at clock across room, late!!)* we have to hurry and pick up Emma from school!! *(super enthusiastic)* And Desmond is already dressed, isn't he? Yes!! And now Mommy needs to get dressed too, doesn't she? Yes she does! Quickly. . . here. . . *(groping in bag, extracting bottle)* You sit here *(sits him)* and drink some juice while Mommy gets. . .

He complies happily.

What a good boy! Thank you.

She stands and begins to wiggle out of her suit, not looking at him.

God! I swear this suit shrinks every time it gets wet.

She squeezes out, notices that he's gone, and looks around quickly.

Desmond? Desmond?

She peers over the screen to see him fleeing back onto the pool deck.

Oh shit!!!

Now naked, she runs after him.

DESMOND!

Sam #3

ALISON: Every day, for three and a half months, we went to the hospital to do what little we could. Change a tiny diaper, take a temperature, take pictures, sing songs, talk to him. Will him to live.

It was an emotional roller coaster. We clung to the highs of successes—"He's digesting one teaspoon of breast milk!"—and waded through the defeat of setbacks—"He's had a brain hemorrhage." It was an education: Learning to decipher the neutral faces and words of doctors. Learning the medical lingo. Learning what each machine, wire, and tube that he was hooked up to did.

I have many memories of days that went on endlessly and yet somehow sped by. But one day, *(voice of doctor)* "You can take him home." *(ALISON's voice)* "What? We're not ready. We're not prepared." A sleepover in the hospital to relieve some of the panic of being the only ones in charge. But during the night Sam slips back and has to go on oxygen again and we wait another five days.

But then, as if none of the three and a half months had occurred, I hold my baby, now just five pounds, in my arms. Quiet goodbyes to the doctors and nurses who are available. No chance to thank the hundreds of people who have been involved in this journey. We walk down the hall, away from that secret, isolated world that has been ours. I glance over my shoulder, half expecting someone to come running after us saying, "Wait, there's been a mistake, you can't take that baby with you." But they didn't.

There have been many trips back. Hospital emergency rooms dreading hearing the words "We want to admit him." Two-day stays. Weeklong stays. But we've never had to give him up for longer. He is ours forever.

Letter #2

ROBIN: Dear Partner,

BARBARA runs across the stage again, naked, calling for the still missing child.

BARBARA: *Desmond!*

Everyone is shocked at seeing BARBARA again.

ROBIN: *(to audience)* Don't encourage her.

Dear Partner,

Don't panic. I know the last time you got a letter from me it was bad news, but I wanted to have this one on record.

Thank you! After you left this morning and I was getting the kids ready to go to the park, I opened the diaper bag and you had already packed it! You get it! You speak my language!

Love, snuggle bum.

Circle Square

DEBORAH: Every once in a while I realize I'm not teaching them enough and I panic. Jeremiah, come here!

She starts drawing on an imaginary chalkboard.

Circle. Circle! Square. Square! Come on. We've got to get this before Granny gets here!

Miracle

JILL: I will never lose my awe over my children's arrival—how all of a sudden at the end of labour, there was another person in the room. And they hadn't come in the door. They arrived. A perfect, glorious angel. Birthing is transcendent, painful, divine, and common. Each baby a miracle. But now I find, as my babies get a little older, that sometimes their wings are hard to see. And other people's children? I can't see their wings at all. Like that horrible little sociopath miracle in the sandbox. Or that "sharing-impaired" miracle next door.

But you know what the biggest miracle about children is?

We keep making them.

Letter #3

ROBIN: Dear Husband, dear Partner, dear Father of our Children,

Just when I thought you actually understood, you go ahead and make the asinine comments of last night! Then when I brought it up this morning you said, "What's wrong?"

Last night you asked me to help you with the kids and I said, "No," I simply needed some time off. You said you "never get any time off" because you work so hard all day and then come home to your turn with the kids. During my day I don't get the choice of taking one moment for myself. With your work you have that option. It's stupid to drive yourself all day with no lunch and no breaks. We need you in reasonably good shape when you come home!

I cannot believe you said, "Looking after children should come naturally"! Who says? About as natural as juggling burning torches or writing a "trucking" symphony. Maybe in a simpler society it was more "natural," but even then I bet it was "naturally" hard work, and many of the children died.

You have "more responsibility" than I do? Let me ask you a question. What would happen if you got up and left your desk for four hours? Now, what would happen if I got up and left the house for four hours?

I am spending all day alone, keeping your children alive with my brains leaking out my ears, and you are going to acknowledge, appreciate, and understand my efforts even if I have to ram it down your throat with the Jolly Jumper!

Love, Robin.

The Other Man

BARBARA: I'm falling in love with another man. I don't know, I was so busy and so caught up in my work I didn't realize it was happening. But my husband did. I mean there's this guy, and his breath is sweet, and his face is smooth, and he's promised me he'll never ever grow any whiskers on it. And I hold him, and I kiss him, and I love him fiercely. And one day I looked up and my husband was staring at us with the most peculiar expression on his face and he said, "It's a strange feeling to sit in the same room with your lover and watch her fall in love with someone else." But we know we'll be all right because I'm watching him fall in love with our son too.

Compassion

DEBORAH: That's sweet. I used to have so much compassion for my husband when he got sick. Now all I can think is, "Get your skinny ass off that couch. I'm not looking after one more needy lump."

Jar Lid

JILL: I hear my husband's voice echoing from the icy chambers of the fridge, "Where the hell's the mayonnaise?"

I elbow past, show him the jar, *(a mega mayo jar glows brightly in the fridge)* and explain. "You couldn't see it because it was behind the milk." He goes to the jar and points at the lid. "Oh yeah, well look at this. You never screw the lids on tight. I can't tell you how many times you've done this and I've been left with a giant mess on the floor."

He's right. "That's because I never simply make a meal. I am usually arranging carpools, packing sports bags, and refereeing arguments while I cook." He then goes on to tell me that he has polled his buddies and made the anthropological discovery that "most women don't bother tightening lids. Every guy I know has to cope with this too."

I tell him, "I'm glad you have found a fault in me that you can complain about with your friends. Because I certainly enjoy many hours complaining about you with mine."

But this doesn't dampen his moment of superiority. Oh no, he's on a roll. He brings our daughter into the conversation and points out all of the attributes she could "with a little effort, inherit from her dad. Pumpkin, you will be able to pack the car for any road trip without wasting an inch of space; remember the lyrics to every Bruce Springsteen song; save precious resources by wearing the same pair of underwear four days in a row: front to back, back to front, then inside out, back to front, front to back; and, most importantly, you will securely fasten every jar's lid."

And my daughter looked up at him and said, "Dad, I'd rather be able to find the jar."

Yes!

School On Time

DEBORAH: It's January. And I am no longer going to be the focal point of other parents' jokes. I am going to get my children to school *on time*.

"Good morning!"

I hear my youngest stirring. *(child's voice)* "Hi Mom."

I use a time-tested method. "Georgia, would you like me to pick out your clothes for you?" She shoots out of bed, tearing through her drawers.

Easy. Next, I ease on the lights for my eldest. "Jeremiah, it's time to get ready for school. We're going to be on time this morning."

"The light is burning my eyes. Shut it off. Get lost. I hate you."

He's never been a morning person. "Get up!"

Going to his drawers I realize I haven't had a chance to fold the eight loads of laundry assembled on the living-room floor.

I head downstairs with my son draped across my shoulders.

I dig like a wild dog through the cloth mountain and stuff his flaccid body into his clothes one noodle-limb at a time and prop him up against a pile of *National Geographics*.

Twenty minutes to be in the car. "Breakfast!" *(in the fridge)* No bread. No eggs. No milk. No cheese. . . *Condiments*! I coat pickles with peanut butter and jam and roll them in taco spice. Two per plate. "EAT." I prepare a lecture on how "many children never get pickles for breakfast," but everyone is eating eagerly.

The momentum is building and the children, energized by the vinegar and sugar, have taken up the torch.

(child) "I don't have time to feed the bird."

(other child) "I'll brush my teeth in the car."

They see the value of corner-cutting. This milestone holds within it the seed of a better future for my children. The opportunity that they will one day hold down full-time employment and not make their living in the arts.

We're heading out. I'm still in my pyjamas but a heavy winter coat sufficiently disguises that. We're in the car and I hear the "Chariots of Fire" soundtrack. The children are whooping with pride.

"Undo your seat belts. Get ready to jump."

I turn the car off and coast the last four parking spots. "Get out. Run. RUN." They are so beautiful when they are enthused.

(looks at watch) Five to nine. Time to spare. Something miraculous has taken place for my family this morning. We have accomplished the impossible.

"Don't wait by the door. Go in. GO IN." They can't. It's locked.

We never had anywhere near as many Professional Development Days when I was growing up.

CMOM

Rumbling "important news" music.

VOICE-OVER: Live from Domestic Studios it's the CMOM Morning News With Bubbly Waters.

ALISON: Good morning. I'm Bubbly Waters, and this is the CMOOOOOOOM news. Today's good-mood index is at a record high due to an unforeseen combination of factors. A mind-boggling number of Facebook entries have come in overnight, the piano teacher has cancelled, and the icky crunchy peanut butter has finally been used up. But first a look at this morning's traffic, with her head in the clouds, in the CMOM chopper, it's our very own Terry Towel.

JILL: Thanks, Bubbly. Traffic is at a standstill in the kitchen thanks to a messy accident during a high-speed chase for the last blueberry Pop-Tart, and we expect high-volume delays as Dad was last seen clutching the newspaper and headed towards the upstairs bathroom.

ALISON: Thanks, Terry. And now to the news. An unexpected explosion occurred at 7:45 a.m. Let's join Brenda Basket at the scene.

BARBARA: I'm coming to you live from under the breakfast table, where earlier this morning a quake measuring 3.5 on the Richter scale was recorded when her brother LOOKED AT HER FOOD!

ALISON: What can you tell us about the brother's present situation, Brenda?

BARBARA: The current peace treaty is clearly on shaky ground. It appears that, if the brother comments on her hair or tells her what to do, hostilities are sure to resume. It is rumoured he will be hosting a farting contest, which will only add fuel to this fire.

ALISON: Be careful under there, Brenda. And now let's go over to Sue Stock with the business report. Sue?

ROBIN rolls in on a BMW scooter.

ROBIN: Thanks, Bubbly. The daughter is looking at some hefty deficit spending unless she can get an advance on next week's allowance. After a flurry of market activity there are some blue chips in the house, but no one will eat them with the no-name salsa.

ROBIN exits on the scooter.

ALISON: Thank you, Sue. The CMOM business report is brought to you by BM. . .

ROBIN crashes off stage and the BMW sign rolls across the front of the stage.

Thanks again, Sue.

A sudden change in music indicates an emergency broadcast update.

Wait, this just in. We interrupt our newscast to bring you coverage of a sudden state of emergency. We go live to Sarah Faucet. Where exactly are you, Sarah?

DEBORAH: I'm coming to you live from inside the bathroom, and holy doodle, Bubbly, if you could see what's coming towards me now.

ALISON: What is it?

DEBORAH: It's an enormous pimple that could be developing into a cold sore.

ALISON: Sounds terrifying.

DEBORAH: It's reaching towards me.

ALISON: Monstrous, Sarah.

DEBORAH: Yes, Bubbly. Are you getting my footage?

ALISON: Yes, I'm just getting it now. Oh my God!

The rest of the news team draws in, aghast at the extremity of the situation.

ROBIN: Catastrophic hormonal flooding.

DEBORAH: The smell is unbearable!

JILL: It's sprouting hair all over.

BARBARA: The end of life as we know it!

ALISON: Sarah, can you sum it up in a single word?

DEBORAH: Yes we can, Bubbly.

ALL: TEENAGERS!

Blackout.

ACT TWO

The Alienators

All come out dressed in distinct, fabulous domestic superhero costumes.

VOICE-OVER: Faster than cash out of your wallet,
Jumping to conclusions from a single glance,
More predictable than pimples on picture day,
It's the Alienators!

DEBORAH: Splitting your infinitives, dangling your participles, it's:

ALL: GRAMMAR GUARD.

ROBIN: STOP! What you meant to say was, "Whom the Hell do I think I am."

BARBARA: Carrying the weight of the world on her shoulders. She's the human doormat, it's:

ALL: MARTYR MOM.

ALISON: I'd feel better if you took the car. I'll double Granny on your skateboard to the hospital for her dialysis.

JILL: And when all you are seeking is a straight answer, in flips:

ALL: WAFFLE WOMAN.

DEBORAH: You are to be through that door by midnight. Okay, two o'clock. Okay, four a.m., but I mean *IN BED*!

ALISON: She's the seductress of the second sense, it's:

ALL: SUPER SNOOPER.

JILL: Oh, is this your diary? You misspelled private.

ROBIN: And just when you've enticed the cool crowd to come over on Friday night. . .

DEBORAH: . . . Your bedroom door opens and in walks:

ALL: THE LOSER.

BARBARA: I love this song. Turn it up.

She dances while singing a hot, hip, inappropriate song. A music selection will be inserted here.

Music blasts and the moms drop their superhero props for a hip-hop number.

They begin to exit, but then return for a model runway Swiffer dance.

All exit quickly except ROBIN, who licks her finger to touch her butt. As her finger nears her rump she notices a stain on the stage and bends to the floor to wash it off with her finger instead. She looks back at the audience and lip-synchs "the Alienators."

DEEP MALE VOICE-OVER: THE ALIENATORS!

BARBARA: We are trained professionals. Please don't try that at home.

Windsock

BARBARA: I started my career early and my kids late and I thought I was brilliant until I realized that they would be entering puberty just as I was hitting menopause.

An older friend said: "Congratulations! You can all be miserable together!"

And we are.

In many ways, it puts us on the same page.

I do really embarrassing things in front of my kids and they point them out for me. Except for last summer. . .

We had this amazing vacation that ended with a family reunion on the Gulf Islands, and then we came home.

The next morning I'm peering into the mirror for what seems like the first time in a long time and I spy with my little eye. . . this long white hair growing out of the side of my face, a good two and a half, maybe three inches long.

I screamed.

They all came running.

What the hell is this?

(as first teenager) "Wow! Mom, that's huge!"

(as second teenager) "Eew, Mom—gross!"

Did ANYONE want to mention this?

Or did you just think it would be fun for me to greet all those people with a windsock growing out of the side of my face?

"We didn't think anyone would notice."

Just like they wouldn't notice the big L on my forehead? Loser!

My daughter grabs the tweezers, leans into my face, and "PINK!"

The second teenager has plucked it out. She beams with pleasure.

She holds her trophy aloft, beaming with pride.

Now this has become a weekly ritual between us.

She pores over my face like she's lost in the Amazon and I am the only map out.

That's one small hair for Mom, one giant leap for motherhood.

Stupid

JILL draws a chalk line diagonally on the ground.

JILL: Today my daughter called me stupid. It's the first time that someone I love has looked me in the face and said, "You're stupid." I can't tell you how much it hurt.

A line has been crossed.

She steps over the line.

I'm on the other side.

My children used to love me, adore me, I was the "best mom in the whole world." Now on this side of the line, they hate me, are embarrassed by me, I'm "the worst mom in the whole world."

I'm stupid.

I know all parents of teens moan about this passage. But today is the day it happened to me. I have to stop. I don't want to just roll my eyes and carry on. I don't want to take another step forward. I want to go back.

She steps back across the line.

To when our family was our world, created day by day with small adventures. Revisiting the Play-Doh village we built over weeks till we had to eat on the living-room floor because every inch of the kitchen table was covered with our concoctions.

Before, people didn't value my role as a mother, but my children did. Fiercely. Now people don't value my role as a mother and my children don't either. Fiercely.

She returns to the stupid side of the line.

Today I am stupid.

Soon to be a stupid bitch.

Only to become a stupid fucking bitch.

Prayer

DEBORAH: Let us pray.

Give me solace and strength. Help me.

Help me to churn out three meals a day. Three different meals. Every day. Every single day. Three nutritious, fibre-filled. Breakfast. Lunch. Dinner. And on days of rest and celebration, help me make bigger meals to feed more people.

Let me hear a Hallelujah.

ALL: Hallelujah.

DEBORAH: Let me hear a HELP ME.

ALL: Help me.

Lights up on the audience.

DEBORAH: Help me resist the eternal fundraiser.

To say, no I do not want your over-roasted coffee beans; I do not need your crap chocolate almonds. Let me hear you say "no."

She walks into the audience to talk to individuals and groups.

Now I want you to be honest with me here. I am going to ask you to reach down inside and admit. Come on, raise your hand. Admit that you have been pushing unwanted commodities on your friends and family. Pushing—until they feel abused and defiled. Pushing things like coupon books, pushing wrapping paper, expensive scented candles, window stickies. Raw cookie dough.

She uses anything that the local parents are selling, improvising with the audience.

Ask for forgiveness and I will heal you. . . If I never find your children at my doorstep ever again.

And please continue to pray with me. If I can't be more compassionate, relaxed, happy, witty, thin, and tall. Let me joyously join the ranks of the medicated mamas. The parade of Paxil parents. Loosing my mothering guilt. Knowing I will only feel this bad about the things I have done. Until I do something far, far worse.

Let me hear an "amen."

ALL: Amen.

Breast Cancer—The Discovery

ROBIN: So, I'm reaching for something over my head and I feel something odd with the inside of my right arm. Jesus Christ. I don't even like to say the word "breast," let alone "cancer."

A quick doctor's appointment followed by a quick biopsy and all of a sudden I'm considering my own quick death, and what's going to happen to my kids—possibly in the very near future. It's actually quite strange how fast you can get used to that. It doesn't leap out at you in nightmares or catch you by surprise while you're having a shower. It just sits on your shoulder.

It's hard to tell people. Nobody knows what to say to me. Here's a tip—if you find out someone has breast cancer, don't say, "I hear you've been sick." First of all, I don't feel sick, and second, "sick" is too. . . normal and too temporary.

I'm suddenly in this world of specialists, each with their own language, and I seem to be the only thing they have in common. I take my husband with me to appointments, which makes me feel like a kid, or a fool, or a woman who can't control what's happening to her.

We tell our kids the bare minimum so they won't worry, which is a joke because the tension level in our house is through the roof, and even the dog is worried. The next thing I know I'm in the hospital counting backwards.

Parent

Queen's "We Will Rock You" pounds during the bleacher set up. All the parents but ALISON are aggressive and having fun. ALISON gets pushed out of the way so others can sit together and talk. When the puck is dropped the mothers turn into yelling demons.

Hockey sounds.

ROBIN, JILL, BARABARA, & DEBORAH: SKATE. SKATE. HIT HIM. OPEN YOUR EYES! KILL 'EM. FIGHT. PUSH! GET IT BACK! GET IT BACK!!

DEBORAH: Offside, ref!!!

The mothers stop in a grotesque freeze.

ALISON: I'm sorry. I'm not very good at this. I'm just not. I mean, I know what an offside is. It just happens so fast I can't see it. They scare me. Parents like that scare me. Why can't they be more supportive?

Dreamland music as ALISON is drawn back to the group.

DEBORAH: Everyone's a winner, sweetheart!

ROBIN: A score is just a number!

BARBARA: The other team has feelings too!

JILL: Remember, share the puck.

ALISON: That's my son in goal!

Back to reality. More hockey sounds. The mothers jump back into their roles as the nasty moms going crazy over the game.

BARBARA: You idiot!

ROBIN, JILL, BARABARA, & DEBORAH: SKATE! AHHHHHH too bad. AHHHH!!!

The mothers freeze.

ALISON: *(scurrying away again)* I can't relate. I never played team sports. Maybe if I had. . . I'm a team player in other things. I do my share of volunteer stuff, at the kids' school and in my community. Even here, I am the 50/50 co-coordinator. But I usually bribe my daughter to actually do the collection because I hate asking for money from people who have already paid hundreds of dollars in fees to enable their child to play hockey and then hundreds of dollars more in equipment costs so their child isn't permanently maimed while playing. And for years I've been the "Jersey Parent." Do you have any idea what the thirty-six sweat-soaked jerseys of eighteen adolescent boys smell like? RUTTING GOATS! Then there are the hours. Now I have always thought of myself as a morning person, but four a.m. isn't morning, it's still the night before. And what about sleep for their growing bodies? Isn't that more important in the bigger picture than available ice time? And I confess that my heart doesn't soar when I am told on Friday afternoon that the team has been lucky enough to pick up an extra game. Tomorrow morning. In Seattle.

More hockey sounds. The mothers unfreeze and watch another play until there is a goal for JILL's team.

JILL: YES! ANOTHER ONE.

ROBIN, BARABARA, & DEBORAH: AHHHHHHH! Defence, defence! *(lots of yelling)*

DEBORAH: THAT GOALIE IS A SIEVE!

The mothers freeze grotesquely again.

ALISON: *(weeping but trying to hide it)* I'm okay. Just because that asshole hotshot on the other team has scored for the eighteenth time on my son and is doing some *(JILL celebrates in slow motion)* stupid hand-slapping, stick-pounding celebratory dance while his teammates and their parents gloat and leap about, satisfying their pathetic need to be the best. . . to win on the back of my child. I know that the goalie is only one player on a team and if the puck gets by him it's already gotten by aaaaaallllllll the other players, *(other mothers slow-motion whisper, pointing and bitching about the goalie)* but tell that to the parents who take the coach aside after a loss and ask why he's playing *that* goalie, or his teammates who won't talk to him if he lets in a goal when the score is tied, or the *fucking* coach who pulls him to put in another goalie, even though he has assured me that he doesn't think winning is everything. IT'S HOUSE LEAGUE. IT'S A SPORT. . . *(turns to address the mothers)* A GAME. IT'S SUPPOSED TO BE FUN. AS A NATION, WE ARE OUT OF SHAPE.

During this, the mothers unfreeze and take in the woman who is screaming at them, then they gradually get up and leave.

SHOULDN'T WE BE ENCOURAGING EVERYONE TO PARTICIPATE? TO MAKE LIFELONG, HEALTHY HABITS? And what about my son in all of this? My nearsighted, asthmatic son? He can't decide whether to focus on getting scholarships for a university career or heading straight to the NHL!

She mouths the word FUCK as she collapses in her chair.

Breast Cancer—The Treatment

ROBIN: It turns out the surgery was the easy part. . . now for the chemo. I sit in a chair and they inject the biggest hypodermic—I mean it has to be eight inches long and an inch in diameter. It's full of bright red liquid and a nurse injects this slowly into an IV tube so that it can slowly mix with saline, and then pour slowly into my vein. It takes about an hour and a half—I guess if she does it too fast. . . it'll kill me? Four doses, with three weeks in between so my white cells have a chance to recover and I don't die from a paper cut.

For some reason I don't feel that nauseated, so instead I have lots of time to think about dying. And about my family, and what might happen to them if I do. How vital am I to my kids becoming functioning human beings?

So my hair starts to fall out within days of the first chemo treatment. Once I realize I'm shedding more than the dog I get a friend to come over and shave off what's left. Kind of a relief, actually, and I become an instant low-maintenance redhead. If my hair ever starts looking limp I just take it off and shake it. My visiting mother comes upstairs one morning to find me wigless in the kitchen. "My God, you look just like your father."

Fast-forward—I've been cancer-free for the magic five years. I no longer live in fear. I'm quite comfortable in denial and my sense of immortality is almost completely restored. There's only one little cloud on the horizon. I have a daughter.

Foreign Language

JILL: I'm a nervous wreck parenting teenagers.
It all began in grade nine.
Mine, not theirs.

I was sitting in French class thinking, "I can't understand a thing. It's like they're speaking a foreign language." Then I started to have that thought during Math and Science too. I got so far behind, I just stopped going. Nobody noticed.

I had to do something to pass the time. So I did drugs. I didn't have any money, so I chose boyfriends who dealt drugs. Now I must have been able to hear some tiny internal voice warning me I was headed for danger, because I decided to try a fresh start, in a new school for grade ten.

I arrive the first day, full of optimism, dressed to impress. Platform shoes, which I have glittered myself, satin pants and blue-streaked hair with matching eyebrows. I walk in and I definitely make an impression.

The students stare at me open-mouthed. They speak about me, *(others whisper)* but never to me. Luckily I meet the only other weirdo in the school—Violet.

ALISON approaches JILL as Violet.

She isn't hard to find. She's wearing a hooded cape, like some Stevie Nicks medieval hippie. I'm a Bowie glitter girl. We become instant friends. She's the first vegetarian I've ever met. I become one, too. Our specialty:

BOTH: Mushrooms.

JILL: Our favourite pastime is creating the perfect outfit and then going dancing.

BOTH: Perfect!

JILL: The only places that will let us in are "after-hours clubs."

JILL knocks on a door and the rest of the cast become the club inhabitants, dancing, handing drugs and alcohol to JILL.

Illegal rooms filled with gays, dealers, users, and misfits who, between the hours of two and five a.m., have found a place where we fit in. We have to pop Bennies to stay awake all night. I get so little sleep that my nightlife seriously begins to interfere with my day life. So I do the only sensible thing I can. I quit school.

My parents were devastated, and rather than face their disappointment I left home. They were good, caring parents, and I cut them off like that. Now my son is sixteen. If I could do it to them, he could do it to me.

When he goes to a party I panic. I don't want to keep smelling his breath, checking his pockets, and scanning his face for lies.

He's a beautiful kid, I believe in him, and I want to trust him, but the coke-snorting, shoplifting slut from my past won't let me.

Atrophy

DEBORAH: What did you ask? My husband?

While cleaning and resetting the stage.

Oh, he's a good father. Kindish. Smartish. Happyish. Doing the best he seems capable of. He used to be more interesting. I can't remember why.

I've been practising my maiden name on contest blanks for new homes and European getaways. Checking the marital status boxes "single," "divorced," "widowed."

I fantasize about him comfortably, instantly, painlessly dead by some unforeseen, freakish, accidental means. I take him to a dark tropical paradise where he punctures his foot on a poisonous coral, and I nurse him to death in the stifling heat. All the bills covered by insurance. No more character-crushing compromises.

I conjure him uncontrollably attracted to another. Maybe even another man, so I could just tell the kids, "It was inevitable. Your dad's gay!"

(as him) "Are you mad at me? Have I done something wrong?"

(as herself) "No! Of course not."

And just to prove it, my yeast infection clears up for the evening and I turn my head to the side while he pushes. And I reassure him of how tremendous it feels. Suggest that we do it more often, while I wash myself and strip the sheets. Not lying there as I had, when the drying semen reassured me of his love, and our promise of forever.

The promise and the semen have become chilly and annoying.

Toys

ALISON brings in the thrift-shop box to pass on the childhood items that are no longer needed.

JILL: My daughter used to play dress-up for hours. Putting on layer upon layer of frilly outfits. Now she goes out wearing more makeup than clothes.

JILL places a pink frilly dress into the box.

DEBORAH: They made it for Mother's Day. It's been on the mantel for years. I told them it broke. Shhhh.

DEBORAH drops in a handmade "god's eye" made of crossed batons, multicoloured hemp, and Popsicle sticks. She covers it up with JILL's dress.

ALISON: *(holding up a preemie sleeper)* He said, "Jesus Christ, Mom. I lived! Get over it!"

She places Sam's preemie outfit into the box.

BARBARA pours in a seemingly bottomless bucket of Lego.

BARBARA: Childbirth hurts, but you don't know pain until you've stepped on a single piece of Lego.

ROBIN, with loathing, brings out a battery-powered singing plush Christmas dog.

ROBIN: My mother-in-law gave this to us.

She pushes a button and it starts to sing. ROBIN contemplates it and becomes sentimental.

It wouldn't be Christmas without it.

She is not going to put it in. DEBORAH grabs it from her and slams it into the box.

DEBORAH: Oh yes it would!

DEBORAH leaves with the box before ROBIN can take the dog back.

Sex

BARBARA: I believe teenagers learn from example, so I've decided to become celibate. My husband and I have a happy, fulfilling, platonic relationship and we've neutered the dog.

JILL: I've discovered a great method of using sex talks to educate my children. . . "I've been hearing a lot of disconcerting news lately about younger and younger kids having oral sex. Can I discuss this with you now, or do you need to study for your science exam?"

DEBORAH: I use the car.

ALISON sets up two chairs as the front seat of a car.

I get out on the highway with him. No exits.

She locks the car doors and starts to drive, talk to the teenager in the front seat beside her.

Sooo. . . Sweetheart, have you had any nocturnal emissions? No, not peeing in your bed. Ejaculating in your bed. Fantasizing, sexually, and ejac— No?! Are you sure? No, I'm not mad! It's perfectly normal. Have you?

BARBARA pops up from the back seat to help with the lesson.

BARBARA: Do you masturbate?

DEBORAH: Masturbate?

ROBIN: *(appears in the car)* Apply pressure and friction to the penis.

DEBORAH: To alleviate sexual tension.

ALISON appears in the car.

ALISON: It avoids the need to pressure a special person.

DEBORAH: Male or female!

ALISON: That you may be attracted to.

JILL appears in the car.

JILL: To perform sexual acts that you are definitely not ready to deal with the consequences of.

BARBARA: Namely sexually transmissible diseases or unwanted pregnancy.

ALL: Whoa!

DEBORAH almost drives off the road at the idea.

DEBORAH: When you're masturbating better throw on a condom.

JILL: Makes cleanup faster.

ROBIN: You need to practise!

ALL: Practise! Practise! Practise.

Rise!

They raise the right arms into a fist.

Rip!

With the left hand, they each reach up to their right fist as if it is holding a condom package and rip it open.

Roll!

They roll the condoms down over their right arms.

Rub!

They use their left hands to rub up and down over their right forearms!

Their right fists burst open and spray gently down like dying fireworks.

DEBORAH: *(to other moms)* Thanks, I think that went well.

ALISON: Sweetheart, waiting won't hurt a relationship, but rushing into sexual intimacy might. Please wait.

DEBORAH: Wait until you're married.

ROBIN: Wait until you're in a committed, caring relationship.

JILL: Wait until you're eighteen.

BARBARA: Wait until I'm dead.

The Morning After

ALISON is in a housecoat doing a crossword puzzle at the table.

ALISON: Sunday morning. I'm enjoying an uninterrupted crossword before everyone gets up. My son's bedroom door opens and a girl, that I don't know, comes out. She appears to be wearing nothing but a T-shirt of Sam's.

"Hello. I'm Sam's mom. You are. . . ?"

(as girl) "Anna."

She scurries back into the bedroom.

I have no words. My pulse is doing something peculiar.

I move to my son's room. I open the door.

Anna and Sam are in bed together. Spooning!

"We need to talk."

(as Sam) "Have you ever heard of knocking? Get out of here."

"We, the three of us, need to talk."

(as Sam) "You are making a fool of yourself, Mom."

"We need to talk. Now! In the kitchen, both of you. Sweetheart, *(calling up to her husband)* I need you down here."

We gather.

"Honey, this is Anna. She and Sam have spent the night together."

My husband is not making eye contact. He is concentrating far harder than necessary on pouring his coffee.

"Anna. Do your parents know you are here?"

(as Anna) "Yes."

She's lying. I know it.

I look at my husband and I catch him giving Sam the thumbs-up! I am alone in this.

"PROTECTION. Did you use protection?"

Am I yelling? I don't want to yell.

(as Sam) "We are just friends, Mother. Besides, it's none of your business. This is beyond embarrassing."

"I think it's important that Anna's parents know and are comfortable with the two of you sleeping in the same bed. I also need to know that if you are having sex that you are protected. Anna, do your parents know you are here?"

(as Anna) "Kinda."

I knew it!

(as Sam) "What are you going to do, Mom? Phone and get her in trouble? No one else's parents would do this. What do I have to do to shut you up? Show you a used condom?"

I choose to take this as a rhetorical question.

(to her husband) "Would you like to say something here?"

But my husband looks as if he would rather be on the dining-room table having a vasectomy. Performed by my mother.

"I'm sorry that I am making you uncomfortable. All three of you! Anna, you aren't to spend the night here again until I've had a conversation with one of your parents. Sam, you are to let me know when 'friends' are sleeping over."

(to her husband) "Sweetheart, we need to talk."

Boot Camp

Marching music. DEBORAH *marches in as a sergeant and whistles everyone into line.*

DEBORAH: Fall in!

More marching music. She tosses army jackets to all on stage. One more whistle.

You all know why you're here? This ain't no candy-ass recreation-centre workshop. When you go face to face with a *teenager,* ain't nobody gonna be standing there holdin' your Crabtree and Evelyn hand. The bottom line: Know your enemy. What did I say?

ROBIN, JILL, BARBARA, & ALISON: *(not in unison)* Know your enemy.

DEBORAH: What did I say!!?

ROBIN, JILL, BARBARA, & ALISON: *(in unison)* Know your enemy!

DEBORAH: Right then. We're going to do a little ROLE-PLAYIN'. You. Step foooorward!

DEBORAH *points at* JILL, *who pushes* ROBIN *forward.*

(teen voice) Maaawwwwwm. Why do you have to dress like that?

ROBIN: *(trying to impress sergeant)* I beg your pardon, honey?

DEBORAH: *(teen voice)* Didn't anyone tell you the eighties are like soooooo over?

ROBIN: I'm comfortable in this. . .

DEBORAH: *(teen voice)* Comfort? What does comfort have to do with what you wear? Aren't you embarrassed? I am.

ROBIN: But these are coming back in style!

DEBORAH: *(as sergeant)* WRONG. You never match wits with a teenager on fashion. You will always be outclassed, underdressed, and overweight. Back in line, Chub-Chub.

DEBORAH: Who's next? YOU! *(points to JILL)* Toothpick!! Get it up here.

JILL: Yes, ma'am!

DEBORAH: *(teen voice)* Mawwm, why do you have to be sooooo stupid!

JILL: Excuse me?

DEBORAH: Everyone else's mother is normal!

JILL: But. . . *(starts crying)*

DEBORAH: I wish you weren't my mother!

JILL: That's so mean.

DEBORAH: *(as sergeant)* You're gonna cry, are you? Who's the baby now?! Suck it up, Wrinkly. How many times do I have to cram it into your rusted, crusted cranium: teenagers do not feel guilt. What did I say?

JILL: Teenagers do not feel guilt.

DEBORAH: What did I say?

ROBIN, JILL, BARBARA, & ALISON: Teenagers do not feel guilt.

DEBORAH: Back in line!

JILL: Okay.

DEBORAH: Who's next? Saggy, at the end!

> DEBORAH *approaches* ALISON *and talks in male teen voice.*

Mom, where are your keys? I need the car tonight?

ALISON: I have a meeting at six thirty. What time do you need it?

DEBORAH: I need it tonight, is that so hard to understand? Dah?

ALISON: Then no, you can't. Can't you get a ride from someone else?

DEBORAH: *(is impressed by response)* Can't *you* get a ride with someone else? Todd's parents bought him his own car so he doesn't have to deal with this kind of hassle.

ALISON: Well, we don't agree with giving our children everything they ask for. . .

DEBORAH: *(as sergeant)* WROOOOOOOOOOOOOOOOONG! Never justify yourself. YOU ARE THE PARENT! Who are you?

ALISON: I am the parent.

ALISON is cringing in terror.

DEBORAH: What did I say?

ROBIN, JILL, BARBARA, & ALISON: YOU ARE THE. . . I AM THE PARENT.

DEBORAH: Well start pretending you are, spineless!

She spots BARBARA.

Oh goody goody, we're down to princess shiny butt. Get your dimples down here, darlin'! Your kids are having a party at your house tonight.

BARBARA: I don't think so. We just had the carpets cleaned. Sir.

DEBORAH: Well looky looky, the little lady would rather have her baby girl attend some crack-smoking, crystal-snorting rave doing the double-back monster on a chopped hog with a thirty-five-year-old guy who hasn't seen soap since September than get her house a little dirty.

BARBARA slinks back to the group lineup, weeping.

All of you, drop down and give me twenty. You gals are in sor-ry shape.

Three parents drop and attempt to do push-ups. BARBARA pulls out a twenty-dollar bill.

Think you can buy your way through these years?

BARBARA: Worked so far.

DEBORAH: Give money on demand and what do you get?

BARBARA: Peace and quiet?

DEBORAH: WRONG.

BARBARA: Love and affection?

DEBORAH: UH-UH.

BARBARA: Gratitude?

DEBORAH: Your kids are gonna drain your RRSPs so fast, the only caviar you'll ever taste is the guck you'll suck outta your guppy's ass. Now, all of you on your feet! To the right! March!

Marching music. The mothers line up and march out while they chant. DEBORAH encourages and threatens the audience to join in.

I don't know but I been told (Lets hear ya.)

ALL: I don't know but I been told

DEBORAH: As a mom, I'm dumb and old. (I can see every one of ya.)

ALL: As a mom, I'm dumb and old.

They exit, marching.

DEBORAH: Grey and wrinkled in the face. *(pointing at people in the audience)*

ALL: Grey and wrinkled in the face.

DEBORAH: I'm my kid's biggest disgrace.

ALL: I'm my kid's biggest disgrace.

DEBORAH: *(to audience)* YOU ARE AAAALLLLLLLL absolutely PA-THET-TIC! Fall out!!

Waiting Up

ALISON: It's four a.m. The time we used to get up for hockey practice before he quit. I don't have a clue where he is. Out getting stoned, impregnating his girlfriend, drinking and driving? So what do I do? He's big, the size of a man; we can't physically stop him from doing anything. You know, when you get pregnant you say, "I'm going to have a baby." You don't say, "I'm going to have a teenager." If you did, the birth rate would be a lot lower.

Affair

DEBORAH: So, as I was saying, I haven't married my soulmate. And my life partner isn't even trying to appreciate me. Besides, his breathing really bugs me. So obviously our relationship has come to an end.

When suddenly I think of all the marriages. And I have to ask myself, am I really that special? Me, and the last two or three generations of Westernized humans? So extraordinary that we can't possibly tolerate the ups and downs of a long-term relationship. Can't keep a family together?

So I'm just getting my head around this "I'm not so special" stuff and "we can raise these two ridiculously conservative kids" stuff, when I meet someone. A man. Who thinks I'm beautiful and smart. And it's lovely to be admired at meetings. In that high-school kinda way. You know, when you wonder if he likes you or if he REALLY likes you and you want to pass him a note to accept his "drinks after work"? *(giggles, blushes)*

So he asks me, "How's your marriage?"

"Right now? Oh. It's a marriage. Doesn't that sort of say it? A marriage? It seems enough when the neighbour asks, 'How are you?' You just answer, 'Married.'"

"You're so funny," he says. "You make me laugh."

He says his marriage is not going well.

I make him laugh, that's all.

And then, suddenly, he's got no marriage to speak of. Oops. Marriage didn't work for him. That's too bad, because it's working for me. I mean, it's working for us. My husband and me. Mr. Married-head and me. Just because it didn't work for *him* doesn't mean it didn't work for *us*. I mean "doesn't work." It doesn't work.

I give him the name of my cleaner. "Money can buy you most wifely services." But not someone who'll make him laugh. We laugh.

"Who could that perfect person be?" "No, no! I don't need a ride."

But my bus splashes by and he insists on driving me to catch it. *(gets into his car)* And we don't seem to be able to think of anything funny to say. And I keep my seat belt unclasped in the international seat-belt "I'm getting out at the next stop" symbol. But I want him to drive away. Speed out of town in this dog-hair filled minivan. But he reads the international symbol and pulls into a bus stop thirty-seven seconds ahead of the bus and he puckers and blows me a kiss. . .

And that tiny piece of pressurized air hits me so hard in the solar plexus I stop. . . breathing.

I'm falling in love with another man.

Sam #4

ALISON: *(a phone rings)* The police. Sam has stolen our neighbour's car and crashed it into the side of a building. He's okay but the car isn't. The police suspect he was high on something but Sam won't say what. He sounded frightened when I spoke to him on the phone and kept telling me how sorry he was. I really want to believe him but his apologies have become so tired. He pleaded with us but we decided to leave him at the station for the night. It's probably safer there anyway, because if he was home he'd run the risk of one of us dropping something heavy on his head trying to knock some sense into him. I looked around the house last night and I will no longer turn a blind eye to all the things that have gone missing. . . money, an iPod, my gold locket. We are going to ask him to leave. This house can no longer be the place where he sleeps instead of going to school, recovering from his all-night parties and binges.

And now here it is, seven a.m. and I have to wake up my daughter and tell her that her brother is in jail before she hears about it on Twitter. Then I will go and apologize to the neighbours. My tiny two-pound bundle. How did we get here?

New Job

ROBIN: I got a job! *(others cheer)* The first full-time, benefits, holidays, grown-up job I've had in thirteen years! So now I'm nine-to-five and my husband is at home. *(others are concerned)* I am starting to feel guilty though, because I realize that days are going by without my emptying the dishwasher, or the garbage, or the compost pail. Or I'll put on a load of laundry and then forget all about it, and shortly thereafter it will miraculously appear dry and folded.

I should check in with the kids. My son's sitting at the table—"Need any help with your homework?"

"No, I'm done. Dad helped me."

To the audience—a brave face.

Well that's great—Dad's better at math than I am, anyway.

I smell something... baking. Baking? My daughter's in the kitchen— "Whatcha making?"

"Cookies"

"I didn't know we had any frozen cookie dough."

"We don't, I made them from scratch. Daad gave me the recipe."

(looks at audience, bewildered) Daaad gave you the recipe.

"Wow, if you've both finished your homework, why don't we all watch TV together?"

(son) "Dad says we can only watch an hour a day and there's nothing good on now so as soon as the cookies are done we're going to walk the dog."

"Together?"

"Yeah."

(to audience, stunned) Aliens have stolen my children.

(recovers) Actually, it's really great how everyone's adjusted so easily to this new routine with Dad. But there are always things that fall through the cracks. On the way home the next day I pick up some milk because I noticed we're running low.

Carrying milk—finds note on fridge—reads it.

"Dear Partner,
I didn't want to have to write this letter, but since we seem to be having a communication issue: Please stop meddling. I can handle this. It's not rocket science. Love, Dad."
At least I got the milk.

She opens and then slams the fridge because it's full of milk.

Thongs

BARBARA: Why would a girl, who does not even have a boyfriend yet, need to wear sexually provocative underwear?

I wear thongs. . . to the beach, on my feet.

But I'm supposed to call them flip-flops because if I say that I wear thongs *out loud,* my daughter goes into a full-body shudder and screams. . . "I don't want that picture in my head!!"

I could never wear one of those teeny little thong things. I mean. . .

Do they make them in my size? King size? The King Kong Thong!

Technically you could argue that I do almost wear a thong, when you consider it's been so long since I bought new underwear I'm down to just the elastic around my waist.

Oh—I surprised husband by wearing one once. . . but it just confused him. . .

He thought I'd taken the kids rock climbing and forgot to give the harness back.

Speaking of harnesses, my bras aren't that delicate, either.

My breasts are large. And yes I have considered breast-reduction surgery, but I dunno. . . I mean, I'm kind of attached to "the girls."

If they had a voice. . . what would they say?

Yeah. What would the girls say?

Dreamland music as BARBARA turns to join ROBIN.

Broadway Boobies

They hold large round photographer's reflectors, painted like giant breasts with holes in the middle for their faces as the nipples.

ROBIN: Hey! Whoa! Wha-oh, oh.

BARBARA: Huh! Wha-what's happening? /

ROBIN: / She's taking the brassiere off again.

BARBARA: Oh no, I'm afraid of heights. . . ahhhhhhhhh!

ROBIN: Whooooo hooooooo!

A fall of several storeys, they scream, bounce like on a bungee cord three times, then settle much lower than before.

BARBARA's eyes are squeezed shut.

Lucy. Lucy, it's over.

BARBARA: That was terrifying! I thought I was going to die.

ROBIN: Don't be such a drama queen. Hey? Is that the water running?

Two of the moms come on with a filmy length of blue cloth that they stretch across the stage in front of the girls and slowly raise as the bath fills.

BARBARA: How I love a bath! And here we go!

They pop up and lean back in unison, floating in the tub.

Ethel. . . Is that the waistline? *(leaning over)* We used to be miles from here!

ROBIN: We've definitely moved south.

BARBARA: Maybe that's why we're—"having a heat wave."

They both sing a bit of "Heat Wave."

It *is* surprising.

ROBIN: What?

BARBARA: Last night, I thought I was going to spontaneously combust.

ROBIN: I think it's the "change."

BARBARA: Oh my gawd, not the change. But, but, but I'm not ready for that. . .

ROBIN: Well you better get ready, because I got a feelin':

Music plays and the two sing to the tune of "Here Comes Santa Claus."

BOTH: Here comes menopause
Here comes menopause
Right down hormone lane
It's a nasty bag of tricks
That'll drive you gals insane
Feel your nerve endings jingle jangle
Makes you cower in fright?
Crawl into bed and cover your head but
You won't be sleeping at night!

Here comes menopause
And peri-menopause
It can last for years

ROBIN: First your memory

BARBARA: Then your libido

BOTH: Tossed out on their ears.
Who's that horny little bald guy?
He's your husband, that's right

BARBARA: When he comes near

ROBIN: You need not fear

BOTH: Your dry HOONEY will snap shut tight!

The rest of the moms enter as golden boobs or cheerleaders, singing and dancing raunchily, to a slow bump and grind.

ALL: Who's that horny little bald guy?
He's your husband, that's right.
When he comes near,
You need not fear
Your dry hooney
Will snap. Shut. Tight.

Follow-Up Call

Removing her Broadway Boobies costume.

DEBORAH: This is not a musical.
This is my life.

All right, I *am* special. And my feelings *are* different. But I don't want to have a cliché. An affair. It would be so trite and obvious.

I don't want to take my clothes off in front of someone else, and that's definitely what would happen, and then I'd end up raising *five* kids, and I can't even deal with these *two*. And my right-wing children would be devastated. My parents would be mortified. Someone should warn my husband.

DEBORAH dials and disguises her voice.

Where is your wife? She's in really big trouble
Bruce! How did you know?
Call display. Crap. Sorry!
I've done something foolish.
No, I mean I thought about doing something really stupid.
How did you know?
But it's not with who you think.
How did you know?
The kids?
How did they know?
Church?!
I'm sorry. I'm sorry.
I don't know. Eighteenth and Cambie.
Yes. Starving.
I don't know.
I don't care. Anywhere.
You decide.
No, we had noodles last night.
Okay, I won't.
Not an inch.
I love y—

He hangs up.

New Bra

JILL: My daughter got her first period. Finding out about it wasn't anything like I had imagined. She didn't run to me confiding and needing advice. No. I found "the evidence" in the laundry, and it was me who ran to her.

"Sweetie, have you started your period?"

"No. . . Yes."

"Wow. Weren't you going to tell me? This is a big event for you in your life. Should we do something to celebrate?"

"No, for God's sake, no. And please don't tell Dad."

"Well. . . I know some mothers who have passed down an heirloom when their daughter started her period, like this ring I have from my grandmother I could now give to you. . . If you could be responsible in looking after it."

But that doesn't interest her.

"Or maybe I could buy you something?"

"Yes. That would be good."

"I know, since you're not a little girl anymore, why don't we buy you a brassiere."

"You'd do that?"

"Yes."

"Okay."

"All right. Let's go to the Bay. That's where I buy mine and they're usually on sale there."

She doesn't seem that happy about being at the Bay. She doesn't like anything, won't try anything on, and I begin to get a little frustrated.

"What don't you like about this one?"

I'm holding up a lovely cotton bra, sort of like a sports bra, only daintier. It would be comfortable, and maybe even flatten her breasts down a little bit, because I imagine she's probably self-conscious about them.

But noooooo, she hates this one too.

"Fine! If you can't find something you like in the Bay's lingerie section, which covers approximately one city block, where would you suggest we go?"

"Victoria's Secret."

Now I think of Victoria's Secret as a place where women shop. When their sex life is dwindling. Or they're in the sex trade. For me, Victoria's Secret is not about underwear. It's about sex, and. . .

"I do not want to go there with my twelve-year-old daughter!"

"All of my friends shop at Victoria's Secret."

"Well, all of my friends shop at the Bay."

"That's because your friends are OLD. OLD people shop at the Bay."

She's right. I am old. What do I know? We go to Victoria's Secret.

It's close to Valentine's Day, so the shop is full of pink and red display ensembles. We pass the anal peek-a-boo undies, with the matching tasselled bra. Then, next to the boa thong, she sees what she wants.

"I like this one."

It is a padded bra, with underwire and rhinestones.

"I'm not buying you that."

"Why not?"

"You don't need padding, and the underwire would be uncomfortable. A bra is. . . something to stop you from jiggling, because that can be painful when you're running or playing sports."

"I like this one."

"Well, I'm not buying you that."

"I don't want one of your ugly old lady bras, or a little girl bra."

"The underwire and the padding are to enhance the breast. It's for sexually active people. It says, 'Yoo-hoo, look at my breasts.' Do you want the boys in your class looking at your breasts? Is that what you want?"

"I just want to go home. You don't understand me at all. You only want to buy me something you want me to wear. If I am grown up, I should be able to choose what I want to wear. You're saying I'm not little, but you're still treating me that way."

This truth hits home.

"Do you think you could let me see what it looks like on? Maybe that would help me."

Now this would be a major concession for her, because she never lets me see her in her underwear anymore.

"All right."

My daughter picks out two bras—the rhinestone one and a black number with red hearts. She goes into the dressing room and I wait outside.

"Can I come in now? Can I see?"

She timidly opens the door and hides behind it to let me in. Then she closes the door and stands in front of me. She looks so vulnerable, so sweet, and even a little bit proud. The bra really does look just like a bathing-suit top.

Open-faced she waits for my response. I love her so much.

"It looks beautiful, let's get them both."

Final Voices

ALISON: My life with kids hasn't been easy, but the other day we had a family gathering that my son agreed to come home for, and at one point I saw him sitting on his dad's lap. All six foot two of him. They were laughing. And the next time I want to ring his bloody neck I hope that image prevents me.

BARBARA: I imagine that when my kids arrived in the world and saw me, it must have been like getting to the front of the slow-moving grocery lineup and seeing the "in training" badge on the cashier. We're growing up together, and I truly love her and he is amazing. So I guess when I finally am grown up, I'll owe them. Big time.

ROBIN: Dear Partner,

You know, I never really liked children. When they're little, they can't carry on a decent conversation, they never laugh at your jokes, and they are hopelessly self-involved. When they get old enough to carry on a decent conversation, they still don't laugh at your jokes, they are bitingly sarcastic, and they are even more hopelessly self-involved. I don't remember how you talked me into this.

But thank God you did.

DEBORAH: I came out as a lesbian to my family the Christmas I turned twenty-one. My parents? They put away their uncertainty and pulled out their support. Two months later? I changed my mind. And arrived home with the marvellous man, who's put up with me for over twenty years. And my parents moved over and welcomed him. And our vegetarianism. And religious variations. And our children. And that's what parenting is. An endless unhinging of my arms and my heart. Banging open. Swinging wildly open. Creaking rustily open. My children offer me the opportunity to unhinge, letting more life in.

Blackout.

DO YOU WANT WHAT I HAVE GOT?
A CRAIGSLIST CANTATA
BY VEDA HILLE, BILL RICHARDSON, AND AMIEL GLADSTONE

Acknowledgements

Thank you to the performers and other folks who lent their talents along the way: Laara Sadiq, David Adams, Karin Konoval, Andrew Wheeler, Meghan Gardiner, Ford Pier, Patsy Klein, Sam Newton, Eric Napier, Fannina Waubert de Puiseau, Rob Kitsos, Sarah Chase, Jennifer Swan, Jeff Harrison, Julie Martens, Stephanie Aitken, Justin Kellam, Sholem Krishtalka, and Mitchell Marcus.

INTRODUCTION TO *DO YOU WANT WHAT I HAVE GOT?*

There is no regular process for developing a play at the Arts Club. My guiding principle is to give the play whatever resources it needs to get to the next draft—everything is open to invention. But developing as many as nine new plays a year and being able to be responsive to each as they come in, draft after draft, means tolerating a little chaos now and then. Play development doesn't happen on a nine-to-five, Monday-to-Friday schedule. It can happen at odd hours and sometimes in odd places, which makes for some memorable, even magical, moments.

One of my favourites was a meeting I had at Veda's home with the other writers, Bill Richardson and Amiel Gladstone. It was a dark, wet fall evening and we were warned when we arrived that Veda's son Anders, then age three, was already in bed. We tiptoed into her bedroom, and Ami and Bill and I sat on the edge of Veda's bed, our knees knocking against the keyboard where she sat, and we listened to her play and sing her way through half a dozen new songs. It was an extremely intimate version of a house concert. And sort of clandestine, as the performance was interrupted by Veda's husband Justin taking a half-asleep Anders to the bathroom for some late-night toilet training. We were shushed so as not to disturb the delicate balance between peeing and waking. We were all like kids in school, biting the insides of our mouths and shaking with silent laughter as we heard Anders complete his task and be returned to bed. Then, without missing a beat, Veda simply resumed playing. After, we crept into their kitchen and drank wine and ate a yummy homemade fruit flan by candlelight (the kitchen lights bright enough to wake Anders if he needed another bathroom excursion) and whispered notes about structure and fussed with some lyrics. The privilege of working with artists I admire has never stopped being a thrill for me.

Every piece in this show works like crazy. The hooks to the songs are as ingenious as the lyrics. It's a true delight. And you simply must hear Veda's music to truly appreciate the absolute genius of these remarkable artists' collaboration.

RACHEL DITOR: For future productions, is there a trick or insight you have about getting this play "right"?

VEDA HILLE: The things that I care about musically are having personalized voices; voices that sound like individuals, like ordinary people. The things I remember Ami saying again and again and again are: "This play should not feel relaxed or easy. You should feel exhausted at the end. You have to work hard and never let it slack."

RD: Do you have a particularly memorable moment from the production?

VH: I remember when we first improvised "Three Hundred Stuffed Penguins" with Laara Sadiq in a workshop; she really sold it. The workshops were so fun, because we just kept writing things and chucking things and seeing what stuck. Seeing what made us laugh dangerously hard. That continued into production too, of course. But the early days had an edge, because we really had no idea if we were doing something useful or not.

RD: Did you learn something working on this play? Did it teach you something about your craft? About process, about theatre, etc.?

VH: I learned I could write a musical! As long as I was surrounded by brilliant writers, actors, and one particular director. Completely surrounded with no escape.

RD: What was the genesis of this play?

VH: Bill and I were sitting in a café in Vancouver in 2008 (S'il Vous Plait, now defunct). We were committed to writing something together for my project with Theatre Replacement called *20 Minute Musicals*. Our options were a play called *Knees!* about the introduction of short pants into the senate (Bill's idea), and some other thing that I brought in but was not particularly into. Bill said that he thought there might be something to do with Craigslist. I said that sounded good and that we could call it *Do You Want What I Have Got?* Then Bill started sending me ads, and verses he was writing about ads. I started writing songs. I secretly thought my part of it was mediocre, but then we put it in front of people and they went a bit nuts. So we kept going. Et voilà!

Do You Want What I Have Got? was originally produced in a twenty-minute version by Theatre Replacement as a co-commission between the PuSh International Performing Arts Festival and Theatre Conspiracy, Vancouver, in 2009. It was developed as part of the Arts Club Theatre's ReACT showcase, Club PuSh, and the Belfry Theatre's SPARK Festival.

The play premiered in January 2012 at the Arts Club Theatre in a co-production by the Arts Club and the PuSh Festival. It featured the following cast and creative team:

Performers: J. Cameron Barnett, Dmitry Chepovetsky, Bree Greig, Veda Hille, Selina Martin, and Barry Mirochnick

Director: Amiel Gladstone
Musical direction: Veda Hille
Set design: Ted Roberts
Costume design: Darryl Milot
Lighting design: John Webber
Dramaturg: Rachel Ditor
Assistant director: Shane Snow
Stage manager: Allison Spearin
Assistant stage manager: Rebecca Mulvihill

This version (for the most part) went on to tour the Lower Mainland, British Columbia, and Whitehorse with Allan Zinyk joining the cast.

A revised version opened in Toronto in January 2013, produced by Acting Up Stage Company and Factory Theatre. It featured the following cast and creative team:

Performers: Dmitry Chepovetsky, Bree Greig, Daren A. Herbert, Veda Hille, Selina Martin, and Barry Mirochnick

Director: Amiel Gladstone
Set and costume design: Robin Fisher
Lighting design: Kimberly Purtell
Musical direction: Veda Hille
Choreography: Monica Dottor
Stage manager: Dustyn Wales

The version published here was produced in April 2013 at the Arts Club with the original team, along with Josh Epstein and Marguerite Witvoet joining the cast.

Set List

Bus Boyfriend
You Dropped Your Bible
Children's Guillotine
Decapitated Dolls
Free Sponges
Clown on Stilts
Cat Hats
Coffin-Jar
300 Stuffed Penguins
Ringneck Dove
Covenant
Heavy Metal Roommate
Rapture
Oh, My Lord
RIP Steve
Salsa Want
Roommates
To My Neighbour
Nighttime Watcher
Noodles
Did Someone See Me Today?
Free Man's Toupée
Dead Deer, Dead Moose
Cow Tatoo
Did Someone See Me Today? Reprise
Flag Me for Removal
Chinese Redhead
Hi My Lady
Chili-Eating Buddy
Do You Waltz?
Missed Connections

Characters

Piano: Piano player/singer, an alto.
Girl 1: A soprano.
Girl 2: A mezzo-soprano.
Boy 1: A tenor/baritone.
Boy 2: A tenor/baritone.
Drums: Drummer/guitarist/singer, a bass.

All=entire cast singing
Ensemble=all cast except soloist singing

Notes

Most regular text is sung. Spoken parts are indicated throughout.

The cast plays a variety of characters with some minor costume changes here and there.

The set is an empty stage. Some chairs. Pipes and rigging. Lamps of all sorts. All settings are created using lighting and the occasional prop.

Bus Boyfriend

On a city bus.

GIRL 1: Bus boyfriend, I want to smell you again.
Bus boyfriend, I want to smell you again.
Bus boyfriend.

(spoken) Craigslist. Missed Connections.

This was months ago.

We only rode the bus together three times. You wore drab, greyish-blue clothes that were slightly baggy. I had chin-length brown hair and cute sunglasses. I was holding a cup of coffee that kept spouting forth like a caffeinated geyser from the tiny sippy hole in the top, scalding my hands as I attempted in vain to dry off with a flimsy recycled-paper napkin.

BOY 2: Bus boyfriend. I want to smell you again.

BOY 1: Bus boyfriend. I want to smell you again.

ALL: Bus boyfriend.

GIRL 1: *(spoken)* You sat next to me. There was genuine sexual tension, which is rare in this city, and even rarer on the bus. You smelled REALLY, REALLY, REALLY, REALLY, REALLY good. I didn't make eye contact, although I took off my glasses so you wouldn't think I looked like a spy. I didn't make conversation. I just smelled you the whole way downtown.

GIRL 2: Want you got and I have and I want and I do you.
Want you got and I have and I want and I do too.

GIRL 1: Do. . .
Do you?
Do you?
You want what I have?
You. . .
Do you?
Do you want?
To?
God I want what
you have.
What I do what you
want you do you do.
ALL: You want what I have got.
Do you want what I have got?
Do you?
Do you?
Do you?

BOY 1 & BOY 2: Wheels on the bus go round and round. Wheels on the bus go round and round.

GIRL 2: What you got and I have and I want and I do you. What you got and I have and I want and I do too.

Holding the overhead pole on the bus, the characters almost connect, but not quite. They all get off the bus and move on.

You Dropped Your Bible

On a street.

GIRL 2: ooo ooo ooo ooo ooo ooo ooo ooo ooo ooo ooo ooo

BOY 1: I can't be held accountable,
I am in no way liable,
I walked behind you just today
And saw you drop your Bible.
I saw you drop your Bible
As we both walked along,
And when you bent to pick it up
I looked and saw your thong.

GIRL 2 drops her Bible and then bends over to pick it up. As she stands up she adjusts her thong.

GIRL 2: ooo ooo ooo ooo

BOY 1: It was pink, it was pink,
All fluorescent, bright, and pink.
I glimpsed your florid butt floss
And couldn't help but think
A thought that scorched my sinner's soul
And left the blackest stain.
I will be your Jesus
If you'll be my Magdalene.

> *GIRL 1 and BOY 2 enter with Bibles and then stand with GIRL 2 as a church choir.*

GIRL 1, GIRL 2, & BOY 2: ooo ooo ooo ooo aaa aaa aaa aaa aaa

BOY 1: Is that the Thong of Tholomon
With which you gird your loins?
That flash of Baptist lingerie
Has stirred my pagan groin.
Perhaps you might invite me
To your Bible study class,
Then shop with me for vestments
That will bifurcate my ass.

ALL: ooo ooo ooo ooo

BOY 1: It was pink, it was pink,
All fluorescent, bright, and pink.
Salvation is within my grasp,
I'm standing on the brink.
I hear the sound of angels' harps,
Their dulcet carols swell
To waft us up to Heaven
Where we'll raise a little hell.

ALL: Raise a little hell
Raise a little hell.

ENSEMBLE: He can't be held accountable.
He is in no way liable.
He walked behind her just today
And saw her drop her Bible.
He saw her drop her Bible,
He knew that it was wrong.
He looked, looked, looked,
And saw her thong.

BOY 1: Sh'ma Yis-ra-eil, A-do-nai E-lo-hei-nu, A-do-nai E-chad
Ba-ruch sheim k'vod mal-chu-to l'o-lam va-ed.
V'a-hav-ta eit A-do-nai E-lo-he-cha,
B'chawl l'va-v'cha, u-v'chawl naf-sh'cha,
U-v' chawl m'o-de-cha.
V-ha-yu ha-d'va-rim ha-ei-leh, A-sher a
No-chi m'tsa-v'cha ha-yom, al l'va-ve-cha.

ALL: It was pink, it was pink,
All fluorescent, bright, and pink.
Salvation is within his grasp,
He's standing on the brink.
He hears the sound of angels' harps,
Their dulcet carols swell
To waft them/us up to Heaven
Where they'll/we'll raise a little hell.

Children's Guillotine

GIRL 2 enters, slightly drunk.

GIRL 2: *(spoken)* Children's Guillotine. Looking to get rid of this childrens'-size guillotine. Only used once. Has been recently cleaned and oiled. Sure to make any child happy. Christmas is coming up soon, so don't miss this one.

Decapitated Dolls

A tired mother.

GIRL 1: My daughter likes
To pull the heads off dolls.
My daughter likes
To pull the heads off dolls.
The therapist says
We should let her.
So we do,
We do,
We do.
We have lots of
Headless dolls.
Some of their heads
May be retrievable,
Most, probably not.
Probably not.
Probably not.
Free to a good home,
To a good home,
Freedom and goodness and free.
Washington, DC.

Free Sponges

PIANO: *(spoken passionately)* Sponges. Free, as promised, will be out on front porch at one p.m. today. Do not come any earlier, they will not be there. Please limit one per person. Do not knock or try to ring the doorbell in hopes of getting an edge on anyone else. NO ONE WILL ANSWER.

(spoken) I am very busy today, so will only be able to repost how many are left every forty-five minutes. Please be respectful and do not make a mess. Remember, only one per person, please.

(spoken) I will take the sponges off the porch at seven p.m. SHARP. Do not try to come later than that. They will NOT be there anymore. So don't even try!

(spoken) PS The stick lying next to the sponges on the porch is not for the taking. It is our family's marshmallow-roasting stick.

Clown on Stilts

A sweet guy and a couple of children.

BOY 2: Dear clown on stilts at mall downtown,
Clown, clown, clown.

You were very cute and I liked your humour.
I was the guy who took your picture.
The kids were my sister's.
Like to take you out to dinner.
Like to take you out to dinner.
Clown on stilts at mall downtown,
Clown, clown, clown.

You were very cute and I liked your humour.
I was the guy who took your picture.
The kids were my sister's.
Like to take you out to dinner.
Like to take you out to dinner and more.
Clown on stilts at mall downtown, clown on stilts at mall downtown,
Clown, clown, clown.

ENSEMBLE: You were very cute and he liked your humour.
He was the guy who took your picture.
The kids were his sister's.
Like to take you out to dinner.
Like to take you out to dinner.

BOY 2: And more, if you are interested.

ENSEMBLE: Clown on stilts at mall downtown,
Clown on stilts at mall downtown.

BOY 2: I am single, living midtown. . .
Clown, clown, clown.

Cat Hats

A lonely woman in a shawl looking out into the darkness.

GIRL 2: *(spoken)* San Diego. Free. Carton of Irregular Cat Hats.

(spoken) I have a big box of used cat and kitten hats that I have collected over the years for various occasions. As of recently my cat, Snowman, is no longer living, and thus I am forced to get rid of these precious memories. I would not feel right asking for money—so, I am offering the whole box for free. There are many styles, from cute and funny to formal.

Snowman.
Me and Snowman.
Me and Snowman.
Snowman.
Snowman.
Snowman.
Snowman.

The ghost of Snowman appears.

BOY 2: Miao miao.

GIRL 2: Me and Snowman.

BOY 2: Miao miao miao miao miao miao.

GIRL 2: Snowman.

BOY 2: Miao miao miao.

GIRL 2: Snowman.

BOY 2: Miao miao miao.

The ghost of Snowman expires.

GIRL 2: *(spoken)* There is a variety of fourteen different hats, total. I just hope you and your pet can find as much joy in these hats as me and Snowman once did.

Thanks. And have a great day.

Coffin-Jar

In a variety of different places. A straightforward man, a boy in a hurry, and a spectral woman.

BOY 2: *(spoken)* Coffin.
Handsome varnish finish. Airtight. Has been used for storing produce. Free to anyone who wants to pick it up.

BOY 1: *(spoken)* Potato Cannon.
It's eight feet long. My neighbours figured out what was happening, so I need to get rid of it today!

GIRL 2: *(spoken)* Large Glass Jar.
Believed to contain a ghost, possibly of George Harrison. If you are into supernatural phenomena, or are a Beatles fan, this is for you.

300 Stuffed Penguins

A young woman looks around her purple bedroom. She brushes her hair and then uses the hairbrush as a microphone, alternating between speaking and singing.

GIRL 1: What I'm offering here
Is about three hundred stuffed penguins
Of various

Shapes, sizes, and species

To a deserving child.

A deserving child.

I'm going through
A pretty weird time in my life right now—
Having just gone through a breakup,
And graduated college,
And temporarily living

In my parent's house,
Before I move out for good in the fall:

(Though I remain unemployed
Because my philosophy degree

Is at such a premium),
And sifting through my room,

Which has become a strange amalgam
Of my adolescence

And burgeoning adulthood,

It's been brought to my attention
That I probably won't "catch a man,"
Or have anyone believe
I'm about to turn twenty-three

With three hundred penguins and a bunch of purple furniture around,
And that looking at my current room, one might think
That some sort of thirteen-year-old

With developmental issues is living here.

I loved penguins as a child,
Long before they were trendy,
And collected them,
Often putting on penguin weddings,
And penguin ballet recitals,
Where I made costumes for individual penguins,
All of whom had names that I kept track of
In my penguin censuses.
I could recite all seventeen species of penguin
In alphabetical order:

Adélie Penguin
African Penguin
Chinstrap Penguin
Eastern Rockhopper
Emperor Penguin
Erect-Crested Penguin
Fiordland Penguin
Galapagos Penguin
Gentoo Penguin

Humboldt Penguin
King Penguin
Little Blue Penguin
Macaroni Penguin
Northern Rockhopper
Snares Penguin
Western Rockhopper
And the Yellow-eyed Penguin.

So yes, I feel justified in saying
I want a deserving child,
A child that will really, well,
Love the penguins,
And cherish his/her youth with them
As it slowly slips away.
It slips away.
It slips away.

Ringneck Dove

A desperate wife.

GIRL 2: *(spoken)* Wanted. Dead ringneck dove. In return for one DEAD ringneck dove, you will receive one LIVE ringneck dove, of unknown age, named Baby.

(spoken) My husband has had Baby for fifteen plus years. We keep thinking it will die one of these days, but it just likes life too much. My husband will not let us get rid of it, nor will he let me help it meet its end.

(spoken) The only way this will work for me is if the death appears to be of natural causes. All I need to do is get your dead dove, and give you my live dove; you're happy, and I'm happy.

(spoken) Pictures are attached, though all look alike to me anyway.

(spoken) I'll be checking emails eagerly, and I'll be ready to act on something with short notice.

(spoken) Time will be of the essence for a successful dove swap.

Covenant

All in different places: a hippie chick, a low-rent hood, an inarticulate flirty gay man, and an enthusiastic woman trying to help.

PIANO: You must recall the story
Of Noah and the flood.
Forty days of ceaseless rain,
Then he released the dove.
It spread its wings, away it flew,
Bereft of tag or band;
It came back to the ark each night
The bad news was:

GIRL 2: No land.

PIANO: Noah, though, was undeterred.
Each day that dove he launched,

GIRL 2 releases a dove.

And sure enough, it brought him back
A telltale olive branch.
Ararat, oh, Ararat,
There foundered Noah's craft.
Beneath an arching rainbow
He abandoned sail and mast.
The rain still falls on last year's man,
It falls on this year's too.
Oh, what are all our postings
But the dove that Noah flew?

GIRL 1: *(spoken)* I was wearing purple polka-dotted crotchless panties, yellow fuzzy tap-dancing shoes, and rainbow knee-high socks. On my tits I had disco pasties. You had a green goatee, sick tatts, and no pants. I saw you hula-ing on the multicoloured flying dragon art car while I was riding my tight cruiser through the sick playa dust. We made eye contact, and I never saw you again. Hope the universe brings us together. Namaste.
PS My name is Raven.
PPS This was at Burning Man.

BOY 2: *(spoken)* I've done many a snatch and grab, but no one has ever stuck in my mind like you. There was a quick moment when our eyes met that I felt something strong. I think you felt it, too. I got your name from your driver's licence. So, Jennifer, if you'd like to have a drink sometime, get back to me.

BOY 1: *(spoken)* To Zellers cashier in the Tillicum Mall.
Umm.
Well.
Snip snip.
Uh.
Duh. Huh. Yup. Mmmmm.
My, my.
XO.

GIRL 2: *(spoken)* I was running to catch the train and saw you on the subway ahead of me. You were sprinting and collided with a support column. Your prosthetic arm flew off. I have it now, and I'd like to meet the rest of you.

ALL: Oh what are all our postings
But the dove that Noah flew?
With glowing hearts we see them rise,
Weighed down with what we crave.
Our prayers in need of answer
And our covenant with Craig.

Heavy Metal Roommate

The PIANO player leaves to have a snack. Everyone else becomes hard rockers.

GIRL 1, GIRL 2, & BOY 1: Looking for a metalhead roommate for our metal house.
Looking for a metalhead roommate for our metal house.
Looking for a sinister and metal roommate for our wicked-ass house, wicked-ass house.
Looking for a sinister and metal roommate for our wicked-ass house, wicked-ass house.
With a jam space and a nice big patio.

Looking for a metalhead roommate for our metal house.
Mountain view!
Looking for a metalhead roommate for our metal house.
Hardwood floors!
Close to transit and stores.
Close to transit and stores.

We don't party all the time, only once in a while and on the weekend.
We don't party all the time, only once in a while and on the weekend.
We don't party all the time, only once in a while and on the weekend.

Rapture

An earnest entrepreneur.

BOY 1: *(spoken)* Have you ever thought of what will happen to your pets after Jesus comes back to claim the souls of the saved during the Rapture and delivers you to Heaven to enjoy everlasting life?

(spoken) I am here to offer you pet-care service for after the Rapture.

(spoken) As an atheist, I will surely still be here on this earth, post-Rapture, and would love to look after your pets and make sure they are well taken care of, after you and your family have been raptured, until the end of their natural life.

(spoken) For a small deposit of only fifty dollars, they will receive adequate amounts of food, water, and shelter, as well as plenty of exercise and socialization as I would imagine there will be a lot of pets abandoned by Jesus, the pet hater.

(spoken) Thanks. And have a great day.

368 | The Arts Club Anthology

Oh, My Lord

The pets. Various species.

BOY 2, WITH ALL: Oh, my Lord, my sweet, sweet Lord,
Your creatures are down here alone.
Oh my Lord, my sweet, sweet Lord,
You've called our families home.
Lord, Lord, Lord. Lord, sweet Lord, oh my Lord, my sweet, sweet Lord,
Now who will take care of our needs?
We do not have hands,
We can't open cans,
At least could you rapture the fleas?
Jesus throw us a bone.
Oh Lord, don't leave us alone.

RIP Steve

The ENSEMBLE is glued to their smartphones.

PIANO: How wondrous is the register
Of famous signings-off,
Those who had the wherewithal
To more than gasp or cough.
Goethe thought to cry "Mehr Licht,"
Of light he wanted more.
Oscar Wilde in Paris dissed
His hotel-room decor.
Death brings out his steno pad
To take down final lines.
"Oh wow" opined the late Steve Jobs;
He said "oh wow" three times.

He spoke his six last syllables,
Took one last look around:
System past rebooting,
Inbox shutting down,

And then stepped into mystery,
And then slipped off the map,
A digit in whatever code
Empowers the cosmic app.
If there's some great beyond to know,
I guess Steve knows it now.
The angels strum their iPhone nines
And sing:

ENSEMBLE: "Oh wow. Oh wow. Oh wow."

PIANO: And as I search on Craigslist,
I do pause to reflect
Without the platform built at NeXT,
We might not have these interwebs.
iMac, iPhone, iPad, I miss you Steve.
RIP I do believe you when you said,

ALL: "For the really big big things you have to trust me."

PIANO: I trust you now.

ALL: Oh wow.
Oh wow.
Oh wow.

Salsa Want

Dance break.

GIRL 2: Want you got and I have and
I want and I do you?
Got I want what you have,
What I do what you want you do.
You want what I have got.
Do you want what I have got?
Do you, do you?
Do you, do you?

ALL: Do you, do you, do you?
Do you feel lonely or empty?
Lonely or empty?

Want you got and I have and
I want and I do you?
Got I want what you have,
What I do what you want you do.
You want what I have got.
Do you want what I have got?
Do you, do you?
Do you, do you?

Do you, do you, do you?
Do you feel lonely or empty?
Lonely or empty?

Roommates

In the style of Kander and Ebb and Bob Fosse.

ENSEMBLE: *(spoken)* Sergei, Vicki, buck naked, salt
Liza, drum kit, Spam, don't call
Sergei, Vicki, buck naked, salt
Liza, drum kit, Spam, don't call.

GIRL 1: I'm just a girl, an ordinary girl,
A girl who's trying to make it on her own.
I've got a flat, a garden-level flat,
Okay, a basement flat, to call my home.
It's pricey in the city,
And to live alone is gloomy,
So that is why I'm posting here:
I'm looking for a roomy,
I'm looking for a roomy.
Someone courteous and clean
Not like the one I'm kicking out,
Or previous sixteen.

I'm living in the city now,
I'm trying to be urban,
I'm open to both genders,
And to yarmulkes and turbans.
I'm not all that particular
Or wedded to perfection.
I just want criminality
A smidge below detection.

I'm looking for a roomy.
I'm looking for a roomy,
Someone courteous, and clean.
Unlike the one I'm kicking out,
Or previous sixteen.

ENSEMBLE: *(spoken)* Liza, drum kit.

GIRL 1: And not another Sergei prone to public self-abuse,
Not another Courtney, always quoting Dr. Seuss,
Not another Vicki, who was vegan to a fault.
She chewed on nuts and berries and gave up caffeine and salt.
Then one weekend something snapped,
some longing breached the dam.
I found her baying in the yard, smeared head to toe with Spam.
And buck naked. Buck naked. Buck naked.

I'm just a girl, an ordinary girl,
A girl who from the plainest cloth is cut.
I have a flat to share, austere and clean spare,
Please call me, please call me, BUT:

No pets, no smokers, no practical jokers,
No phobias, no allergies, no sleepovers, no parties,
No drugs, no drink, anything else, let me think:
If you listen to Metallica, don't call,
If you wish that you were Liza, don't call,
If you come with a well-used drum kit, don't call.

(spoken) Beat it.

GIRL 1 kicks the DRUMMER *offstage and* GIRL 2 *sits down behind the drum kit. She drums as best she can for the rest of the number.*

GIRL 1: *(spoken)* NEXT!

GIRL 2: *(spoken)* Drei, vier, fünf!

ALL: If you're moving because of bedbugs,
If your address is now your car,
If you've got an imaginary friend,
Or poop with the door ajar,
If you're partial to Stephen Sondheim
Whenever you're feeling down,
And take on a hangdog, distant look
Then bellow, "Send in the Clowns."
Or think a drain's the perfect place
To amass your fallen hair,
Or if the CD you perpetually play
Is *The Best of Sonny and Cher,*

Don't call, don't call, don't call. Don't call, don't call. Don't call. . .

GIRL 1: I'm just a girl, an ordinary girl,
Plain and average, that's my strongest suit.
I've got a flat to share, I'd love to have you there,
Would suit someone who's celibate and mute.

ALL: Don't call!
Don't call!
Don't call!
Don't call!

GIRL 1: Don't
Call!

To My Neighbour

The Corrector, a spectacled, officious woman, along with two neighbours out in their yards.

GIRL 2: I log on every morning,
I cannot comprehend,
Who taught these people spelling, grammar, punctuation?

BOY 2: To my neighbour, who I saw pooping in his yard yesterday—

GIRL 2: Whom. Whom I saw.

BOY 2: Pooping in his yard yesterday. I saw you couched down with your pants around your ankles.

GIRL 2: Crouched down. I saw you crouched down with your pants—

BOY 2: Your pants around your ankles. I asked, "Hey. What are you doing?" Your reply was—

BOY 1: "Pooping in a groundhog hole. I read about it online. It's supposed to trick the groundhog into thinking another animal has moved into it's lair."

GIRL 2: It's not it's.
I.T.S. No bloody apostrophe!

BOY 2: Since you are normally a sane person I refrained from calling the police. But I
saw you, saw you, saw you, saw you. . .

ALL: Saw you saw you saw you saw you
Saw you saw you saw you saw you.

Nighttime Watcher

A nervous man in his bed.

BOY 2: Nighttime watcher required.
Thirty dollars per hour.
I would like to say this is not a joke,
Please no time-wasters.

Nighttime watcher required.
Thirty dollars per hour.
I would like to say this is not a joke.

ENSEMBLE: What is required?

BOY 2: To sit in my room at night
And watch over me while I sleep.
I have a lot of trouble sleeping.
It would be comforting to know someone was there.

Nighttime watcher required.
I would pay forty an hour if
You could wear a small owl costume.

I would like to say this is not a joke.
Please no time-wasters.

ENSEMBLE: See you see you see you
See you see you see you
See you.

Noodles

A demonstrative young man.

BOY 1: I will pay you, pay you, pay you, pay you;
I will pay you, pay you, pay you, pay you, pay you
One dollar
To sit in my bathtub full of noodles
While you wear a one-piece bathing suit.
I will not be home nor will anyone else
While you do this.

Dancing dancing dancing dancing dancing dancing dancing.

I will pay you, pay you, pay you, pay you, pay you
One dollar.
I will leave the key for you
And you will sit at your leisure.
I will require at least a five-minute stay.

A neighbour will watch the front door from across the street,
And using a supplied stopwatch
Will time your entrance and departure.
Please, bring your own footwear.
The noodles will be cooked and therefore slippery.

I will pay you, pay you, pay you, pay you, pay you
One dollar
To sit in my bathtub full of noodles
While you wear a one-piece bathing suit.
I will not be home nor will anyone else
While you do this.

> The ENSEMBLE joins him in a dance.

> Dancing dancing dancing dancing dancing dancing dancing.

I will season season season season season
The pasta
When I return home prior to dinner.
Do not bring any sauce.

Did Someone See Me Today?

> The women in a coffee shop.

GIRL 2: You know me from the Starbucks.
I go there every day.
They've got that fast, free wireless
And no-fat soy lattes.
I tap-tap-tap on my laptop.
I cultivate the look
Of someone who is polishing
The last draft of her book.
A latter-day de Beauvoir.
A novel on the go,
Waiting, say, for Sartre,
Or Camus at Deux Magots.

In fact, the Gap employs me.
I work there, stacking jeans.
In fact, it's Missed Connections
That illuminates my screen.
My mission's ontological.
To prove that I exist,
I've got to be a pulse point
On the radar called Craigslist.

Did someone see me today,
Did someone see?
Did anyone by chance remark me,
Standing, waiting for the light.
I was queuing for the bus
At half past three.
By four I was at yoga,
Slate-grey top, magenta tights.
Did someone see me today
And sense a spark?
On the Winner's escalator,
At the Japadog on Fourth,
On the seawall,
Or jogging in the park?
Do I have to go Godiva,
Flash my boobies from a horse?

PIANO: Did someone see me today
While passing by?
Like they saw the blond jaywalker
Give the finger to a cop,
Or the waitress
Who popped out her glass eye,
And who buffed it with her dishrag
And then wiped your table top
And said, "What the fuck's your problem?"
When you asked her, please, to stop,
And her name tag said "Miranda,"
But the hostess called her Dot,

And the import of your message
Is that you found Dot hot, hot, hot, you found Dot hot,
I guess I'm not.
I guess I'm not.

GIRL 1: Will someone see me, will someone see?
I am slightly ectomorphic
But I'm steady on the ground.
I've no prior commitments,
Always free,
And I wouldn't mind eschewing lost
And saying yes to found.
Will someone see me today
And come through.

GIRL 2: Saw you writing in the Starbucks,
Saw your anorak was peach,

GIRL 1: Saw you're someone who likes sunsets,
Who likes walking on the beach,

PIANO: Saw you're someone who's in hiding
Looking for someone who seeks.

Back on the transit bus, in the same formation as the top of the show.

PIANO, GIRL 1, & GIRL 2: Can that be true?
Can that be you?
Because that is me, too.

Did someone see me today,
Did someone see?
Did anyone by chance remark me,
Standing, waiting for the light?

GIRL 2: I was riding on the bus at half past three.

GIRL 1: I've no prior commitments, always free.

Off the bus.

GIRL 2: I was topless on a horse, yeah, that was me.

PIANO, GIRL 1, & GIRL 2: Did someone see me today?
Did someone see me today?
Did someone see me?
Did someone see me?

GIRL 2: You know me from the Starbucks,
I go there every day.

The noodles man is back.

BOY 1: Do you want what I have got?
Do not bring any sauce.
Do you want what I have got?
No sauce.

Free Man's Toupée

The follicly challenged.

DRUMS: Free man's toupée.
Only worn twice, from the House of Frank.
Only worn twice, from the House of Frank.

PIANO, GIRL 1, & GIRL 2: A gorgeous, gorgeous shank.

DRUMS: Brownish blond with a sprinkling of grey.

PIAINO, GIRL 1, & GIRL 2: Too-ra-loo-ra-lay.

DRUMS: Easy to trim and easy to wash.

PIANO, GIRL 1, & GIRL 2: Gosh golly golly gosh.

DRUMS: Need to get rid of it,
Need to be free,
Whenever I wear it dogs growl at me.
Whenever I wear it I can't be discreet,
Squirrels attack me on every street.

He swats at a couple of squirrels.

PIANO, GIRL 1, & GIRL 2: On every street, on every street.

DRUMS: Wash in machine.

PIANO, GIRL 1, & GIRL 2: Keep it clean, keep it clean.

DRUMS: Real human hair.

PIANO, GIRL 1, & GIRL 2: Never despair, never despair.

DRUMS, PIANO, GIRL 1, & GIRL 2: One size fits all.

Dead Deer, Dead Moose

A hunter in Massachusetts, a dude in Alaska. The wife and kids back home.

BOY 1: I'm in Massachusetts. I need a dead deer.

BOY 2: I'm in Alaska, with one dead moose.

BOY 1: I said I was out of town hunting for the last three weeks, but really I was with my other girl.

BOY 2: I have a dead moose, free for the taking. It died yesterday, apparently of natural causes.

BOY 1: With my other girl, and my wife thinks. . .

BOY 2: I called Fish and Game to come and get it.

BOY 1: My wife thinks I landed a big buck.

GIRL 1: I think he landed a big buck!

BOY 2: Apparently, moose are a natural resource and belong to everybody. . .

BOY 1: She thinks I landed a big buck and the kids. . .

BOY 2: Belong to everybody until they die, then they belong to whoever's property they died on.

GIRL 1 & BOY 1: The kids love to get their pic taken with a dead deer.

BOY 2: So, according to Fish and Game, the moose now belongs to me. Sweet.

BOY 1: Sweet.

GIRL 1, BOY 1, & BOY 2: Sweet.

GIRL 1, GIRL 2, & PIANO: Love to get our pic taken with a dead deer!

BOY 1: So if you have a dead deer. . .

BOY 2: So if you want a dead moose. Please.

BOY 1: Please let's make a deal.

BOY 2: Please come and get it before the bears do.

BOY 1: Do you have a dead deer?

BOY 2: I have a dead moose.

BOY 1: Thanks.

BOY 2: Thanks.

GIRL 1, BOY 1, & BOY 2: Sweet.

Cow Tatoo

A woman jogger and the Corrector pop up.

GIRL 1: *(spoken)* Hot guy with cow tatoo running on Lakeshore Drive.

GIRL 2: *(spoken)* Tattoo? T. A. T. O. O.?

GIRL 1: *(spoken)* I see you running on Lakeshore. You usually run without your shirt on and have a tatoo on your shoulder. I think maybe it's a cow tatoo.

GIRL 2: *(spoken)* To spell "tattoo" you've got to know
It's double T and double O.
There's nothing quite so grim to see
As "tattoo" with a single T.

GIRL 1: *(spoken)* Interested in grabbing a coffee?

GIRL 2: *(spoken)* Pre-emptively, I'll just add too
That cappuccino's like tattoo.
Cappuccino's got to be
With double P and double C.

GIRL 1: *(spoken)* PS I have a boyfriend and need to be discrete.

GIRL 2: *(spoken)* Oh my God!
Dear person who is seeking carnal fumbling on the sly,
Good luck in getting laid. I'll end off with this slight aside:

You might have better fortune nailing down a tasty piece
By noting that discreet's not spelled like the country next to Greece.
Dis-C.R.E.T.E. applies to figures, numbers, ratios.
Dis-C.R.E.E.T. is good for sordid situations.
Thought you'd like to clarify the thrust of your intentions,
No need at all to thank me for this kindly intervention.

Did Someone See Me Today? Reprise

A couple of male joggers, one of them turning out to be the man looking for the clown on stilts.

BOY 1: Did someone see me today, did someone see?
I go jogging on the Lakeshore
and I do have a tattoo.
It's not a cow,
It's a yin-yang.
It can't be me,
But I do like cappuccino
Even though you've got a boyfriend.
LOL. BTW. MSG me.
Winky-face emoticon.

He releases a dove.

BOY 1, BOY 2, & DRUMS: Did someone see me today?
Did someone see me today?
Did someone see me?
Did someone see me?

BOY 2: Dear clown on stilts at mall downtown.
The guy who took your picture, that was me.
I am single living midtown. . .

He releases a dove.

BOY 1: You know me from the Lakeshore.

BOY 2: Clown clown clown.

BOY 1: You know me from the Lakeshore.

Flag Me for Removal

A couple more of the grammatically challenged. The Corrector in her home. Two guys' guys.

GIRL 1: *(spoken)* I will write you essay.

BOY 2: *(spoken)* We are looking for a smart or more person to help un with our company.

GIRL 2: The cats are old,
The dogs are old.
Just once, even once, did you think
It would turn out like this?
You'd be living alone,
And eating ice cream at the sink.

Flag me for removal, Lord,
I'm weary of this earth.
The planet's gone to rat shit
Since they cancelled *Mary Worth.*
Her daily dose of common sense,
Her decency, her tact,
All of these were pivotal
In keeping me on track.
Now *Mary Worth* is dead and gone,
And *Blondie* has gone bust;
Charlie Brown has crossed the bar,
Prince Valiant bit the dust.
All my friends have disappeared,
There's no one left I know.
So flag me for removal, Lord,
It's time for me to go.

BOY 1 & BOY 2: Three pink plastic lawn flamingos.
We got the momma and the daddy and two babies.
In good shape except momma's got a bullet hole.
Will trade for a good dog or weed eater.
Will also consider any kind of alcohol
As long as it ain't been opened up.

Chinese Redhead

In different places: a sweet gal, an enthusiastic man, and a foot fetishist.

GIRL 1: *(spoken)* My boyfriend and I came into the sex shop you (used to) work at, and you gave us some stellar customer service! You were totally adorable, had just moved to Canada, and were working your last shift, which is really too bad. I was too shy to make a move. . . I was the skinny redhead browsing giant fake cocks, and you were the super friendly redheaded Chinese girl.

(spoken) Anyway, you were awesome and we'd love to see you again!!

(spoken) Oh, and the dildo is AWESOME, thanks for your help! Come try it out!

BOY 2: Why ddn't I have a kindergarten teach as hot as you? Oakridge Mall.

(spoken) Damn, I would never imagine myself posting here, but damn you had that cosmic energy that left me in suspension. i didn't know whether I wanted bear mace or a bear hug. . .

GIRL 2: *(spoken)* I saw you in Langley. You were trying on special shoes to fit your six toes on your left foot. I thought the extra toe was very special, and I would like to massage it with baby oil. It was so sweet, the way you waved it at me. Rawr.

Hi My Lady

A foreign man.

BOY 1: Hi, my lady,
Hi-hi, my lady,
Hi, my lady,
Hi-hi, my lady
In black and black.
Black and black.

GIRL 1, GIRL 2, & BOY 2: Hi. Hi-hi.

BOY 1: Please, my beauty,
Please, please, my beauty,
Please, my beauty,
Please, please, my beauty,
Reply,
I beg you to reply.

GIRL 1, GIRL 2, & BOY 2: Please. Please-please.

BOY 1: You were about to enter your compound
When you saw me in my blue van.
My blue van.
I did wave my hand.
My hand I waved,
And you saw,
But I drove away.

I got chickened, my lady,
Hi-hi, my lady,
I got chickened, my lady,
Hi-hi, my lady
In black and black,
Black and black.

I got chickened, my lady,
Hi-hi, my lady,
I got chickened, my lady,
Hi-hi, my lady
In black and black,
Black and black.

With your sweet, sexy figure
That I can't forget:
I am a gentleman. I am a gentleman.

(spoken) I turned around and pulled towards your house, saw you were not there, waited a little, but no sign of you. I don't know what has happened to me on that moment as I missed my golden opportunity. My beautiful lady. My beautiful lady.

GIRL 1, GIRL 2, & BOY 2: My love, my love.

BOY 1: *(spoken)* Please forgive me for not stopping. For instance, I thought we could both get into trouble. Now, I realize I am in love with you. I will take care of you my whole life.

I cannot forget that unbelievable scene.

GIRL 1, GIRL 2, & BOY 2: He cannot forget that unbelievable scene!

BOY 1: Please, my beauty,
Please, please, my beauty,
Please, my beauty,
Please, please, my beauty,
Reply,
I beg you to reply.

Please, my beauty,
Please, please, my beauty,
Please, my beauty,
Please, please, my beauty
Take care, from someone special,
And for now,

Goodbye, my lady,
Bye-bye, my lady,
Goodbye, my lady,
Bye-bye, my lady

In black and black,
Black and black.

GIRL 1, GIRL 2, & BOY 2: He is a gentleman.

Goodbye, my lady,
Bye-bye, my lady,
Goodbye, my lady,
Bye-bye, my lady

In black and black,
Black and black.

He is a gentleman.

Goodbye, my lady,
Bye-bye, my lady
Goodbye, my lady,
Bye-bye, my lady.

(spoken) Goodbye.

Chili-Eating Buddy

A midnight toker with a sweet side.

BOY 2: *(spoken)* Here's the 411.

I made a big pot of chili yesterday.

ENSEMBLE: A big pot,
A big pot of chili.

BOY 2: Should be aged by now.
I'm bored and broke.
I'll swap a bowl of chili
For some 420.

ENSEMBLE: A big pot,
Some 420,
A big pot,
Some 420.

BOY 2: Come on over,
Eat my chili,
Smoke your weed.
Play some tunes.
Tell some jokes.
And fart away.
Fart away.
Fart away.

ENSEMBLE: A big pot,
Some 420,
A big pot,
A chili-eating buddy.

BOY 2: Age and race and looks are unimportant.
Age and race and looks are unimportant.
Age and race.
I'm serious about this.

Also looking for a guy
Who'd like to get together now and then
To drink coffee and hug.
I'm not gay
Or anything like that.
Just enjoy a cup of java
With another guy
In our underwear.
Kind of a male bonding, sipping thing.

ENSEMBLE: A big pot, some 420.
A big pot, a chili-eating buddy.
Age and race and looks are unimportant.
Age and race and looks are unimportant.
Age and race and looks are unimportant.
Age and race and looks are unimportant.

    BOY 2 horn solo.

    GIRL 1 flute solo.

    BOY 1 chest-slap solo.

    ALL jam.

Age and race and looks are unimportant.
Age and race and looks are unimportant.

BOY 2: Age and race.
I'm serious about this.

Also looking for a guy
Who'd like to get together now and then
To drink coffee and hug.
I'm not gay
Or anything like that.
Just enjoy a cup of java

With another guy
In our underwear.
Kind of a male bonding, sipping thing.

Send a picture and your favourite blend for a response!

Do You Waltz?

The clown on stilts. A guy who knows his penguins. The girls on the bus.

BOY 1: Want you got and I have
And I want and I do you,
Got I want what you have
What I do what you want to.
Do you want what I have got?
Do you want what I have got?
Do you? Do you? Do you?

BOY 2: Adélie penguin
African penguin
Chinstrap penguin
Emperor penguin
Erect-crested penguin
Fiordland penguin
Galapagos penguin
Humboldt penguin
King penguin
Little blue penguin.

BOY 1: Want you got and I have
And I want and I do you,
Got I want what you have
What I do what you want to.
Do you want what I have got?
Do you want what I have got?

Do you?
Do you?
Do you?

BOY 2: Erect-crested
penguin
Fiordland penguin
Galapagos penguin
Humboldt penguin
King penguin
Little blue penguin.

BOY 1: Want you got
and I have
And I want and I
do you,
God I want what
you have
What I do what you
want to.
Do you want what I
have got?
Do you want what I
have got?

GIRL 1 & GIRL 2:
Wheels on the bus go
round and round.
Wheels on the bus go
round and round.
Bus boyfriend, I want to
smell you again.

BOY 1: Do you?
BOY 1: Do you?
BOY 1: Do you?

GIRL 1: Again.
GIRL 1: Again.

Missed Connections

Everyone in different places.

ALL: Are you the one?
Am I the one?

BOY 1: This is crude, this is seamy,
But I saw you and I wondered,
Did you see me?

GIRL 1: Are you free? Unencumbered?
Send a message
And I'll send you back my number.

BOY 1: I was the one who borrowed *War and Peace.*

BOY 2: You were the one who wore the worn-out fleece.

GIRL 2: I was the one who had the pink beret.

GIRL 1: You were the one I saw at IGA.

BOY 1: I was the one who bought the instant noodles.

GIRL 1: You were the one who had the mohawked poodle.

BOY 2: I was the one who had the box of Rogaine.

GIRL 2: You were the one who threw up on the SkyTrain.

ALL: Am I the one?
Are you the one?

GIRL 2: What's the chance
That you'll see this?
If you do you'll only shrug
And say, "Who needs this?"

BOY 2: Did you glimpse me behind you?

GIRL 1: I was right behind you.

BOY 2: It's insanity to think that I will find you.

PIANO: It's a castaway's notion,
Just a note, inside a bottle, in the ocean.

BOY 1: I was the one who had the psycho friend.

GIRL 1: You were the one who robbed the ATM.

GIRL 2: I was the one who asked to sign your cast.

BOY 2: You were the one who fixed my broken mast.

PIANO: I was the one who said your hat was hokey.

BOY 1: You were the one who sucked at karaoke.

GIRL 1: I was the one who ordered lemon Jell-O.

GIRL 2: You were the one with the pimped-out cello.

BOY 2: I was the one who tried to sell you blow.

PIANO: You were the pilot of the UFO.

BOY 1: I was the vampire with the fear of bats.

GIRL 2: You were the one who found my missing cat.

GIRL 1: I was the one who stole the English tabloids.

GIRL 2: Snowman!

BOY 2: You were the one with the infected adenoids.

GIRL 2: Me and Snowman!

GIRL 1: I was the one you drank under the table.

ALL: You were the one who gave birth in the stable.

GIRL 1 releases a dove.

I was the one who borrowed *War and Peace.*
You were the one who wore the worn-out fleece.
I was the one who had the pink beret.
You were the one I saw at IGA.
I was the one who bought the instant noodles.
You were the one who had the mohawked poodle.

GIRL 2 & BOY 2: Me and Snowman.

ALL: I was the one who had the box of Rogaine.

Back in the same transit tableau as in the opening number.

You were the one who threw up on the SkyTrain.

Everyone moves apart, alone again.

The one you are, the one I am, the one you are, the one I am.

PIANO: The one you are the one.
Did someone see me today?

GIRL 1: Did someone see me today?

GIRL 2: Did someone see me today?

BOY 1: Did someone see me today?

BOY 2: Did someone see me?
Today?

End.

ARTS CLUB THEATRE COMPANY PREMIERES 1970–2015

Now Mercutio by Bill Millerd and Daphne Goldrick

The Enchanted Forest by Bill Millerd and Daphne Goldrick

Alice in Wonderland by Jim and Judy Walchuk

Vancouver Revue Renewed by ACME Theatre (Beth Kaplan, Annabel Kershaw, Mario Crudo, Lani Ashenhurst, Alec Willows, Andy Rhodes, Don Adams, and Donna BeLisle)

Cruel Tears by Ken Mitchell

Walls by Christian Bruyere (co-production with New Play Centre)

Journey to Kairos by Ann Mortifee

Ned and Jack by Sheldon Rosen

Mabel Leaves Forever by Andrew Rhodes and Alec Willows

Talking Dirty by Sherman Snukal

Genuine Fakes by John Lazarus

Reflections on Crooked Walking by Ann Mortifee

A Musical Evening with Ruth Nichol and Leon Bibb

The Late Blumer by John Lazarus

Family Matters by Sherman Snukal

It's Snowing on Saltspring by Nicola Cavendish

Welcome to the Planet by Ann Mortifee

Only in Vancouver by Bruce Kellett and Daphne Goldrick

Rattle in the Dash by Peter Anderson

Don Messer's Jubilee by John Gray

Another Morning by Steve Petch

Black and Gold Revue by Dean Regan

Gunga Heath by Heath Lamberts

It's Snowing on Saltspring Tra-La by Nicola Cavendish

Only in BC by Bruce Kellett and Daphne Goldrick

7 Stories by Morris Panych

A Little Show conceived by Leon Bibb, Bruce Kellett, and Ruth Nichol

Dead Serious by Doug Greenall

Tightrope Time: Ain't Nuthin' More Than Some Itty Bitty Madness Between Twilight & Dawn by Walter Borden

Maniac Bride by David King

Fair Game by Karen Wykberg

The Necessary Steps by Morris Panych

Mixed Blessings by Sherman Snukal

A Closer Walk with Patsy Cline by Dean Regan

Make Up Your Mind by Kurt Vonnegut

Celestina by Fernando de Rojas, translated by Steve Petch

The Ends of the Earth by Morris Panych

Santa's Got Soul conceived by Joe Chappel, Candus Churchill, Lovie Eli, Jay Krebbs, and Marcus Mosel

All Grown Up by Leslie Mildiner

The Wild Guys by Andrew Wreggitt and Rebecca Shaw

Blowin' On Bowen by Nicola Cavendish

World's Greatest Guy by Shawn Macdonald and Gary Jones

When the Rains Come by Ann Mortifee

More Sex Tips for Modern Girls created by Edward Astley, Susan Astley, Kim Seary, John Sereda, Hilary Strang, Christine Willes, and Peter Eliot Weiss

Vigil by Morris Panych

It's Blowin' Growin' & Glowin on Bowen by Nicola Cavendish

Denis Anyone? by Denis Simpson

Alice: Play With Music by John Lazarus

Red Rock Diner by Dean Regan

Joey Shine by David King

Fear Knot by Shawn Macdonald and Gary Jones

Swing by Dean Regan

Wang Dang Doodle, book by Leslie Mildiner

Easy Money by Mark Leiren-Young and Bruce Kellett

A Town Called Hockey by Leisl Lafferty, Gary Jones, and Richard Side

Hotel Porter book by Dean Regan

Under the Influence by Michele Riml

The Ginkgo Tree by Lee MacDougall

Gold Mountain Guest by Simon Johnston

Flying Blind Creative team: Lois Anderson, Peter Anderson, Debra Iris Batton, Manon Beaudoin, Colin Heath, Veronica Neave, Carl Polke, Brendan Shelper, Wayne Specht, and Roy Surette.

Girl in the Goldfish Bowl by Morris Panych

Carol's Christmas by Kathleen Oliver

The Matka King by Anosh Irani

The Dishwashers by Morris Panych

Unless by Carol Shields and Sara Cassidy

Sexy Laundry by Michele Riml

Mom's the Word 2: Unhinged by Jill Daum, Alison Kelly, Robin Nichol, Barbara Pollard, and Deborah Williams

Into the Heart of the Sangoma by Ann Mortifee

Griffin and Sabine adapted by Nick Bantock

Back Kitchen Release Party by Trevor Devall, original music by Alison Jenkins, Don Noble, Tracey Power, and the Back Kitchen

Up Island by David King

His Greatness by Daniel MacIvor

It's a Wonderful Life adapted by Philip Grecian

Poster Boys by Michele Riml

Cyrano adapted by James Fagan Tait

Mom's the Word Remixed: For Crying Out Loud by Linda A. Carson, Jill Daum, Alison Kelly, Robin Nichol, Barbara Pollard, and Deborah Williams

Mrs. Dexter and Her Daily by Joanna McClelland Glass

My Granny the Goldfish by Anosh Irani

Paradise Garden by Lucia Frangione

Tear the Curtain! by Kevin Kerr and Jonathon Young with Kim Collier

Don Quixote by Peter Anderson and Colin Heath

The Patron Saint of Stanley Park by Hiro Kanagawa

Do You Want What I Have Got? A Craigslist Cantata by Veda Hille, Bill Richardson, and Amiel Gladstone

Scar Tissue adapted by Dennis Foon from the novel by Michael Ignatieff

Henry and Alice: Into the Wild by Michele Riml

The Unplugging by Yvette Nolan
My Turquoise Years adapted from the memoir by Marion Farrant
How Has My Love Affected You? by Marcus Youssef
Armstrong's War by Colleen Murphy
Helen Lawrence by Stan Douglas and Chris Haddock (co-production with the Canadian Stage Company, Toronto, and The Banff Centre)
Sister Judy by Shawn Macdonald
Farewell, My Lovely by Aaron Bushkowsky (co-production with Vertigo Theatre, Calgary)
The Waiting Room by John Mann and Morris Panych
Onegin by Veda Hille and Amiel Gladstone

NOTES ON CONTRIBUTORS

Linda A. Carson, a graduate of Vancouver's Studio 58, has performed in theatres across Canada and written several plays, including *Dying to Be Thin*, *Here To Hear* (with Cathy Nosaty), and *Jack and The Bean*. Some of her most memorable acting credits include roles in *Synthetic Energy*, *Mom's the Word*, *Patty's Cake*, *Brighton Beach Memoirs*, and *Where The Wild Things Are*. Linda's favourite role has been that of "Mother" to Julian and Timothy and "Dear Partner" to Kim Selody. Linda's parents, Ron and Isabel Carson, once told her that children take you to places that you would never normally go and she thanks her two sons for doing just that.

Sara Cassidy's poems and short stories have been published in many literary publications. She is the author of six books for children and teens and two chapbooks of poetry and fiction, and is a graduate of the MFA in Writing program at the University of Victoria. She has written hundreds of feature articles and columns for magazines and newspapers, including the *Winnipeg Free Press*, the *Halifax Chronicle Herald*, Victoria's *Focus Magazine*, the *Victoria Times Colonist*, and the *Globe and Mail*, and has won a National Magazine Award (Gold). Sara teaches writing and is the artistic director of the Victoria Writers Festival.

Jill Daum is a graduate of the Studio 58 Theatre Program at Langara College. She has worked professionally as an actor in theatre, film, and TV for over twenty-five years. She is proud to be a founding member of the Mom's the Word Collective and co-writer of *Mom's the Word Remixed: For Crying Out Loud*. Jill also works at Kidsbooks in Vancouver, promoting children's literature as a bookseller. You can catch her reviews of the best reads for children on BC's Global TV.

Rachel Ditor is a freelance director, dramaturg, and the literary manager of the Arts Club Theatre in Vancouver, where she commissions and develops new plays for the company. Rachel began her work in play development in 1992 at Playwrights' Workshop Montréal and has since worked in the field with companies across the country, including the National Arts Centre and the Banff Playwrights Colony where she was a faculty dramaturg. She has published articles on new-play dramaturgy, teaches dramaturgy at UBC, and is a member of the Literary Managers and Dramaturgs of the Americas. Rachel is also the director of the Canadian Women and Words Foundation. She makes her home in Vancouver and in Victoria with her husband, Ken, and kidlets Jonah, Mira, and Toby.

Amiel Gladstone is a West Coast–based playwright and director who has worked with many of the major theatre companies across the country. On Craigslist he has bought hockey tickets; computers; couches; vintage suitcases; rugs; lamps; chairs; a coffee grinder; wallpaper; a DVD player; headphones; car rides in and out of Montreal, Toronto, Kelowna, and Vancouver; as well as a flat in Paris.

Veda Hille was born on August 11, 1968, into a nice family in Vancouver, BC. She started playing piano in 1974 and her childhood interests included plants, books, microscopes, science fiction, and psychiatry. She attended art college in the late '80s and started writing music. Now she makes records, writes musical theatre, scores films, teaches songwriting, tours, and generally keeps busy.

Anosh Irani was born and brought up in Bombay, India, and moved to Vancouver in 1998. He is the author of the acclaimed novels *The Cripple and His Talismans* and *The Song of Kahunsha*, which was a finalist for CBC Radio's Canada Reads and the Ethel Wilson Fiction Prize, has been published in thirteen countries, and was a bestseller in Canada and Italy. His play *Bombay Black* was a Dora Award winner for Outstanding New Play. Irani was nominated for the Governor General's Literary Award for Drama for his anthology *The Bombay Plays: The Matka King & Bombay Black*.

Alison Kelly is an actor, writer, and theatre instructor. Aside from the *Mom's the Word* trilogy, she is the co-creator of the plays *Conversations With My Mother*, *Wince*, and *The Stay Fresh Special*. She is also a co-creator of the comedy website *Ranting Parent* (rantingparent.com) which takes a quirky look at the world of today's parents, and is a proud contributor to *Between Interruptions*, a collection of essays about motherhood by Canadian writers. She has taught theatre and physical theatre to people from ages three to seventy-three and has been on faculty at Vancouver's renowned Studio 58 for twenty-five years. Her latest adventure sees her joining the therapeutic clown team at BC Children's Hospital in Vancouver. Alison lives in North Vancouver with her husband. Her now-grown children appear to have forgiven her any indiscretions she may have committed in writing the *Mom's the Word* plays.

Robin Nichol has been acting, directing, stage-managing, writing, and dramaturg-ing for the last twenty-five years. She holds a BFA from UVic, an MFA from UBC, and has been teaching acting and directing for the theatre program at Thompson Rivers University in Kamloops, BC, since 2004. She has directed for the Playwrights Theatre Centre, Studio 58 at Langara College, Douglas College, Drayton Entertainment, Project X Theatre, and at Thompson Rivers University, and had an extensive acting career for six years playing herself across Canada and in Australia. She would like to thank her child-bearing comrades Jill, Linda, Ali, B, and Deb for an amazing ride that shows no signs of stopping!

Playwright, actor, and director Morris Panych has been described as "a man for all seasons in Canadian theatre." He has appeared in over fifty theatre productions and in numerous television and film roles. He has directed over eighty theatre productions and written over a dozen plays that have been translated and produced throughout the world. He has twice won the Governor General's Literary Award and has won the Jessie Richardson Theatre Award fourteen times for acting and directing. He has also been nominated six times for Toronto's Dora Mavor Moore Award and three times for the Chalmers Award.

Barbara Pollard's career began with five seasons at the Stratford Shakespeare Festival and in 2014 she played Gertrude, Queen of Denmark, in a ground-breaking production of *Hamlet* at Bard on the Beach. Barbara has worked all across Canada on many regional stages, and with *Mom's the Word* she was blessed to work in Scotland, Ireland, Chicago, and London's West End, as well as appearing with the team at Just for Laughs and the Melbourne

International Comedy Festival. Besides live stage, Barbara has appeared in feature films, TV series (*The X-Files, Da Vinci's Inquest, The Haunting Hour*), and just played a lead in the television film *Far From Home*. She also teaches and directs. Barbara is the proud mother of a daughter, Emma, and a son, Desmond.

Bill Richardson is a Vancouver-based writer and broadcaster and the host of the CBC Radio shows *Saturday Afternoon at the Opera* and *In Concert*. His books include *Bachelor Brothers' Bed & Breakfast*, which won the Stephen Leacock Medal for Humour, and *After Hamelin*, a novel for children and winner of the Silver Birch Award.

Carol Shields was one of Canada's most-acclaimed writers, receiving in her lifetime the Pulitzer Prize for Literature, the National Book Critics Circle Award, and the the Governor General's Literary Award for Fiction. Her nine novels, three collections of short stories, three volumes of poetry, and six plays have been received with acclaim the world over. She taught English at the University of Manitoba for many years before moving with her husband to Victoria, BC. Carol passed away in 2003.

Sherman Snukal is a playwright, television writer, and producer. He's had six of his plays produced professionally in Canada, the United States, and Europe. His comedy, *Talking Dirty*, is one of the most successful plays in Canadian history and won the prestigious Floyd S. Chalmers Canadian Play Award. Sherman has written and produced over thirty hours of television that have been broadcast throughout Canada and around the world. His performing arts documentaries have won a Gemini and many international awards, including the prestigious Czech Crystal Award at the Karlovy Vary International Film Festival.

An actress, writer, comedienne, and producer, Deb Williams began her professional career at the Arts Club in *The Granville Island Revue, Comedy of Errors*, and *School for Wives*. She has gone on to perform, tour, and develop many productions at the A.C., including *Clybourne Park, The Importance of Being Earnest*, and *Becky's New Car*, for which she received a Jessie Richardson Award. She is an artistic associate for Solo Collective and the Belfry Theatre, and co-founder of the Flame, the hit monthly Vancouver storytelling event, celebrating its fifth season at the Cottage Bistro in 2014. As a comedian she is regularly on TV and radio and can be found mouthing off on rantingparent.com. She is in development with a number of new plays and feels grateful to have made her living as an artist in Canada for twenty-eight years. Deb is a proud graduate of Studio 58 and proud mother of two scientific adults.

First edition: January 2015
Printed and bound in Canada by Imprimerie Gauvin, Gatineau

Cover design by Blake Sproule

**PLAYWRIGHTS
CANADA PRESS**

202-269 Richmond Street West
Toronto, ON
M5V 1X1

416.703.0013
info@playwrightscanada.com
playwrightscanada.com

RECYCLED
Paper made from
recycled material
FSC
www.fsc.org   FSC® C100212